**Rich Nations and Poor
in Peace and War**

Rich Nations and Poor in Peace and War

Continuity and Change in the Development Hierarchy of Seventy Nations from 1913 through 1952

Henry Barbera
City College, CUNY

Lexington Books
D.C. Heath and Company
Lexington, Massachusetts
Toronto   London

Library of Congress Cataloging in Publication Data

Barbera, Henry.
    Rich nations and poor in peace and war.

    Bibliography: p.
    1. War—Economic aspects. 2. Economic development. 3. Economic his-
tory—20th century. I. Title.
HB195.B33   338.9   73-2003
ISBN 0-669-86900-7

Published simultaneously in Canada.

Printed in the United States of America.

International Standard Book Number: 0-669-86900-7

Library of Congress Catalog Card Number: 73-2003

Si cambia il maestro di cappella,
ma la musica e sempre quella.

Italian proverb

Contents

List of Tables

Acknowledgments

My earliest intellectual debts are to William Cornell Casey, who sought to show to any who would listen something about the beauty and potentialities of political sociology and to C. Wright Mills, who exemplified the realism and imagination necessary for an engaged view of social stratification.

In planning this project, Theodore Caplow's accepting response to it sustained my initial motivation, as did W. Phillips Davison's smoothing of an anticipated tangle near its end. It is a pleasure to have been in contact with them; they embody the highest professional standards.

Several scholars have read this manuscript, raised questions about it, and have even tried to help it along: if I did not heed each suggestion, it reflects less on their value and more on the constraints of an inner voice. These generous people include: Allen Barton, Robert Bierstedt, Karl W. Deutsch, Kurt Finsterbusch, William T.R. Fox, Richard Hartshorne, Morris Janowitz, Robert M. Marsh, Donald Puchala, and J. David Singer.

I would like to single out for special mention an always-gentle critic and comrade, Rita Udell, whose resourcefulness at a critical juncture saved me considerable time and energy.

My greatest debt can hardly be discharged adequately. It is to my wife, Penny, for moral support in all kinds of weather.

March 1973

**Rich Nations and Poor
in Peace and War**

1 Argument

Omnia mutantur nos et mutamur in illis.
Latin proverb

Development refers to a level of mastery over the environment or furthering the potential for such mastery. It cannot be properly understood unless it is translated into significant material details in the life of the average man, especially in terms of his health, education, and welfare.

As the eye roves the earth, it is caught and held by both obvious and subtle material differences between men variously located in the development hierarchy of nations. By accident of birth, the average man in one nation lives a life somewhat different from the average man in another nation. The man in a rich nation knows more because he has more formal education; he communicates more and with more people because of the operation in his nation of more mass media and mass transport; he works more hours with less fatigue because he consumes a more protein-filled diet each day and because he operates more power-driven tools; he lives longer and has less death in the family because more public health programs and public welfare facilities are available. His counterpart in a poor nation, however, has a much less materially satisfying life because he is bound by the limitations of time, space, and energy. Can war account for these differences?

War may be strictly defined as organized fighting between at least two politically independent nations in pursuit of goals. It represents one of the several ways available to settle disputes. It is the nation that contends for world goals (security, autonomy, territory, prestige, allies, and ideology), not individuals or races or continents or subunits of the nation. War is made and unmade by the nation, and only the nation has this prerogative.[1]

The phenomena popularly referred to as "war" and "peace" differ not in the goals nations pursue but rather only in the means used, diplomatic or military, to attain those goals. Peace, therefore, does not mean the end of struggles between nations or the settlement of disputes. Behind these phenomena of war and peace lies the broader dimension of power, which must also refer to the prosecution of goals. While one nation attempts to achieve its goals, it must watch and resist another nation competing with it, and it may occasionally need to block the achievements of still another nation. Thus a context of rivalry surrounds nations as a normal and perennial condition of power politics or the mobilization of collective strength to meet opposition over goals. If this context

1

is the general condition of power politics, then war may be seen as a particularized aspect of that process. War is an historically episodic event, circumscribed by time; and, unlike power, it is discontinuous.

From the perspective of any government, then, the nation is concerned first with power and secondarily with development. "Economic development has always been one of the concerns of government, if only as a means of increasing the internal and external power of the state, but that concern is almost always subordinated to other more pressing concerns of the state. Higher priority is usually given to the attainment of power in comparison with other states."[2]

While development and power are conceptually distinct phenomena, the former may influence the latter much more than vice versa. For example, the greater a nation's mastery over the environment, the more it may decide upon the things that matter most in the world. But an addition of power in a nation may mean only an addition to the size of its population, for potential power is measured by level of development plus size of population. In any case, the story of power resides in the wars fought, the range of diplomatic representation maintained abroad, the favorable treaties signed, the extent of territory held, the spheres of influence established, the threats issued and believed, the length of boundaries protected, and the number of interferences in the quarrels of other nations.

In contrast, the story of development can be told in terms of increases in schools and teachers, in transportation and communication systems, in quality and quantity of housing units, in skill of the labor force and degree of urbanization, in agricultural yields and protein counts, in hospital beds, in energy consumed or produced, in infant mortality rates, and in a variety of other statistical series all of which indicate a significant mastery over the environment.

A nation develops by using increasingly sophisticated technologies applied by increasingly complex organizations. Ideas and principles, communication and contact, along with centralization and cooperation, promote mastery of the environment. (These general variables lie behind the more specialized ones of capital formation and investment.) A nation does not develop in a vacuum, however; it is always relative to other nations. The level of development of a nation depends on the accumulated body of its instrumental culture, the density of its network of communication, and the degree of its internal cohesiveness. The greater the magnitude of these variables, the higher the level of development of a nation.

In this work, I am interested in determining whether or not war affects development and, if so, to what extent. Although there will be occasional references to power, my main interest is in the state and direction of world development and inequality before and after world war. For war to affect development and inequality between nations, it must affect the variables of culture, communication, and cohesion. For example, it must add to, or subtract from, given amounts of useful information, it must facilitate or frustrate the channels which diffuse that information, and it must strengthen or weaken the mechanisms that administer it. These variables will receive extended commentary in the chapters to follow. Together they form the conceptual frame of reference out of which a theory of development and inequality will emerge.

War has been consistently advanced throughout history as an explanation of development and inequality. No other explanation of rich nations and poor has received as much attention, if the sheer number of volumes on the subject is any indication. Yet no other explanation appears so confused.

War, for example, causes an escalation in output, even those outputs normally associated with development; at the same time war consumes men, minds, materials, and money. Hence the question naturally arises, will a nation at war be so boosted in its output as to compensate for war destruction or will the reverse be so? What about nations officially neutral in war, how will they fare? To the extent that a development hierarchy can be effectively objectified, can war explain such inequality between the nations?

There are basically four possible hypotheses about the relationship between war and development. War is either productive, destructive, unpredictable, or irrelevant to development. The relationship between the factors is either direct, negative, variable, or lacking; that is, war associates positively, inversely, occasionally, or not at all with the development of nations.

My aim throughout this work will be to test these hypotheses in the light of statistical measures which would indicate the degree of socioeconomic development over a long term. In order to do so, I will attempt to show the extent to which the First and Second World Wars affected rich nations and poor. This will involve examining all nations as they struggle together for more health, education, and welfare in this crowded and bloody century; accordingly, the combatant and the neutral, the occupied and the nonoccupied, the developed and the underdeveloped will be compared by measures reflecting their prewar and postwar situation. The proof will not be conclusive, for no one study could promise that, but it will still add to the degree of confidence one may store in these hypotheses as alternative explanations of war and development.

These hypotheses depend on one assumption for the nonce and that is continuity in development. An example of continuity can be seen in energy production over time. According to some observers, figures on energy may be considered as the chief measure of development.[3] An increase in energy means greater mastery over the environment. Since record keeping on energy production began, the world has exhibited a fairly constant upward trend. This can be seen in Table 1-1, which shows the rise in the production of energy by decades from 1860 through 1950. Although the data are presented in aggregate form, it may be assumed that the rate of growth of energy has outstripped the rate of growth of population.

Table 1-1

World Production of Commercial Sources of Energy (Electricity Equivalents, in Million Megawatt Hours)

Year	Energy	Year	Energy
1860	1,079	1910	9,387
1870	1,674	1920	11,298
1880	2,623	1930	13,053
1890	4,056	1940	15,882
1900	6,089	1950	20,556

Source: PROCEEDINGS OF THE INTERNATIONAL CONFERENCE ON THE PEACE-FUL USES OF ATOMIC ENERGY, HELD IN GENEVA, 8 AUGUST-20 AUGUST 1955, VOLUME I, THE WORLD'S REQUIREMENTS FOR ENERGY: THE ROLE OF NUCLEAR ENERGY (New York: United Nations, 1956 IX.I, vol. I, Tables XXIIIB and XXIIIC, pp. 28 and 30; these figures represent all energy figures and summarize the following fuels converted: coal, lignite, petroleum, natural gasoline, natural gas, and water power. These figures do not reveal the great and steadily increasing efficiency in either production or use of energy over this time period.

What Others Have Said

In the remainder of this chapter, I shall present many views about the relationship between war and development. A rich body of literature exists on the subject and it yields readily to sorting. So from the perspective of the four possible hypotheses, some of that literature will pass in review. But one fact will immediately become apparent. The exemplars classified under the various hypotheses bring different emphases to bear on their understanding of the subject; that is, those under the productive formulation emphasize gains; those under the destructive formulation emphasize costs; those under the unpredictable formulation emphasize circumstances; and those under the irrelevant formulation deny any relationship, positive or negative, between the factors. No calculus known to man can handle all of the authors to be cited on their own terms, so contradiction runs rampant. A way out of that dilemma will be one of the tasks of the next two chapters, where the problem will gain increasing specificity. The only purpose of the present classification is to provide some notion of the astonishingly wide range of what is thought to be possible in the relationship between war and development.

Subscribers to the Productive Hypothesis

According to the productive hypothesis, war helps development whether a nation wins or loses because of measurable gains from the translation into nonwar use of such immediate solutions to military problems as psychological testing, field surgery, radar, and sanitation; from the upgrading of the work force through on-the-job training, diffused job techniques, and increased managerial skills; from credit expansion and capital concentration, resulting in fuller exploitation of natural resources and in the enlarging and, in fact, the creating of needed industries (textile for uniforms, metallurgical for cannon and tank, shipbuilding, aircraft, and engineering are the most obvious); and from the expansion of the use of fixed equipment like factory buildings and machinery to two and three shifts a day to achieve greater and more standardized outputs, the important idea of rationally organized systems thus gradually becoming even more institutionalized. Thus war affects minds, men, money, and materials positively rather than negatively under the productive possibility.

Mumford, for example, describes the stimulation of invention and innovation by military needs. Napoleon III offered a reward for "a cheap process of making steel capable of withstanding the explosive force of the new shells. The Bessemer process was the direct answer to this demand."[4] But the most profound invention was the gun; "the gun was the starting point of a new type of power machine: it was, mechanically speaking, a one-cylinder internal combustion engine." Because of it, a number of events followed: first, it increased the consumption of iron and stimulated mining; second, "war established a new type of industrial director who was not a mason or a smith or a master craftsman—the military engineer. . . . It was to the Italian military engineers from the fifteenth century on that the machine owed a debt quite as high as it did to the ingenious British inventors of James Watt's period"; third, heavy fortifications were developed, and road-building, canal-building, and bridge-building became necessary adjuncts of warfare; fourth, it increased the demands on industry for standardized arms and equipment, thus accelerating factory organization: "In terms of the barracks, the routine of the factory seemed tolerable and natural. The speed of conscription and volunteer militia forces throughout the Western world after the French Revolution made army and factory, so far as their social effects went, almost interchangeable terms." "The army is in fact the ideal form toward which a purely mechanized system of industry must tend"; and fifth, such production efficiencies stimulated the growth of armies: and as armies grew, so did the costs of armament, food, and clothing, compelling rulers to have recourse to bankers and so fostering capitalism: "As security for the loan, the lender took over the royal mines. The development of the mines themselves then became a respectable avenue of financial enterprise, with returns that compared favorably with the usurious and generally unpayable interest. Spurred by the unpaid notes, the rulers were in turn driven to new conquests or to the exploitation of remote territories: and so the cycle began over again." And so Mumford sums up by asking "How far shall we go back in demonstrating the fact that war has been the chief propagator of the machine?"

Perhaps the greatest proponent of the productive hypothesis is Sombart, who claimed that war first helped development during the sixteenth century and continued to do so up through the nineteenth.[5] War helps industrial organization, commerce, and finance, each in several ways. War helps industrial organization in two ways: first, it leads to the building of larger factories and machinery in order to increase armament outputs; and secondly, it increases the demand for iron, steel, and copper, thereby stimulating mining and metallurgy firms which respond by developing larger and more complex forms of organization. War helps commerce primarily because troops need uniforms and food. With the advent of mercantilism, the job of clothing and feeding men under arms, no longer accomplished through the decentralized expedients of the prior era, was undertaken by careerists of rising national states who ordered goods to be gathered and stockpiled for later distribution; thus there emerged a class of private military traders who could provide the capital and handle the multiple arrangements of supplying the military forces with standardized products. War helps finance in two ways: first, state capitalism is advanced because increasing its taxing programs so concentrates money that the state is able to build monopolies in saltpeter and gunpowder manufacturing, cannon and musket production, and in the construction of fortifications; and, second, private capitalism is advanced by state encouragement of certain industries, for example, metal-working and textiles, through such devices as credit extensions and secured markets.

After China disputed the northern borders of India in 1961, an Indian economist made the following prediction: "Our finding is that the potential economic strength of our country is so tremendous that we can fight even major wars, and keep on fighting, if forced to do so, over a long period of time without weakening our productive power and in fact, adding simultaneously to its strength and size."[6] This kind of prediction is neither novel nor unsupportable. For example, a number of Japanese authors argue that the development of Japan was greatly aided by her participation in the Sino-Japanese War, the Russo-Japanese War, and the First World War. Thus,

The economic development after the Sino-Japanese War was in general so extraordinary that the phenomena which attracted attention before the war [i.e., the aggressive spirit of the Meiji Restoration] were no longer noticeable. . . . The Sino-Japanese War was, indeed, a test of our national strength and resulted in the self-realization and awakening of the nation, thereby bringing in its train a notable economic development.[7]

Another author states:

The economic growth of Japan in the last twelve years [1904-1916], in short, has been stimulated by the Russo-Japanese War. . . . The war marked a turning-point in every branch of our industrial and commercial growth, foreign trade and transportation service in particular having been completely reorganized through the war. If we may judge by superficial observation, it may be safely said that as a result of the war industry in Japan progressed with leaps and bounds.[8]

Of the impact of these two wars on transportation and communication, the following is asserted:

It may be admitted that their improvement was splendidly attained owing directly or indirectly to the expenditures for war and armament, on account of the imperative utilization of railways, ships, telegraph, telephone, etc., for military purposes; that is, owing to the government's protective policy for the shipping trade, the munificent bounties allowed to railway constructions, and the nationalization of private railway lines. . . . Concisely stated, great development arose in economic circles regularly subsequent to each of the great wars. . . .[9]

Speaking of the effects of the First World War, still another author says that Japan

derived many benefits from the War, as it furnished occasion for the building up of her productive industries. The difficulty experienced in importing goods forced her people to face the necessity of a self-sufficing economic existence; while order after order for munitions and other commodities found their way from other countries to Japan. Under the circumstances it is no wonder that her industry grew more and more active, culminating in the promotion of many extensive business projects; indeed her economic condition in general, during the War, might be said to be incomparably the most prosperous in her history.[10]

To consider war as an instrument of national policy resulting in measurable gains accords with the productive hypothesis; the greater those gains in the things that matter most, the more is that hypothesis confirmed. This final citation represents the point of view fairly well:

The means for a nation to obtain wealth and satisfy its cravings is found in waging war. . . . The German victories of 1870 have enriched the individual German. Every German has a share *in the profits,* and is directly interested *in the firm, in the constitution, and in victory. That is what is now meant by a people's war.*[11]

The author then refers to the Sino-Japanese War, the Spanish-American War, the Russo-Japanese War, the Boer War, and the Franco-British quarrel over Fashoda, and asks:

What were we all seeking? For commercial outlets to an industrial system which produces more than it can sell, and therefore is constantly smothered by competition. What happens then? New markets are opened by force of arms.[12]

Subscribers to the Destructive Hypothesis

According to the destructive hypothesis, war hinders development because it imposes identifiable costs: in minds, by shortening the training time of students, by emptying universities of younger faculty, and by turning the thoughts of scientists away from "pure" science and its application to health, education, welfare, and industry, toward military topics; in men, through the loss of those killed and those maimed or diseased whose later productive labor is thereby impaired, and through the loss of the unborn of the dead and crippled; in money, through the interruption of "normal" production due to military conscription and shifts in products, through the interruption of trade due to blockades—overcoming a blockade makes routes circuitous and dangerous and raises the real cost of imports and exports—and the cost of allocating protection by a fleet, and through the near-absolute interruption of luxury industries as a source of gain due to rapid tax increases; and, in material, by the destruction of crops, railways, bridges, factories, houses, and the contents of buildings including works of art and libraries.

That war imposes a cost in minds is argued by Staley.

Misdirection of inventive genius and organizing genius into the arts of war instead of the arts of peace. This . . . may be the greatest economic cost of war, in the long run, and it affects neutrals almost equally with participants in war. War stimulus sometimes produces inventions that are also serviceable in peace, but incidental benefits of this kind are not nearly so large as the progress that could be made if more talented persons were working on the problem of bombarding atoms and fewer on bombarding cities. The real progress of invention comes from fundamental science, which requires peace and quiet and funds for research rather than armaments.[13]

Nef claims that any science activity flourished least in war, if at all, and that the invention of gunpowder and many other weapons of war was a by-product not of military but of industrial needs. He also claims that normative restraints on war, rather than war itself, are part of the set which may lead to social and technical advance. This is what he has to say about war and the industrial revolution:

As had happened before and as was destined to happen again, the wars [of Coalition against France] contributed less than nothing, while the preparations for war contributed relatively little, to the economic progress of those nations on the Continent which bore the brunt of the destruction. The industrial revolution started in Great Britain in the 1780's, just before the new [fierce wars with huge armies] began on the Continent. There the industrial revolution started later, after 1815, when the guns had ceased to fire. War was an important cause for the delay.[14]

More hesitantly stated is the following view.

The direct stimulus of war to inventiveness and to creative investment by no means appears to compensate for the losses in blood and treasure and capital. On the other hand, it is impossible to envisage, for example, the evolution of the era from Elizabeth to Napoleon's defeat outside the context of war. Mercantilism is, after all, a reasonable pattern of economic policy for societies at war or living in the shadow of war. On balance, however, a rough economist's calculation must rate war a negative force in economic change.[15]

The most equivocal statement classifiable as a destructive hypothesis reads as follows:

The most outstanding features of the history of mankind are the accumulation of technical knowledge and the increase in the scale of societies. The examples of how war stimulated inventions range from the improvement in early metallurgy to the construction of interplanetary rockets, but on the other hand, by causing wholesale destructions and retrogressions of civilizations, war has often acted as a brake upon rather than a stimulant of technical progress and evolution towards increasing complexity and scale.[16]

That war imposes a cost on men is a fact so well-known and grim that it warrants only mention here. Viallate makes an excellent statement. "The Great War by its unprecedented scope and by its duration, which no one at the beginning of hostilities would have believed possible, has had consequences more disastrous than the worst predictions that any one dared formulate. Consequences disastrous because of the great number of men at the age of full productivity killed or injured beyond rehabilitation during the course of those fifty-two months; because of the wealth representing the savings of many generations back, consumed with such swiftness for a task economically unproductive; and because of the amount of work performed during this long period in a task of pure destruction."[17]

Several authors assert that economic depression invariably follows upon war. For instance, Condliffe says,

Whatever the intervening secondary causes may have been, the ultimate cause of the great depression that has lasted since 1929 is to be found in the impoverishment and economic dislocation caused by the war which began in 1914. It is, of course, obvious that many complicating factors have intervened since the war ended. No one would contend that financial crises and economic depressions are solely consequences of war. But the economic history of the modern world affords abundant proof that the distortion of economic activity occasioned by a great war inevitably increases the severity and lengthens the distress of these periodic fluctuations of industry.[18]

And another author notes that depressions followed both the Wars of Coalition against France and the First World War. "What a striking parallel! Eleven years and a few months from peace to crash a century ago; eleven years almost to the day history repeats itself."[19]

A number of other authors assert that war adversely affects neutrals, victors, and even civilization.

If even one-fifth of the loss in the depression years is counted as an indirect loss from war, that alone would exceed the direct costs of the American participation in 1917-1918. There is no reason to think that the United States would have escaped much of the rigors of the world depression had we stayed entirely neutral in the World War.[20]

Victors in war, contrary to what might be popular opinion on the matter, do not seem to fare any better than the vanquished.

Nations that lose wars suffer economically. Victor nations, of which Britain is an example, may lose far more than they gain. Even in the case of the United States, which suffered little physical war damage, there is reason to believe that war debits will over-balance war credits and that the net result for United States economy will be a loss. If a comparison is made between the combined economic positions of the six chief warring nations in 1938 and in 1946 it must be apparent that the net economic losses for all six combined are prodigiously high. . . . Modern total war does not seem to be a paying proposition economically. Looked at from any angle, its losses seem to outweigh its gains.[21]

And it is said that war adversely affects civilization.

Indeed, the threat of war, as well as actual war, is the greatest present impediment to advances in civilization both in Western culture and in all the leading cultures of the world.[22]

Subscribers to the Unpredictable Hypothesis

According to the unpredictable hypothesis, war helps development occasionally, hinders it occasionally and may even do both simultaneously. The factors determining whether or not development results from war seem to be whether the war occurred in the past or the present, and whether the nation concerned was victor or vanquished. In the unspecified past a gain in development could result for the victor from conquest and colonization which brought about an increase in territory, a greater population base brought under taxable control, an enlarged land route or sea lane, a new sphere of influence, and a wider market. The factors of occurrence in the unspecified past and of victory have been further detailed to include the availability of booty (from a rich or recently unravished state) and a rapid rate of growth on the part of the winner, if an old nation, or the formation by the winner of a new nation. These statements and conclusions are drawn from the authors to be cited below; however, the full variety of expressions of the unpredictable hypothesis, specifically in terms of mixed and variable consequences, remains far from exhausted by this sample of the literature.

"If war enriched some of the peoples of antiquity, it impoverishes and makes miserable the peoples of modern times."[23] That statement was made in the eighteenth century and many like it can be found to have been made in other centuries as well. Here is one made in the twentieth century: "War was then still something it has no longer been since about the time of the French Revolution— good business."[24]

"During a long succession of centuries, the chief concern was to discover and improve military apparatus, and these efforts were not entirely without value for the progress of industry, which often drew valuable lessons from these warlike preparations. In this matter the social condition of the ancients should be regarded as the reverse of our modern condition. In antiquity the greatest industrial efforts were related primarily to war, which gave rise to prodigious inventions, especially in connection with sieges. In modern times, on the contrary, the system of armaments is relatively less perfected than in Greek and Roman times, when we take into consideration the great industrial development."[25] But according to two other authors it is precisely because of development of new weapons, that future war appears impossible.

When we say that war is impossible we mean that it is impossible for the modern state to carry on war under the modern conditions [of the perfection of the cannon and the magazine rifle] with any prospect of being able to carry that war to a conclusion by defeating its adversary by force of arms on the battlefield. No decisive war is possible. Neither is any war possible . . . that will not entail, even upon the victorious power, the destruction of its resources and the breakup of society. War therefore has become impossible, except at the price of suicide.[26]

In contemporary dress, the other author continues the argument:

It is safe to assume that future armed conflicts will not be dominated by the strategy of attrition that determined the character of World Wars I and II. The destructiveness of present (and a fortiori, future) weapons is such that strategic decisions can no longer center upon the gradual wearing down of the enemy's mobilizable potential. Hence, we no longer can visualize terminal situations of the "classic" World War I and II type, essentially representing the last stage of a siege. The main feature of that pattern was the unimpaired cohesive structure of the loser's residual forces (and, in World War II, even of his political and social fabric), together with the drying up of sources of supplies and reinforcements. What present weapons portend, however, is an extreme disruptive effect, which goes far beyond the disruption achieved by earlier "battle" strategies. Full-scale nuclear warfare threatens its target with a level of destruction so high that coordinated activities must largely come to a stop. In such a situation, the loser cannot offer "surrender," in the shape of handing to the winner control over cohesive residual capabilities and over a society that is still a going concern.[27]

Two specifications of the conditions under which "the economic gains of the victors justify the war effort which they put forth in order to win" have been suggested: first, booty is available; for example, "war-making might be economically profitable at the beginning of a period of intensified military activity when movable property was abundant, which later, after considerable war damage and looting, the available booty in rival states might not balance war costs. . . . As a region is denuded by successive military campaigns it yields less and less plunder to the victor"; and, second, expansion is occurring; for example, "the wars waged by Britain against Holland and France in the 17th and 18th centuries paralleled British economic expansion and gave British business control of the desired markets and sea lanes. The wars waged against Germany from 1914 to 1945, after British economy had reached and passed its expansion maximum, weakened the British economic position."[28]

On the first specification, available booty, two instances may be cited from the literature.

The loss of power and booty are seen here in classic union. When, in 1066, William and his Norman chivalry conquered England, the whole land was made King's property and fee and it remains so in name to this day. Here is a true Viking delight in "having," the care of an Odysseus who begins by counting his treasure [i.e., the Domesday Book] ... after 1066 England was organized as booty, with ruthless reduction of the Anglo-Saxons, to serfdom. ... England was broken up into 60,251 fiefs, catalogued in the Domesday Book of 1084 (consulted even to-day upon occasion). ...[29]

And the second instance follows.

As a rule devastation is only resorted to to reach a specific end. Ravages such as we effected in the Transvaal are rare: we performed them *in terrorem*: to dishearten the Boers by burning their homes, and by famishing their wives and children; by thus exterminating whole families we hoped to leave untenanted lands on which our colonists might establish themselves later.[30]

On the second specification, existing expansion, two statements from the literature may be cited. Identifying a type of war called regional expansion, Rostow claims that it arises "from the dilemmas and the exuberance of newly formed national states, as they looked backward to past humiliations and forward to new opportunity, while confronting the choices open to them in the early stages of modernization."[31] Toynbee presents the idea quite eloquently.

In the early stages of a civilization's growth, the cost of wars in suffering and destruction might seem to be exceeded by the benefits accruing from the winning of wealth and power and the cultivation of the "military virtues"; and, in this phase of history, States have often found themselves able to indulge in War with one another with something like impunity even for the defeated party. War does not begin to reveal its malignity till the war-making society has begun to increase its economic ability to exploit Physical Nature and its political ability to organize "man-power"; but, as soon as this happens, the God of War to which the growing society has long since been dedicated proves himself a Moloch by devouring an ever larger share of the increasing fruits of Man's industry and intelligence in the process of taking an ever larger toll of life and happiness; and, when the society's growth in efficiency reaches a point at which it becomes capable of mobilizing a lethal quantum of its energies and resources for military use, then War reveals itself as being a cancer. ...[32]

Subscribers to the Irrelevant
Hypothesis

According to the irrelevant hypothesis, war does not affect development. This hypothesis is frustrating to those who would like to pin down a relationship between war and development. The idea that there is no such relationship runs counter to conventional wisdom. "After all, war must have some effect on development." Yet there are a handful of authors who claim that war has an insignificant effect on development or, more strongly, that it has no bearing on development whatsoever either in the long or short term. Another obvious difficulty here is the lack of a frame of reference. The other hypotheses emphasize certain additional factors: the productive hypothesis is in terms of gains; the destructive in terms of costs; and the unpredictable in terms of circumstances. Unlike these other hypotheses, however, the irrelevant naturally lacks a special referent.

Nations continue to improve their material situation regardless of war according to the irrelevant hypothesis. Therefore development tolerates conflict. To note the rapidity with which populations recover from war, or to attempt to assess how many people could be destroyed in war without effect on the course of development, is to think in terms of the capacity of nations to absorb the costs of deadly quarrels and still maintain their functioning and their growth.[33]

Linton says, "Civilization was . . . developed in the face of war and has had it as a constant accompaniment. In spite of this it has grown and flourished. Surprisingly few civilizations have been destroyed by war and most of those which have succumbed were already so ill from other causes that war merely administered the *coup de grace*. It may be urged that modern war is so different from its predecessors as to invalidate all comparisons, but actually its uniqueness, especially as regards potentialities for destruction, has been greatly overrated."[34] This view is expressed by Bryce, writing at an earlier date. After surveying history with the question, does war affect development, he arrives at two conclusions. "One is that war does not necessarily arrest progress. People may advance in thought, literature, and art while they are fighting. The other is that war cannot be shown to have been a cause of progress in anything except the wealth or power of a state which extends its dominions by conquest or draws tribute from the vanquished."[35]

"It can easily be proved that, in our land, the national wealth has, during at least six centuries, been almost uninterruptedly increasing; that it was greater under the Tudors than under the Plantagenets; that it was greater under the Stuarts than under the Tudors; that, in spite of maladministration, of extravagance, of public bankruptcy, of two costly and unsuccessful wars, of the pestilence and of the fire, it was greater on the day of the death of Charles the Second than on the day of his Restoration. This progress, having continued during many ages, became at length, about the middle of the eighteenth century, portentously rapid, and has proceeded, during the nineteenth, with accelerated velocity. . . . The consequence is that a change to which the history of the old world furnishes no parallel has taken place in our country. Could the England of 1685 be, by some magical process, set before our eyes, we should not know one landscape in a hundred or one building in ten thousand."[36]

Most of the nations of Europe during the fifty years from 1735 through 1785 were characterized by growing prosperity; that is, before and after the War of the Austrian Succession, 1740-48, and the Seven Years' War, 1756-63. More specifically: "This war like the other inconclusive wars of the half century 1740-89, hardly interfered with the remarkable increase in French industrial production."[37]

War neither helps nor hinders development according to the irrelevant hypothesis, and Kuznets considers this especially true since the Wars of Coalition against France. "Apparently, short of breakdowns of the social system, modern conditions permit a steady growth, even in per capita product, that was not possible in premodern times. And except during periods of violent revolutionary change in institutions and of major wars—both necessarily limited—modern growth rates are steady; successive subperiods (say of one or two decades) rarely show a drop in the rate of growth below a fairly high positive minimum."[38]

The existence in the literature of interpretations consistent with each of the four basic hypotheses about war and development indicates that a one-to-one relationship does not obtain. None of the authors cited has provided sufficient evidence on which to base a judgment of the alternatives which cannot all be true and which may all be false. Yet their commentary as a corpus exists as a reminder of what is inherently possible in the relationship between war and development. The whole range of what is possible will inform each of the later chapters.

Some of the reasons that explain the variety of possibilities seem clear: the authors have not selected the same wars or talked of the same nations or considered the same time units before and after war or used the same kind of data as measures or even agreed on the meaning of development. Under these circumstances, a set of alternative possibilities would seem inevitable.

Clearly, the factors in the relationships invite further specificity if any headway in understanding is to be made. This is precisely the task of the next two chapters. First the subject of development will be discussed in terms of measuring rich nations and poor in detail; then the components of the dependent variable will be identified. Second, in Chapter 3, nations will be classified in terms of the degree to which they have participated in the two world wars of this century. After this task is attended to, we will be in a more suitable position to analyze and interpret the results of this study of world war on world development.

2 Development

Salus populi suprema lex esto.
Latin proverb

The key difference among nations is their capacity to extend mastery over the environment. The difference is key because this capacity affects the ability to weather crises like war, revolution, or depression; it is the chief determinant of the distribution of world power and the lever behind foreign relations. Other differences like type of economy or polity, regional location, religious conviction, historical singularity, or racial mystique, appear peripheral from this point of view. On relative development, and only on relative development, hang the differing material fates of men.

The material differences between nations are considerable. The average differences in level of living between nations are greater in some cases than the differences among individuals in the same nation. Of all marginal Frenchmen, for example, none are as badly nourished today as the typical Chinese. This is because the average Frenchman produces more in the same time, and produces a more valuable output in less time, than his counterpart in China.[1]

While it may be fashionable in some places to talk of over-development, no nation has enough health, education, and welfare, although certainly some nations have more than others. While all nations control a portion of the environment, some exercise greater control than others; if a handful of nations appears to possess considerable mastery, many more are frequently victimized by the environment. Inequality in development therefore appears as the central drama of our time.

Yet little can be found in the scholarly literature on hierarchies of organizations of similar types—on the hierarchies of brothels, or that of country clubs, or those of criminal syndicates, diplomatic missions, fraternities, gambling houses, hospitals, labor unions, monasteries, police departments, restaurants, retail stores, and steamship lines; even less an identification of what criteria would determine such hierarchies, let alone an identification of what mechanisms affect them and what dependent variables are supposed to be affected by them. This seems to be a somewhat neglected area and potentially of wide concern. At any rate, since organizations of the same type can be located in a hierarchy, obviously nations, as a special illustration of social organization, should be amenable to placement in one. The only requirement for arraying nations is agreement on the culling device. Development would easily win approval as a relevant criterion by which to grade nations.

15

Measuring the State of Development

Measures reflecting the material differences between nations are available, and nations can be unequivocally arrayed in a development hierarchy by them. The state of development is indicated by statistical findings that represent mastery over the environment. Statistics on the health, education, and welfare of a population are indicative of an achieved level of development. However, such statistics have value for study only if they satisfy certain criteria; that is, they must be comparable, sensitive, standardized, and coincident. A series is comparable if it has the same meaning from nation to nation; sensitive if it permits fine discriminations with which to locate nations on a development hierarchy; standardized if it remains unaffected by size of population and territory; and coincident if it matches, rather than leads or follows, turning points in most other series measuring development.

Without comparable data it would be difficult to assess the consequences of war or of any other factor for development. Before uniform measures were devised, analysts had to weigh up roughly very different items representing costs and gains of war. Such costs as the death of soldiers and the number of unborn babies; destroyed and unbuilt roads, bridges, and housing; a slowdown in money circulation, luxury industries and foreign trade are examples; all these costs had to be weighed against such gains as innovations in field surgery; rapid diffusion of sanitation practices; and stimulation of the metallurgical industry for the building of cannon and tank. Obviously, such an evaluation was a difficult task at best. More often, however, analysts studied the more pressing consequences of war from a problems perspective. Discussion of such purported consequences of war as a rise of unemployment in one nation, a drop in industrial output in another, and inflation or recession in still another, illustrate the method of approach.[2] This method, using unique details, is not at all conducive to comparing the consequences of war for a large number of nations. In other words, the first requirement for a measure for this study is that it be capable of application across the board of rich nations and poor so as to yield strict comparisons in development. Fortunately such measures now exist both in abundance and variety.

Without a sensitive measure it would be impossible to study the inequalities in development among nations. Before sensitive measures came onto the scene, analysts had to think in terms of rarity of stones or metals, size of monuments, availability of coins, quality of literary works and paintings, style of life; also, they relied heavily on personal observation recorded in available documents. Now investigators can unequivocally array nations in terms of quantity of hospital beds, school teachers, and high-protein diets. It is assumed, of course, that the quality of the items the series represent are equal from nation to nation; that is to say, the hospital beds are just as useful, the teachers are as well trained, and the diets are just as nourishing. Contemporary measures of relative development, then, are obviously far more sensitive than the more traditional measures, even though they still have limitations. In recent years, moreover, a number of studies have appeared, independent of each other, in which a convergence can be identified in the various series listed as measures of development, despite different theoretical aims and different data-handling practices of different investigators from different fields of inquiry.[3]

Without a standardized measure it would be impossible to evaluate the consequences of war for development. Before standardized measures were developed, analysts thought in gross rather than in per capita terms primarily because they were concerned with power and plenty. A rise in gross figures, however, cannot reveal to anyone whether the rise is due to a move in development or in population size, or how much of a move in each. Perhaps the first to insist on per capita output as a measure of development was Adam Smith.[4] Although his suggestion was not followed up until the twentieth century, it is now commonly agreed that any measure of development requires standardized figures in order to control for the effect of population. A nation is developing, then, only when the increase in its output in, say, health or education or welfare outstrips its rate of population increase. What differentiates one nation from another in development, therefore, is not the gross but the proportionate amount of these items. The most abstract way of viewing a nation is by considering its per capita output. Although most of the complexity, flavor, and mystery of a nation necessarily remain hidden, there is still something to be gained by focusing thought on per capita output: all nations may be viewed together both historically and comparatively at any point of time. This is an important advantage because it frees the analyst from considering the many different internal aspects of a nation (for example, the kind of resources it possesses) and permits him to evaluate nations solely in terms of output measures in health or education or welfare.

Without a coincident measure it would be difficult to assess the consequences of war for development. Before coincident measures were identified, analysts, wittingly or unwittingly, used series with very different growth patterns. There are some series, for example, like literacy rate, newspaper circulation, and steel consumption that grow rapidly at first and then taper off; there are other series, like road length, the consumption of household appliances, and airline travel that start slowly and then pick up in time; there are still other series, like the number of radios, high-protein diets, and hospital beds that have a fairly constant rate of increase; and finally there are some series, like energy consumption, mortality rate, and urbanization that have an erratic growth pattern. If gaps in per capita steel consumption have widened among nations, gaps in mortality rates have narrowed. If the more developed nations have been moving ahead of the less developed in their per capita consumption of household appliances, the less developed nations have been drawing closer to the more developed in per capita consumption of food proteins. If the inequalities among nations in road networks have increased, the inequalities in levels of primary school enrollment have decreased. In general, however, levels of development in the various measurable items are obviously highly correlated. This means that the relative amount of any one item will not stray far out of line for long without creating tensions for modifications. And this is consistent with the integration of any nation: each sector assisting and depending on the others, railways relate to ports as ports relate to cities, cities create markets for farms, and factories provide goods to each other and to all. Only a coincident measure can represent the central movement of a nation, and it may be defined as one that grows in line with most other series.

The Search for a Working Measure
of Development

Inequalities in development among nations are established by figures.[5] The abundance and variety of contemporary information is a technological miracle much appreciated by the ambitious but unwary investigator who decides to track back almost any series in time. Extinctions of series, unaccountable interruptions of series, reductions in the number of nations covered, emergence of new nations, fabrications or questionable entries, unstandardized reporting procedures, altered assumptions or improvements in data and coding methods, are common and mar most of the several hundred currently accessible series. These problems of reliability severely restrict the scope of available and useful historical statistics.

A useful statistical series satisfies a number of criteria. It provides consecutive annual entries for individual nations; extends forward into the forseeable future and back into the past with nearly uniform reliability; covers nations at various levels of development and on all continents; reports verifiable enumerations of objects or events; shuns arbitrary estimates or conversions; avoids weakening by the development process; and eschews a built-in preference for a type of government or economy.

A careful search of known sources uncovered only five series with broad coverage from the beginning of this century. These annual series include: rail-track length, rail-freight kilometers, rail-passenger kilometers, mail volume, and number of telephone instruments. Other series exist but with far less coverage; for example, iron and steel production.

The problem with rail-track length is that once the rails are laid in a territory, the length does not vary appreciably thereafter; that is, growth is rapid at the start and then it levels off absolutely. Rail-freight kilometers and rail-passenger kilometers have been weakened as measures of development by the invention of the internal combustion engine which gave rise to truck, bus, automobile, and airplane traffic. Mail volume is marred by uneven reporting procedures: sometimes a distinction is drawn between domestic and foreign mail, sometimes mail sent is distinguished from mail received, and at all times mail traffic fluctuates by migratory patterns. Only a telephone series satisfies all the criteria and makes methodological sense as a useful measure by which nations can be meaningfully compared.

Defending the Telephone Series

The telephone series shows the relative quantity of a communication facility in any given nation or region or city or status group. The significance of this measure is that telephones provide accessibility and hence enlarge the sphere of social interaction and division of labor, and at the same time increase the diffusion of information. The telephone thus represents mastery of the environment. Not unreasonably therefore has the telephone been identified as one of the ten inventions that shaped the modern world.[6] And it will remain as a significant measure until another form of two-way communication undermines it.

The modern nation is an extraordinarily interdependent phenomenon. The place of the telephone system in the nation should reflect that interdependency. While there is often some degree of uneven growth even in the most integrated nation, one sector does not move much out-of-line without creating stresses and constraints on the other sectors which tend to force them to catch up. The single decision to increase, for example, the amount of line wire in the telephone system has a number of immediate and obvious implications. It means for one thing that copper usage and imports will be stimulated and this further means that metallurgical practices will be affected as will existing factories producing the finished product. It means also that the lumber industry will be influenced; the highway and railroad systems must be strengthened or expanded to meet the need of increased movement in material and men; linemen must be trained and so must operators, which means increasing the burdens on the school system to upgrade the level of skill of entrants to the labor force. All this is to say that the telephone series may well be considered as a central measure of contemporary development and should parallel other measures of development over time.

The value of the number of telephone instruments as a measure has been recognized by others. Christaller said that the number of telephones is the best single indicator of the number of socioeconomic relationships between two places, and used the series effectively to measure the centrality of urban areas. The telephone series was used as one of the twelve consumption categories by Bennett and was also used as one of the nine indexes of the level of living by Fourastie. It has been used by Lipset and Cutright in their separate studies of development and polity. Finally, it was selected as one of the twenty key series by Caplow and Finsterbusch in their building of the development rank of nations and taken as one of the eighteen core indicators of development by McGranahan.[7]

The telephone series can be carried back to 1913 for a majority of nations, and to just after the First World War for most other nations whose telephone systems were then installed. The principal problem in carrying the series back through the past half century is the estimation of national population for various dates. The numerator—the number of telephones in a nation at a given date—is almost invariably more accurate than the denominator—the total population of the nation.[8]

The telephone series is capable of extending forward indefinitely; that is, so long as its usefulness as a measure is not called into question by another yet unheard-of device which accomplishes the same ends more effectively.

A variety of statistical series exist that have little or no value today because they have been substantially weakened as a result of the development process itself. Figures on literacy rates, automobiles, radios, calories, and the like, are indicative; they no longer differentiate the more advanced nations from one another meaningfully. The telephone series has yet to be weakened by any such ceiling effect and its future as a measure appears promising. At present, the number of telephones is not even close to what might be looked upon as an upper limit. If it is assumed that one thousand telephones per one thousand individuals of a national population is an upper limit, then even the United States of America still has about half way to go before it reaches that point. But there is no need to think in terms of this arbitrary limit. It is conceivable that some day the United States will have more telephones than people; after all, every service store, business firm, church office, labor union, government office, farm, club, school, and military camp is a multiple user and even every household is a potential multiple user.

Because all telephone systems generate directories, the enumeration of telephones is simple and accurate. Annual directories are printed and adjusted for changes—in user address and number when changed and in additions and subtractions to the system. If the telephone system is to function, these directories must be valid and reliable. Thus the potentiality of governmental manipulation of these data is much less of a problem than it might be for other statistical series.

The telephone series is built on verifiable enumerations of instruments and not on arbitrary estimates or conversions like such series as energy consumption or gross national product. Economists now find that GNP, for example, is loaded with insurmountable conceptual difficulties, inaccurate with respect to the rich nations, worthless as regards the poor nations, and impossible as a measure of comparative growth rates;[9] misleading when converted into a standard unit;[10] internally subject to several exchange rates (those for tourists, commercial transactions, and their own citizens desiring foreign currencies);[11] and hopeless in predicting future level of development in terms of annual rates of change.[12]

These charges by economists concerning the character of the GNP cast doubt on the usefulness of that measure for development by anyone outside that profession.[13] The telephone series, in contrast, is enumerable, unequivocally clear, meaningful from one nation to another, and useable as a measure by any social scientist.

Unlike steel production, which requires possession of or proximity to iron and coal reserves, and unlike the share of national income of the top 5 percent of income-receivers, which include only a handful of nations, the telephone series covers nations at various levels of development and is dependent neither on natural resources nor a money economy.

Contrary to still other statistical series, telephones do not have a built-in preference for a given type of government or economy. One cannot rate capitalist and socialist nations, for example, on such measures as the proportion of home ownership or the ratio between public and private expenditures on a ladder of development. Telephones however are unencumbered by these other considerations. They are equally useful and equally significant in a capitalist or socialist economy, in a democratic or totalitarian polity, and thus being free from ideological implications they can serve as an honest means of grading nations in terms and only in terms of their relative mastery of the environment.

Testing the Telephone Series

Now that the number of telephones has been urged as a workable series, it remains to be shown that the series is a reasonably good measure of development at all levels. There are several tests that can be devised which will provide a clear basis for judging and deciding on the usefulness of the series as a measure of development.

In the first test, the telephone series is compared with a recently established index of development. It is an ordinal measure based on a single bundle of twenty quite diverse socioeconomic series all approximating the year 1960. When the mean value of the twenty scores for each nation is taken and arrayed, each nation's development rank is obtained. This carefully worked out index has been applied to the first sixty-six nations in population size for the year 1960 and found to work quite well.[14] Almost all of the relationships to be proposed in Table 2-1 are curvilinear and so would be underestimated by the Pearson product-moment correlation technique. The scores of each series therefore were converted to ranks and the result correlated by the Spearman rank-order correlation method.

Telephones per one thousand of the national populations has a Spearman rank-order correlation coefficient of near unity ($r = 0.97$) with the index of development.[15] Or put differently, the single series of telephones per one thousand alone assigns almost the same development rank to each of the first

Table 2-1

Spearman Correlations: Telephones per 1000 with an Index of Development (and Each of the Foregoing with the 20 Component Series of the Index)

Series	Index of Development	Telephones per 1000
Telephones	0.97	1.00
Age, % of pop. age 5-14 (reversed)	0.67	0.61
Air travel	0.74	0.79
Calories	0.81	0.78
Energy consumption	0.94	0.91
Fertilizer	0.79	0.72
Hospital beds	0.92	0.91
Motor vehicles	0.81	0.87
Movies	0.83	0.73
Newspaper circulation	0.96	0.91
Nonagricultural employment	0.93	0.92
Physicians	0.92	0.88
Printing paper	0.96	0.94
Processed material	0.71	0.64
Radios	0.96	0.94
Railroad network	0.77	0.54
Road network	0.80	0.57
Steel consumption	0.96	0.92
Teachers	0.86	0.80
Urbanization	0.90	0.88

Note: All data are in per capita terms, approximate the year 1960, and refer to the first 66 nations in population size.

sixty-six nations in population as the vastly more intricate measure represented by the averages of the scores for the twenty highly diverse socioeconomic series which go to make up the index. The telephone series, moreover, correlated nearly as well with each of those component series as does the index itself which is based on all of them. With sixteen of the twenty components, the two sets of correlations differ by 0.07 or less, as shown in Table 2-1.

In the second test, the scores of the sixty-six nations on the twenty series were plotted against each other. The purpose of these plots was to determine the boundaries and thresholds of the relationships between each of these series; or more exactly, to determine the extent to which the telephone series may be considered as a coincident measure of development. Three series of the twenty showed very little scatter: urbanization, nonagricultural employment, and teachers. Together they tend to condition the remaining seventeen series. These three series moreover establish the conditions for a substantial telephone system defined for this statistical purpose as one telephone per ten people: that is, the requirements of a substantial telephone system in the year 1960 include the location of at least 13 percent of all dwelling units in urban areas, the utilization of at least 60 percent of the labor force in nonagricultural employment, and a distribution of at least three elementary-secondary school teachers in every thousand of the population. Additionally, the number of telephones grows closely in line with all other series; that is, the telephone series neither conditions nor is conditioned by any of the remaining sixteen series. This means that the growth of the telephone series over time will be proportionate to the growth in these other series. On the basis of this test, therefore, the number of telephones per thousand can be referred to as a central measure of the contemporary process of development.

In the third test, the issue of whether or not this series will work as well through time can be squarely faced. If the number of telephones per thousand of the population predicts with reasonable accuracy the performance of other standardized series, at different points in time, then the telephone series will be conclusively demonstrated as a measure of much more than annual increments of stock or growth of a communication facility. This lone series then would not only represent a fairly good measure of contemporary development but also serve as an accurate substitute for the aforementioned index of development through time. The result of this final test can be seen in Table 2-2.

It will be noted that in Table 2-1 the correlation of the telephone series with the steel series is 0.92; and, in Table 2-2, the correlation is 0.60 in the year 1952.

Table 2-2

Spearman Correlations: Telephones per 1000 with Other Standardized Series at Selected Points in Time (The Number of Nations is in Parentheses)

Telephones	Railroad-Freight Kilometers	Railroad-Passenger Kilometers	Real Income (I.U.)	Iron Production	Steel Production
1913	0.64 (17)	0.69 (16)	0.69 (25)	0.65 (22)	0.67 (22)
1920	0.63 (15)	0.47 (15)	0.66 (14)	0.84 (21)	0.77 (21)
1925	0.62 (17)	0.41 (16)	0.76 (25)	0.70 (22)	0.74 (22)
1938	0.85 (50)	0.86 (44)	0.89 (32)	0.73 (28)	0.63 (29)
1947	0.86 (49)	0.83 (43)	0.90 (31)	0.78 (27)	0.67 (28)
1952	0.84 (49)	0.82 (44)	0.92 (32)	0.71 (28)	0.60 (29)

Sources: Gross figures on rail freight and passenger kilometers, iron and steel for 1913, 1920, and 1925 are taken from appropriate tables in League of Nations, INTERNATIONAL STATISTICAL YEAR-BOOK (1926); for 1938, 1947, and 1952 the figures are from United Nations, STATISTICAL YEARBOOK (1954); national real income for all years is from Colin Clark, THE CONDITIONS OF ECONOMIC PROGRESS (New York: Macmillan, 1957). Only total figures were taken from these documents. All these figures were then divided by the same population figures found in Appendix Table A-1 before the results were correlated.

The reason for this difference is that the former is a steel consumption series while the latter is a steel production series. Again, in Table 2-1, the correlation of the telephone series with the rail-freight-kilometers series is 0.54 and in Table 2-2, the correlation is 0.84 in the year 1952. This difference is due to a greater standardization imposed on the 1960 data. In 1960 the rail-freight-net-ton-kilometers series was controlled for both population and distance, while the series for 1952 and prior in Table 2-2 was controlled only for population.

In summary, the use of telephones as a measure of development is probably the most valid and reliable series now available for the serious consideration of any large number of nations in the twentieth century. It stands up to the most rigorous of procedural criteria, it correlates highly with other selected and diverse measures of development, it is a central measure of contemporary development, and it closely associates with other measures of development over time. Although the number of telephones per 1000, being a single series, cannot be a perfect measure, it is nevertheless thus far the only measure fully tested that will permit detailed national comparisons and the study of world trends at all levels of development and at different points in time.

The Development Hierarchy

It is assumed that each of the world wars of the twentieth century created a sustained massive impact on nations. In principle, therefore, every sovereign or colonial nation becomes a candidate for study: the combatant and the neutral, the occupied and the unoccupied, the rich and the poor. In practice, alas, some nations must be excluded because relevant information is lacking either in number of telephones or in size of population. Of the many nations that had 5 million people or more in the generation following the Second World War, historical statistics were lacking, for one reason or another, for the following: Afghanistan, Ethiopia, East Germany, North Korea, Pakistan, Nepal, Saudi Arabia, North Vietnam, South Vietnam, and Yemen. The resulting selection of nations for study, then, is limited by the extent of coverage of the telephone and population series.

In Table 2-3, seventy nations are located in a development hierarchy, as arrayed by the number of telephones per thousand of their national population, for the year 1952. The nations in the table sort conveniently into upper, middle, and lower strata of development or developed, developing, and underdeveloped nations.

Several features of this hierarchy of rich nations and poor for the year 1952 invite comment.[16] First, proximity to Europe, that is, to the sources of the scientific revolution and nation-building, appears to be the dominant influence. With the exception of Japan and South Africa, every nation in the upper stratum is European or is inhabited by a population of predominantly European origin.

Table 2-3
The Development Hierarchy: 1952 (Based on Telephones per 1,000)

United States	Cuba	Taiwan
Sweden	Chile	Bolivia
Canada	Portugal	Ecuador
New Zealand	Venezuela	Kenya
Switzerland	Soviet Russia	Ceylon
Denmark	Rhodesia	Zambia
Australia	Hungary	Ghana
Norway	Greece	Iran
United Kingdon	Algeria	Philippines
Finland	Brazil	Madagascar
Netherlands	Mexico	Mozambique
Luxemburg	Morocco	Uganda
Belgium	Colombia	Sudan
Austria	Poland	Tanganyika
France	Yugoslavia	Indonesia
West Germany	Romania	Congo
Argentina	Bulgaria	So. Korea
Czechoslovakia	Peru	Malawi
So. Africa	Egypt	India
Uruguay	Malaya	China
Ireland	Iraq	Nigeria
Italy	Turkey	Thailand
Spain	Paraguay	Burma
Japan		

With the exception of Bolivia and Ecuador, no nation in the lower stratum has ever had a large European minority. This pattern emphasizes the fact that contemporary development involves methods of mastering the environment which have diffused from Western Europe to the rest of the world and that still continue to diffuse from a few well-marked nodes.

Second, there are pronounced regional patterns. With the exception of Portugal and Greece, all the nations of Western Europe appear in the upper stratum. Nine out of the thirteen Latin American nations appear in the middle stratum. The Arab nations of the Mediterranean—Algeria, Morocco, Egypt, Iraq, Turkey—are in the middle stratum. Almost all of Asia and tropical Africa are in the lower stratum. India and China occupy adjacent ranks; so do some of the Communist bloc nations; Poland, Yugoslavia, Romania, and Bulgaria.

Third, wealth does not at all depend on national population size or extent of national territory.[17] For example, the array of nations in Table 2-3 correlates insignificantly with the array of nations in extent of territory, 0.24. Change in population size and extent of territory over time therefore will not be taken into account because neither relates with level of development. The crucial standard of comparison will always be expressed in terms of averaged measures of development. So one does not really need, logically or empirically, to know, for example, that the German people and land have expanded and contracted in size within a short span of time; what is essential to know is the achieved level of development at several points in time. Therefore it is quite legitimate to compare West Germany in 1952 with the Third Reich in 1938, with the Weimar Republic in 1925, and with Imperial Germany in 1913.

Fourth, development appears unrelated to type of polity or economy. This is not to suggest that a government lacks effect on the course of development; it is only to suggest that there is nothing causal about type of polity or economy for material improvement. Science and technology are among the chief factors accounting for development, and they have as much influence under a single as under a multiparty system of government, in a capitalist as in a collectivist state. A nation may develop, therefore, in spite of its political regime, although rulers naturally and usually take credit for any such material improvement. Even becoming newly independent matters little one way or the other in terms of either economic or political development.[18] The reason for all this seems clear enough. The nation, or more precisely the government, is concerned first with power or collective strength to meet opposition and secondarily with development or average individual welfare.

Fifth, the same proportions of telephones in nations of vastly different size will set differing social processes in operation if only because they involve greatly differing numbers of people. From the standpoint of effects upon the world, it is often the absolute numbers and not the comparative proportions that matter. This can be illustrated by presenting the 1952 figures for Soviet Russia and Rhodesia. It can be seen in Table 2-4 that the number of telephones per thousand of the Russian population is extraordinarily close to the corresponding figure for Rhodesia. But the total or absolute number of telephones in Soviet Russia is greater than the entire population of Rhodesia. The inference is that the organization of the Soviet Russian telephone company is considerably more complex and differentiated in status and role relationships than that of the Rhodesian company; and, further, that the chance of creative innovation and environment control is greater in Soviet Russia than in Rhodesia.[19]

Table 2-4
Population and Telephones in Soviet Russia and Rhodesia: 1952

Nation	Telephones per 1,000	Total Number of Telephones	Population Size
Soviet Russia	13.17	2,636,600	200,200,000
Rhodesia	13.03	31,666	2,430,000

And sixth, the ranking of a nation in development may be quite different from its ranking in power. This may be illustrated by referring to Soviet Russia again. She appears in the upper stratum of power but in the middle stratum of development. Because Soviet Russia is in the middle stratum of development, this does not mean that she is incapable of sending rockets around the moon, developing airplanes, intercontinental missiles, and all the rest. Such capabilities do not come from averaged but from aggregated figures which show the full effect of population size. Averaged figures (in this instance, telephones per thousand) indicates the relative degree of material welfare of the ordinary man in the nation. In contrast, aggregated figures (or the total number of telephones in the nation) indicates the gross amount of surplus that could be strategically converted in a real or potential demonstration of force: it is this which inevitably stands behind all diplomatic gestures and negotiations.

On the basis of the correlations, the number of telephones impartially sorts the rich nations and poor, or the consumer- and production-oriented nations. It might be argued, however, that Communist governments tend to discourage individuals from having private telephones and this in itself would cripple the value of the series. But such discouragement that exists would exist for all nations, Communist and non-Communist alike, at the same level of development. (For example, according to several informants, the government of Brazil is in conflict with its telephone company and middle-class Peruvians tend to move only into those houses that already have telephones installed in them.) Significantly though, there is not a single Communist nation that added more people than telephones to its territorial unit in the last generation. This obviously means that all Communist nations are developing, even though their rates of improvement may differ, and the telephone series along with many others shows this.

In this research design, I sought a reliable and valid measure which would unequivocally array the largest collection of nations possible as the unit of analysis for study. Telephones per thousand is that measure, it does the job, and by it the development hierarchy of nations can be clearly objectified. While there are, doubtlessly, idiosyncratic features from one place to another, on balance, the measure does reliably reveal the main contours of development and the hierarchy of nations validly.

**Specifying Characteristics of the
Development Hierarchy**

To know where a nation stands in the development hierarchy is to know the principle features of the level of living for the average man of that nation. Such knowledge suggests, moreover, the exchange value of a potential migrant at diverse frontiers, the probable amount of his job skill, the average size of his town and work place, his general lifestyle as a consumer, and his life chances. When a man moves to another nation he willy-nilly moves up or down the development hierarchy. Any such move involves a qualitatively different set of material and psychic consequences for the mover. In either direction, the move often means an absolute personal advancement (or why move?). But in relative terms, the move means something else. If, for example, an Iraqi moved to Italy, his exchange value would be less than the average Italian worker and so he would command less, even though in absolute terms he commands more compared to his point of origin. If, however, he moved to India his condition differs. In Italy, he would become a small fish in a big pond of transportation and communication, education and health, central government and industry; in India, in contrast, he would become a large fish in a small infrastructure pond of rare resources and few facilities. Position in the development hierarchy, therefore, counts absolutely and relatively, materially and psychologically, just as it counts socially and politically.

Nations in terms of relative development line up like beads on a string today, as they did yesterday, and will tomorrow. There is always a top, middle, and bottom to it. But rich nations and poor are not locked in place; change exists. Any change in the position of a nation on such a hierarchy will have ramifications not only for the average man with regard to each of the variables listed above but also for the average man in adjacent nations. Thus millions upon millions of people are affected when only one nation displaces another in the development hierarchy.

Change may best be viewed in terms of the characteristics of hierarchy, any hierarchy of organizations of the same type. As with change, so with persistence: both may be similarly viewed. The four characteristics of hierarchy that may be identified are order, integration, progress, and satisfaction. Each of these characteristics, as specifications for study, may be defined as follows:

1. *Order* refers to the relative rank stability of nations in the development hierarchy over time. The hierarchy exhibits order in the degree to which its members collectively maintain their positions.
2. *Integration* refers to the diminishing of relative spread of nations in the development hierarchy through history. The hierarchy exhibits integration in the degree to which its members as a whole reduce the gaps between their positions.
3. *Progress* refers to the relative speed of material improvement of individual nations in the development hierarchy over time. The hierarchy exhibits progress in the degree to which the average of its members results in increasing mastery over the environment.
4. *Satisfaction* refers to the reduction of relative stress felt by nations in the development hierarchy through history. The hierarchy exhibits satisfaction in the degree to which its members gain internal agreement and external acceptance about their positions.

War is taken as a cause of change. Whether the change is for good or bad, most observers are apt to relate it to war. In all the theoretical possibilities about the relationship between war and development that were discussed in the previous chapter, except the irrelevant—that is, the productive, destructive, and unpredictable—war is taken as a cause of change. So it is natural to inquire if any of the characteristics of the development hierarchy depend on war as an engine of change. More precisely, does war cause nations to retain or lose their positions, narrow or widen the gaps between them, uniformly or unevenly improve their material situation, increase or decrease the amount of stress they have to bear?

These questions that relate to the impact of war on the four characteristics of the development hierarchy most clearly specify the dependent factor of this study. To my knowledge they have not been posed ever before either individually or collectively in quite this manner. They seem worthy of attention and are sufficiently interesting in and for themselves to pursue because next to nothing is known about them and answers, however partial and tentative, will provide far more information about the workings of war on development and world inequality than is presently available. Additionally, to the extent that answers are forthcoming, a basis could be laid for a greater degree of confidence with which to judge the various theoretical possibilities advanced earlier. These questions, then, will be systematically explored in the light of the telephone measure throughout later chapters.

But war affects order, integration, progress, and the satisfaction of nations only indirectly—that is, through other variables. What it affects directly are the values of certain mechanisms thought to determine the existing magnitudes of these characteristics of the development hierarchy. In my opinion, the mechanisms that serve the specifications of the dependent factor are culture, communication, cohesion, and consensus. In subsequent chapters, I shall endeavor to substantiate this claim of relationship between each mechanism and each specification by referring to a vast literature. Once that field is surveyed, an emerging theory of development and world inequality will hopefully result. At this point, however, I can only identify and discuss these mechanisms; I will do so ad seriatim.

1. *World culture.* The application of ideas and principles, values and beliefs, to the effort to master the environment enables nations to maintain or secure their positions over time. Differential application of this culture explains the inequalities among nations in development. Continuous differential application through history explains the structure of rank stability.

2. *Global communication.* The utilization of tourists, mail, telegrams, money, trade, and migrants to diffuse the principles and products of culture enables nations to conserve or decrease the distance between their positions over time. Differential utilization of the means of such communi-

cation accounts for the variance of dispersion among nations. Continuous differential utilization through history accounts for the degree of rank spread.

3. *National cohesion.* The mobilization of organizational components within nations under the ubiquitous condition of world competition enables nations to strengthen or further their mastery over the environment through time. Differential mobilization explains varying rank speeds of material improvement by nations. Continuous differential mobilization through history explains the patterns of such speed.

4. *Foreign and domestic consensus.* The achievement of agreement and acceptance from diverse sources to the effort to reduce rank stress enables nations to conserve or increase their satisfaction with positions over time. (But the more such consensus required for the attainment of satisfaction, the more dissatisfaction will be expressed.) Differential achievement of consensus accounts for the extent of rank stress reduction among nations. Continuous differential achievement through history accounts for the shape of stress.

Into these ongoing mechanisms—culture, communication, cohesion, and consensus—that sustain the development hierarchy, comes war. Qualitatively put, order in the development hierarchy either increases or decreases or stays the same as a result of war; if order decreases, for example, the relative rank stability of nations in the hierarchy would depend less on the differential application of world instrumental culture and would reflect significant discontinuities in the influence of science and technology. Integration in the development hierarchy either increases or decreases or stays the same as a result of war; if integration decreases, for example, then the relative spread of nations in the hierarchy would become less susceptible to the influence of global communication and would reflect a considerable diminution of international contact through rises in border impermeabilities or other barriers. Progress in the development hierarchy either accelerates or decelerates or stays the same as a result of war; if progress decelerates, for example, then the relative speed of improvement of nations in the hierarchy would cancel out prewar differences created by the amount of cohesion mobilized and would reflect internal breakdowns in the workings of complex organizations. Satisfaction in the development hierarchy either increases or decreases or stays the same as a result of war; if satisfaction decreases, for example, then the relative satisfaction of nations in the hierarchy would depend less on the structures of consensus and would reflect the unresolved stresses and strains which arise from war-induced rank changes.

If war is to affect development and world inequality, positively or negatively, then it must alter or warp these mechanisms by either stimulating them to higher levels or stalling their work. War must bring important increases or decreases to world culture; it must create or crash through barriers of global communication;

it must build up or break down national cohesion; and it must add to or subtract from the sources of foreign and domestic consensus. For example, an important piece of information on how to control the environment must be gained or lost, an important method of diffusing that information must succeed or fail to penetrate national borders, an important organizational technique for administering that information must be shown to have improved or faltered, and an important source of internal agreement or external acceptance about position in the hierarchy must have arisen or disappeared. These possibilities exist and war can only affect development and world inequality through them.

Nations in the development hierarchy may be differentially affected by war depending on whether or not they participate actively and depending on their prewar level of development. A detailed specification of the independent factor, war, is presented in the next chapter.

3 War

*As long as there is anything to
divide or take, there will be wars.*
Baron Dietrich Heinrich von Bulow

The world wars of the twentieth century have been designated by many observers as total. Perhaps the details of that designation were first presented by Ludendorff, who argued that preparation for war must come before the fighting, that the military command must have unchallenged authority, that the war should be fought by the whole nation and not merely by the armed forces, that it should be fought over the whole area of the enemy territory, and that all methods of propaganda should be used to strengthen the home front, provided the information distributed was based on truth.[1]

Since Ludendorff, a number of analysts have seen the close correspondence between the military and society with increased clarity. For example, Fuller says that "the larger armies grow the more dependent do they become on industry to equip, arm and supply them both in peace and war. Industry, the postal and telegraph system, etc., are organized for war, for a nation in arms demands a nation of armourers and technicians to sustain and maintain it."[2] And Hawtrey writes that "if a country is to provide equipment for its military forces from its own resources, it must have a great and adequately organised manufacturing population, and this manufacturing population must be changed over from the peace-time industries to the production of munitions and other warlike requisites."[3]

Total war, moreover, means total utilization of social and motivational resources. Utilization of social resources is surely total if the nation recruits artists, engineers, farmers, financiers, inventors, manual laborers, manufacturers, organizers, propagandists, scientists and teachers; and mobilizes communication, education, family, health, production, recreation, religious and transportation systems.[4] Utilization of motivational resources must be total, according to Beveridge, because the "one thing that matters now is immediate output, both in quality and quantity. . . . Moreover, being total in war is not simply a question of how one behaves at work; one can wage total war or fail to wage it in one's home, by being a saver or a waster, a cheerer or a grouser."[5]

The outcome of total war in the twentieth century depends more on the availability of men, minds, money and material than on the inequality of initial mobilization, skilled troops and daring generals. In this century, "The significant relationship has been that of *total* resources. Hence the outcome of battles has tended to become less important than the security of the belligerents' mobilization bases." Thus, such wars are won not by battles in the open field, but by attrition of resources: "the gradual wearing down of the enemy's mobilizable potential . . . essentially representing the last stage of a siege."[6]

The Impact of Total War Upon the Nation

War creates a sustained massive impact upon the nation which accelerates four key social processes promoting cohesion: (1) centralization, or increasing the amount of control; (2) consociation, or increasing the amount of conformity; and (3) cooperation, or increasing the amount of consensus. These three social processes determine (4) completion, or increases in the amount of per capita output contribution. The acceleration of these processes as a result of war has been noticed by others.

The higher the level of centralization in a nation, the more control government exercises over its members. The autonomies or semiautonomies of the localities seem unjustified to the bureaucratic services that distribute food, raw materials, or instructions. Two rules forced upon a nation at war are organization and rationalization. Rules which in time of peace are applied only to certain sectors are in time of war applied to the whole nation. Leaders work against all hindrances and move to bring uniformity into localities for the concentration of powers of decision at the center. One of the earliest sociologists to take the process seriously was Herbert Spencer, who asserted that war leads to an expansion of governmental control, to its centralization, to its despotism, to an increase of social stratification, and to a decrease of autonomy and self-government of the people. In this process, war tends to transform a nation into an army, and an army into a nation.[7]

The higher the level of consociation in a nation, the less conflict over problems, procedures, and policies. War not only stimulates more contact between segments within a nation, it also clearly divides members from nonmembers. "The relation of comradeship and peace in the we-group and that of hostility and war towards others-group are correlative to each other. The exigencies of war with outsiders are what makes for peace inside, lest internal discord should weaken the we-group for war. . . . Loyalty to the group, sacrifice for it, hatred and contempt for outsiders, brotherhood within, warlikeness without—all grow together, common products of the same situation."[8]

And the higher the level of cooperation in a nation, the more willing are members (individuals and organizations) to consent to the common cause. "War puts the nation in a strained condition, and the burden of armament expenditures stimulates the people to the self-consciousness of an effort on a firmer basis of nationalism. Such a state of the national spirit gives the best opportunity for improvement in national economy, and how much more should it be the case with the high-spiritedness of the nation elevated through a victory in war?"[9]

War relaxes the usual limits operating on these social processes and so occasions higher completion rates. The higher the level of cohesion in a nation, the higher its contribution in per capita outputs. "For it can be demonstrated, I am confident, that there is only one purpose to which a whole society can be directed by a deliberate plan. That purpose is war, and there is no other."[10] This increased cohesion permits nations to work more effectively to meet its two basic objectives. "The first is to make the national output as big as possible, by bringing into employment all available labour and material resources and by increasing the efficiency of those who are already employed. The second is to make radical changes in the sort of things which are produced, to divert resources away from non-essentials and into the service of the war-machine."[11]

Departures from Cohesion during War

But these processes do not ever operate unrestrictedly. Change in one is limited by its dependency upon the others. As centralization increases, for example, it must impinge upon consociation and cooperation; and vice versa. The problem of the independence and dependence of social processes, however, will not be pursued, primarily because sufficient evidence is lacking. The more modest problem of identifying departures from simple linear increases in each process will be presented briefly instead as a guard against thinking that these key processes operate without restriction.

War tends to strengthen and extend the amount of government control in a nation. But this acceleration of centralization is not uninterrupted, and from nation to nation there is opposition to government during times of war. For instance, the Moslems and Tartars inhabiting the Yaila Mountain Range in the Crimea "rebelled against the Soviet regime even before the German armies drew near." The West Ukrainian population near the Carpathian Mountains were "bitterly anti-Soviet." This feeling of opposition applied to a number of Volhynia Ukrainians and to almost all Galician Ukrainians.[12] During times of war, a government can usually expect resistance for varying reasons from almost any quarter of the population: business and labor, church and school, pacifists, and fifth columnists. Postwar movements in favor of decentralization have been more frequently discussed in the literature and they range from Magna Charta to the Republican victory in the American congressional elections of 1946; other forms of postwar reaction range from revolution, through civil war, through minor internal disturbances, to change in political parties.

War tends to strengthen and extend the amount of conformity in a nation. But this acceleration of consociation is not uniform, and from nation to nation there is group factionalism during time of war. For instance:

There is some evidence that the French Right was lukewarm in its determination to push the war effort and to win at any price. Moreover, the feeling that "Hitler was better than Blum" was widespread among the French bourgeoisie. . . . They found no justification for a war waged in order to consolidate the rule of the Left. In many bourgeois quarters, the struggle against the Left with its "creeping socialism" ranked higher than the struggle against Germany.

But the bourgeoisie was not alone in putting class interest above national interest.

The most extreme antiwar stand was taken by the Communists: to them, fighting was a sacrilege once Moscow had hurled its anathema against the "imperialist" war. In the French Socialist Party, too, there was a strong faction, led by Paul Faure, which opposed the war on pacifist and Marxist grounds. This group believed that the war would arrest social progress and enrich the bourgeoisie while placing all the burdens on the lower classes. The domestic class struggle was an absolute; to suspend it in favor of the war effort was to betray the workers. Here, too, domestic political objectives took precedence over the patriotic motive of winning the war at any cost.[13]

War tends to strengthen and extend the amount of consensus in a nation. But this acceleration of cooperation is imperfect, and from nation to nation there is some lack of willing participation during times of war. Extreme individual departures from the classic *dulce et decorum pro patria mori* are well known and they range from Alcibiades to Quisling. Perhaps equally well known are the milder forms of departure, for instance, the following:

My patriotism is of the kind which is outraged by the notion that the United States never was a great nation until in a petty three months' campaign it knocked to pieces a poor, decrepit, bankrupt old state like Spain.[14]

The more interesting departures however are those of organizations within a nation. Some organizations are so set against the establishment that no amount of persuasion or even coercion gains their willingness to go along for the duration. Organizational departures are important because they wield counter-vailing power. The justification for such departures among the German social democrats in the First World War has been put forth by Liebknecht.[15] Publics, whether organized or not, do not respond to appeals for support automatically, and when they do finally show interest, it has been observed that consensus fluctuates through sets of interposing conditions, for example, a new or renegotiated foreign treaty, a market change, a horror story, an invasion, and so forth.[16]

And war tends to strengthen and extend the amount of per capita output contribution in a nation. But this acceleration of completion varies from one nation to another in war. For example, "Hitler demanded far less from his people than Churchill and Roosevelt did from their respective nations. The discrepancy between the total mobilization of labor forces in democratic England and the casual treatment of this question in authoritarian Germany is proof of the regime's anxiety not to risk any shift in the popular mood. The German leaders were not disposed to make sacrifices themselves or to ask sacrifices of the people. They tried to keep the morale of the people in the best possible state by concessions."[17] Contrary to popular impression, then, Germany during the war years did not operate like a frictionless machine; conflict was rife between various ruling elites of big business and the state, the army and the party, and this conflict was complicated at every turn by the inordinate needs of government bureaucracy that moved at a snail's pace even during escalating emergencies. The consequence of such conflict in Germany can be objectified in per capita output contribution: armaments and steel production in any year of the Second World War lagged behind the per capita figures for any comparable year of the First World War.[18]

Within any nation tensions exist that hold it together and split it apart. The key social processes do not exhibit simple linear increases, for the situation of war, while easing the usual restraints on the patterned operations guiding those processes, simultaneously creates other restraints on them. This naturally inhibits any nation from realizing its own potential. Cohesion varies from one nation to another, and each stands in relative approximation to an idea of perfect organization during war and peace. On the whole, however, and despite identifiable departures, war tends to accelerate each social process and functions to increase cohesion.

The enormous stimulus that war gives to national cohesion and thus to completion is perhaps the most ironic fact of war. In spite of the withdrawal of many young men and in spite of the shifts from one good or service to another, wartime control of output often yields astonishing results relative to peacetime conditions. But while the nation works harder to raise its production, the costs of war are also rising. Hence, war consumes much of the product it stimulates. So at this point, it is not clear how the scale would look once gains and costs are placed on it. It will be the purpose of this study to find out which one outweighs the other, under various circumstances.

Specifying the Independent Factor

The foregoing commentary on the character of total war and its impact upon the nation suggests two specifications of the independent factor. The first is the extent of a nation's participation in war and the other is its prewar level of development. Various combinations of these will be introduced when appropriate as well as the interesting phenomenon of military occupation. These specifications are assumed to be the limiting condition that could determine which nations might be affected, in what way, and by how much. Nations are obviously not all alike—they differ importantly in terms of these two specifications. But whether these differences actually make a difference in postwar recovery will have to be seen. If postwar recovery differences exist, then they will be indicated by the carefully selected measure of the number of telephones per thousand of national populations.

Note well, however, that in neither specification of the independent factor—degree of war participation and prewar level of development—was losing or winning a war introduced as a further refinement. Victory and defeat under twentieth century conditions possess more of a political than a developmental flavor. Politics refers to collective strength to meet opposition in which the outcome is either victory or defeat. Development refers to the material welfare of the average individual, and it is measured in terms of increases or decreases over time. These notions are clearly distinct phenomena. In this work, I am interested in determining whether or not war affects development and, if so, to what extent.

Degree of War Participation

The first specification of the independent factor, war, is the extent to which a nation is involved in war. The importance of participation lies in the degree to which a nation mobilizes its processes of cohesion in order to increase its rate of completion under the condition of war. And it is rate of completion both in absolute and in relative terms that differentiates one nation from another in postwar recovery.

A number of good measures of participation exist, at least, in theory. For example, degree of manpower mobilization, battle-death ratios, and percentage of defense expenditures would certainly qualify as reasonably good measures of participation despite any and all attending qualifications one might append to each. These measures would reveal, either singly or in combination, something about the extent to which men, minds, money, and material are committed in war. These measures exist, however, only in thought. Many documents were combed in order to construct such a series for all nations but the search proved fruitless.

Still some measure is required with which the extent of participation could be indicated. Although the main fighting of the world wars tended to be localized in a handful of areas, the threats and gestures, the preparations and supplies were worldwide in scope. If both wars present the same global impacts and have simultaneous global repercussions, then it could be assumed that the longer any one nation actively participated, the greater its mobilization. It was on this basis that I thought of time as an indicator of participation; that is, a nation's time in war can be used as an accurate and trustworthy measure by any investigator, even though it may be taken as an approximate measure of participation.

Viewed in terms of other possible criteria rather than time in war, some of the nations would line up differently. I am inclined to believe, however, that the difference would not be significant for the purposes at hand. Regardless of the few important exceptions, which I readily assume, time is still an interesting variable in terms of which to think about participation. So even though it is a rough measure in the sense that a few exceptions exist, it is perhaps the best available measure of participation. Its other qualities are that it is simple, objective, convenient, and universally applicable.

But astonishingly enough, given the enormity of the world wars, the amount of ink used to recount them, and the high visibility of nations in the twentieth century, a single or even a handful of sources does not exist which contains this information on the number of years of participation. As a matter of fact, many books and articles were consulted in order to obtain this one detail on the nations that appear in Table 3-1. Inasmuch as the list of references would exceed a typewritten page, none will be referred to here.

With a few exceptions, nations signing a declaration of war are considered to be participants. Some nations, while declaring war, however were not participants. Such nations as Bolivia, Ecuador, Peru, and Uruguay were officially neutral until the last few months of World War I. The entry of these nations on the side of the Allies at this late date, involving little or no real contribution to the war effort, makes their participation virtually a paper one: their inclusion in the category of participants would unduly reduce the meaning of the distinction being attempted. Another exception is Iran, which, contrariwise, did not declare war but was nonetheless occupied and the scene of extensive fighting in the First World War and occupied during the Second World War; the occupations lasted seven and five years, respectively, and Iran is therefore classified as a full participant in each war. A final exception refers to those nations who merely severed diplomatic relations with Germany or Italy or Japan but did not otherwise participate in the Second World War; such nations include Argentina, Chile, Colombia, Ecuador, Peru, and Turkey.

The colonies presented a special problem. Although they technically participated in the declarations of war signed by the mother nations, it was apparent from such data as were readily available that their participation ranged through every gradation from negligible to significant. It seemed reasonable, therefore, to classify as participating all colonies of participating mother nations, but to make some modification in the extent of participation in the case of colonies whose participation seemed clearly to differ in intensity in terms of some ulterior indicators—like troop commitments, fighting on home soil, or occupation—from that assigned to their mother nations on the basis of time. Thus, regardless of the duration of participation of the involved mother nations, those colonies whose participation in a war was clearly important—for example, Algeria—were classified as full participants; and those whose participation was not revealed by any data to be of great extent—for example, Zambia—were classified as marginal and

Table 3-1
Years of Participation in World War (Nations to Be Studied)

Nation	Duration		Nation	Duration	
	The First World War	The Second World War		The First World War	The Second World War
Algeria	3	4	Madagascar	3	4
Argentina	0	0	Malawi	1	1
Australia	4	5	Malaya	0	3
Austria	4	5	Mexico	0	3
Belgium	4	5	Morocco	3	4
Bolivia	0	2	Mozambique	1	0
Brazil	1	3	Netherlands	0	5
Bulgaria	3	3	New Zealand	4	5
Burma	*	3	Nigeria	2	2
Canada	4	5	Norway	0	5
Ceylon	2	5	Paraguay	0	0
Chile	0	0	Peru	0	0
China	1	5	Philippines	0	3
Colombia	0	1	Poland	*	5
Congo	3	3	Portugal	2	0
Cuba	1	3	Rhodesia	2	2
Czechoslovakia	*	4	Romania	2	4
Denmark	0	5	South Africa	4	5
Ecuador	0	0	Soviet Russia	4	3
Egypt	0	2	Spain	0	0
Finland	0	4	Sudan	1	2
France	4	5	Sweden	0	0
Ghana	1	2	Switzerland	0	0
Greece	2	5	Taiwan	3	4
Hungary	4	4	Tanganyika	*	2
India	4	5	Thailand	1	3
Indonesia	0	3	Turkey	4	0
Iran	4	4	Uganda	*	1
Iraq	1	3	United Kingdom	4	5
Ireland	*	0	United States	1	3
Italy	3	3	Uruguay	0	0
Japan	4	5	Venezuela	0	0
Kenya	*	1	West Germany	4	5
Korea	3	4	Yugoslavia	4	5
Luxemburg	4	5	Zambia	1	1

*The asterisks in the table signify that other data are missing for these seven nations before or after the First World War.

Note: This is the same roster as that of Table 2-3.

are arbitrarily classified as having participated for one year. This still creates an element of noncomparability within the participation classification, but it is felt to comport as closely as practicable with reality.

Nations are easily distinguished by the number of years they have participated as combatants in war.[19] If a nation officially participated in a world war for three years or more, it will be classified as active in that war; if it participated less, it will be classified as marginal. All other nations will be considered neutral. This last designation is obviously residual and includes all those nations that did not officially participate in a world war. The categories of war involvement for either world war, then, are active, marginal, and neutral. The resulting classification of nations can be seen in Table 3-2.

Both world wars can be considered as a single event or what is here called the Thirty-One Years War: 1914-45. Nations are distinguished by the number of years they have participated as combatants in that long war. To qualify for maximum participation in the Thirty-One Years War, a nation must have officially participated for six or more years; for medium participation, three or more years; for minimum participation, less than three years. The neutral category is a residual one and includes any nation that did not officially participate in either world war. The result of classifying nations by participation in the Thirty-One Years War can be seen in Table 3-3.

Table 3-2
Arrays of Nations, by Degree of War Participation: The First World War and The Second World War

The First World War: 1914-17

Active: Algeria, Australia, Austria, Belgium, Bulgaria, Canada, Congo, France, Hungary, India, Iran, Italy, Japan, Luxemburg, Madagascar, New Zealand, South Africa, Soviet Russia, Turkey, United Kingdom, West Germany, and Yugoslavia. ($N = 22$)

Marginal: Brazil, Ceylon, China, Cuba, Ghana, Greece, Iraq, Korea, Malawi, Morocco, Mozambique, Nigeria, Portugal, Rhodesia, Romania, Sudan, Taiwan, Thailand, United States, and Zambia. ($N = 20$)

Neutral: Argentina, Bolivia, Chile, Colombia, Denmark, Ecuador, Egypt, Finland, Indonesia, Malaya, Mexico, Netherlands, Norway, Paraguay, Peru, Philippines, Spain, Sweden, Switzerland, Uruguay, and Venezuela. ($N = 21$)

The Second World War: 1939-45

Active: Algeria, Australia, Austria, Belgium, Brazil, Bulgaria, Burma, Canada, Ceylon, China, Congo, Cuba, Czechoslovakia, Denmark, Finland, France, Greece, Hungary, India, Indonesia, Iran, Italy, Japan, Korea, Luxemburg, Madagascar, Malaya, Mexico, Morocco, Netherlands, New Zealand, Norway, Philippines, Poland, Romania, South Africa, Soviet Russia, Taiwan, Thailand, United Kingdon, United States, West Germany, and Yugoslavia. ($N = 43$)

Marginal: Bolivia, Colombia, Egypt, Ghana, Iraq, Kenya, Malawi, Nigeria, Rhodesia, Sudan, Tanganyika, Uganda, and Zambia. ($N = 13$)

Neutral: Argentina, Chile, Ecuador, Ireland, Mozambique, Paraguay, Peru, Portugal, Spain, Sweden, Switzerland, Turkey, Uruguay, and Venezuela. ($N = 14$)

Table 3-3

Array of Nations, by Degree of War Participation, The Thirty-One Years War: 1914-45

Maximum:	Algeria, Australia, Austria, Belgium, Bulgaria, Canada, Congo, France, Greece, Hungary, India, Iran, Italy, Japan, Luxemburg, Madagascar, Morocco, New Zealand, South Africa, Soviet Russia, United Kingdom, West Germany, and Yugoslavia. ($N = 23$)
Medium:	Brazil, Ceylon, China, Cuba, Denmark, Finland, Indonesia, Korea, Malaya, Mexico, Netherlands, Norway, Philippines, Romania, Taiwan, Thailand, Turkey, and United States. ($N = 18$)
Minimum:	Bolivia, Colombia, Egypt, Ghana, Iraq, Malawi, Mozambique, Nigeria, Portugal, Rhodesia, Sudan, and Zambia. ($N = 12$)
Neutral:	Argentina, Chile, Ecuador, Paraguay, Peru, Spain, Sweden, Switzerland, Uruguay, and Venezuela. ($N = 10$)

The relationship between participation in war and subsequent recovery is not easily determined by merely viewing Tables 3-2 and 3-3. That will require testing by examining arrays of nations in each category of participation over the same time span.

The theoretical possibilities presented in the first chapter that obtain between war and development also obtain here. The only difference is taking into account this intervening variable of participation. If development associates positively with degree of participation through war, that is, if the more war-involved nations exhibit greater postwar recovery, then this confirms the productive hypothesis; if it associates inversely, this confirms the destructive hypothesis; if it associates variably, this confirms the unpredictable hypothesis; and if it remains unaffected, this confirms the irrelevant hypothesis. All of these hypotheses, and others, will be tested in the following chapters.

One of the salient features of the Second World War was the phenomenon of military occupation of many nations over long periods of time by both Allied and Axis armies. Occupied nations warrant close inspection because the event of occupation appears overwhelmingly coercive. It does not matter in this instance how occupation was accomplished: by force and violence or fear and terror or some combination of each. The situation for the nation, as soon as it comes under steady occupation, not temporary invasion, is that it loses its ability to select from instrumental world culture, it loses its contact with the network of global communications, it loses its claim to foreign and domestic consent, and it loses its control, however partially, over the key social processes like centralization, consociation, cooperation, and completion (of output).

Occupation is defined in this study as the exercise of effective control by a foreign power over an existing government and its territory. This definition thus excludes such extensive land occupations as those suffered by the Russians and the Chinese because the governments were never brought under effective control. Any nation occupied in the time period extending from 1939 through 1945 becomes a candidate for study. This time limit naturally excludes the postwar occupations of Germany and Japan. Lastly, in order for an occupied nation to be considered for study, it must appear in Table 3-1. This important consideration excludes such occupied nations as Vietnam and Ethiopia.

The control exercised by a foreign power may be understandably strict, as in the case of the German occupation of Norway during the Second World War, or necessarily loose, as in the British occupation of Madagascar during the same war. Nevertheless, occupation means that the government of the occupied nation has lost control to the point where it can no longer make decisions independent of the occupying power.

As a result of an occupied nation's swings from autonomy to occupation and back to autonomy again, the capacity for recovery might be weakened. It has frequently been supposed that such a loss of autonomy must have some deleterious effect on the occupied nation's postwar recovery capacity. Occupied nations might bear costs that outweigh the gains and opportunities resulting from contact with occupying forces; then, too, the reverse might be true.

Prewar Level of Development

Continuing the job of specifying the independent factor of war, we may now turn to the prewar level of development of the nation. I am guessing that a nation's postwar recovery depends on its prewar level of development for the following reason. A more developed nation exhibits greater mastery over the environment than a less developed nation; and despite war, it should thereby be better able to apply the cultural heritage in order to maintain its position, be better able to utilize the communications network in order to conserve its distance between adjoining nations, be better able to manage foreign and domestic consent in order to cope with rank change, and be better able to mobilize the internal cohesion processes in order to improve its material

Table 3-4
Active Nations, by Whether Occupied or Not

The Second World War

Occupied: Algeria, Austria, Belgium, Bulgaria, Burma, China, Czechoslovakia, Denmark, Egypt, Finland, France, Greece, Hungary, Indonesia, Iran, Iraq, Italy, Luxemburg, Madagascar, Malaya, Morocco, Netherlands, Norway, Philippines, Poland, Romania, and Yugoslavia. ($N = 27$)

Nonoccupied: Australia, Brazil, Canada, Ceylon, Congo, Cuba, India, Japan, Korea, Mexico, New Zealand, South Africa, Soviet Russia, Taiwan, Thailand, United Kingdom, United States, and West Germany. ($N = 18$)

situation. Such is the nature of mastery. But nothing is given, and the rutted road of history is strewn with fallen nations that were high and mighty in their time, who were apparently unable to ameliorate the evil consequences of war.

The importance of relative prewar development as an independent factor can be illuminated by comparing the postwar recovery of the German people at two very different historical periods; that is, after the first Thirty Years War (1618-48) and after the second Thirty Years War (1914-45). After the first Thirty Years War, recovery seemed impossible as it proved to be slow, thwarting, and brutal for about a half a century. After the second Thirty Years War, in contrast, a quick recovery was not unexpected and the Germans took in fact about a decade to regain their prewar level of development. This noteworthy difference in postwar recovery can be accounted for by a difference in prewar level of development and not by the Marshall Plan and other forms of aid which are usually insignificant in proportion to the resources of nations, or even in relation to the inputs associated with normal growth. Although the facts of twentieth century Germany probably require no comment, a word appears in order on the earlier Germany. Output declined in Germany from about 1550 to 1618 and so, relative to itself and, more importantly, to other nations, its growth was decelerating even before the war started; and all observers agree that the war might have contributed to an even but slow rate of development for the remainder of the seventeenth century (with the possible exception of the Palatinate from 1652 to 1680); consequently, Germany only began to expand its output sometime during the early eighteenth century.[20]

It would be seriously misleading to account for the difference in German postwar recovery by referring merely to time, the seventeenth versus the twentieth centuries, or by reference to any relevant time-bound aspect like the then existing state of the world instrumental culture, the then existing breadth and intensity of global communication, the then existing level of international awareness and consent, the then existing structure and function of imperial organization, or even to the then existing character of war. Prewar level of development seems the best available explanation of postwar recovery capacity. The idea may be further illustrated. Another participant in the first Thirty Years War, Spain, also suffered losses in power and prestige—which incidentally France acquired as a result of that fighting. In contrast to Germany, however, Spain's ability to recover was much stronger because its prewar level of development was higher. Apparently Spain began to level off in rate of growth just before 1600, and this trend was not interrupted until the first quarter of the eighteenth century. But although Spain's path roughly followed the same curve as that of Germany, it was not as bad as that of Germany.[21]

One last example will suffice to demonstrate the importance of prewar level of development as an independent factor determining postwar recovery capacity. The story of Italy during the fifteenth and sixteenth centuries is so well known that it need only be mentioned to evoke a vision of the most developed area of

Table 3-5

Active Nations, by Development Stratum

The Second World War

Upper: Australia, Austria, Belgium, Canada, Czechoslovakia, Denmark, Finland, France, Italy, Japan, Luxemburg, Netherlands, New Zealand, Norway, South Africa, United Kingdom, United States, and West Germany. ($N = 18$)

Middle: Algeria, Brazil, Bulgaria, Cuba, Greece, Hungary, Malaya, Mexico, Morocco, Poland, Romania, Soviet Russia, and Yugoslavia. ($N = 13$)

Lower: Burma Ceylon, China, Congo, India, Indonesia, Iran, Korea, Madagascar, Philippines, Taiwan, and Thailand. ($N = 12$)

Europe: its industries were the most productive; its trade was the most extensive; its banking facilities were the most used; its universities were the most populated; its people were the most literate, travelled, and consulted; and its cities—Palermo, Naples, Venice, and Rome—were the largest and their division of labor the most complex. Its demonstrated capacity for immediate war recovery can therefore be explained by its unparalleled place in the development hierarchy of that time. "From 1490 to 1560 Italy was the prey of foreign invaders; but she was doing more for human progress in art and letters than all the other European nations put together."[22]

Several propositions can be derived from the hypothesis that difference in postwar recovery depends on prepwar level of development. The first should be obvious: it is likely that postwar recovery time for warring nations unequal in prewar development will be longer for the poorer and shorter for the richer nation. The second follows naturally, that the variation in postwar recovery time for warring nations nearly equal in prewar development will probably be slight. The third assumes, not unreasonably, that world war influences neutral nations too, so that among neutral nations the more developed will likely find in war an opportunity to increase their production and the less developed will probably find war a hindrance to their single export and multiple imports and thus be adversely affected, largely as a result of blockades. And the fourth assumes that among occupied nations, also, differences in postwar recovery time depend on prewar levels of development, longer recovery for the poorer and shorter for the richer occupied nations. (See Tables 3-5 and 3-6.)

No discussion of even a single nation's postwar recovery is meaningful or acceptable without referring to the postwar recovery of other nations as well. A relationship exists between a nation's prewar level of development and its rate of postwar recovery relative to other nations. To simplify what could be a difficult statement about how the rate of a nation's postwar recovery relates to its achieved prewar level of development, through war, four possible hypotheses will be formally identified. The possibilities in the relationship between war, level of development, and rate of postwar recovery include:

Table 3-6
Occupied Nations, by Development Stratum

The Second World War

Upper: Austria, Belgium, Czechoslovakia, Denmark, Finland, France, Italy, Luxemburg, Netherlands, and Norway. ($N = 10$)

Middle: Algeria, Bulgaria, Greece, Hungary, Iraq, Egypt, Malaya, Morocco, Poland, Romania, and Yugoslavia. ($N = 11$)

Lower: Burma, China, Indonesia, Iran, Madagascar, and Philippines. ($N = 6$)

1. The productive hypothesis—that rate of recovery associates positively with achieved level of development through war; nations in the upper stratum of development recover faster than nations in the lower stratum, even when the material situation of poorer nations has improved in absolute terms. According to this formulation, war causes prewar differences in development among nations to redound in further inequalities;

2. The destructive hypothesis—that rate of recovery associates inversely with achieved level of development through war; differences among nations will persist only until the plateau of full recovery has been realized. According to this formulation, the effect of war is in the reduction of prewar differences in development among nations (though not necessarily to the point of equalization);

3. The unpredictable hypothesis—that rate of recovery associates variably with achieved level of development through war; occasionally nations in one stratum of development will improve their material situation faster than nations in another stratum and vice versa. According to this formulation, the prewar differences in development among nations are less important than certain concomitant war conditions which produce postwar variations in recovery;

4. The irrelevant hypothesis—that rate of recovery does not associate with achieved level of development through war; nations in the upper stratum of development do not exhibit significantly different rates of postwar recovery than nations in other strata. According to this formulation, the effect of war is indiscernible in both prewar level of development among nations and in their postwar rate of recovery, thus prewar and postwar differences remain unaltered by war.

My aim, in the chapters to follow, will be to explore these hypotheses in the light of a measure (the number of telephones per thousand of national populations) which indicates socioeconomic development. I will attempt to show the extent to which the First and Second World Wars affected the rich nations and the poor. In order to do so, I must set the points in time for study. This will be the final requirement to be met before an analysis of the results can begin.

Setting Points in Time for Study

As war has a beginning and an end, so its effects should be roughly parallel to that time sequence. I shall assume that it is reasonable to trace these time-bound effects for only a handful of years after the termination of war but no further, because other factors loom up to weaken or strengthen whatever changes war has wrought.[23]

War is either official or unofficial: official, when declarations of intent to start and cease are exchanged between opposing nations; and unofficial, when organized fighting starts and ceases without prior notice between combatants. The wars of 1914-18 and 1939-45 are considered official wars; they are also designated as world wars and in this writing that convention will be adhered to. Within those time periods there were many nations fighting many wars for many reasons. In the first time period, 1914-18, 44 nations were variously involved in 79 bilateral wars; in the second time period, 1939-45, 75 nations were variously involved in at least 161 bilateral wars. (A bilateral war is one between two nations and so recognized by the opponents; for example, the German-Russian war of 1941-45 is called "The Russian Campaign" by the Germans and "The Great Patriotic War" by the Russians.) With so much going on in each period involving so many nations directly and indirectly, it is not unreasonable to inquire into the effect all that activity had on the inequalities in development among nations.

The unit of time utilized in studies of world development varies from one investigator to another, thus failing to establish any basis for comparability. So until different investigators begin to agree on the significant units of time for the short and the long terms before and after important events, little continuity will be achieved and hard-earned results will remain discrete and noncumulative.

The first point in time selected for purposes of this study is the year prior to war. The year prior to war will serve as a natural base for postwar comparisons. In selecting a postwar year, it is necessary to consider that there must be time enough given for the concomitant war effects to erode but not too long after to miss the supposed reactions in development. With this consideration in mind, I have arbitrarily selected the second and seventh years after war as the appropriate later points in time for my purposes. While it might seem preferable to collect data representing all years, I decided against that in the interest of parsimony and personal judgment. Statistical information for the years of war and all the intervening years, therefore, will be left unexamined.

Thus for a study of the world wars of the twentieth century, statistics for the following years should be included: 1913, 1920, 1925, 1938, 1947, and 1952. The long term, then, is defined as the forty-year period extending from 1913 through 1952. The short term includes a world war and the period before and after it: from 1913 through 1925 and from 1938 through 1952.

For the first three selected years, sixty-three nations are considered; for the next three selected years, the original sixty-three plus an additional seven, or seventy nations, are to be studied. No other nation will be introduced in later stages of this work. As mentioned in Chapter 2, the selection of nations for study is limited by the extent of coverage of the telephone and population series. The appendix tables contain all the relevant information; in particular, see Table A-3.

The development hierarchy is the dependent factor to be explained. Each of its specifications—order, integration, progress, and the satisfaction of nations—will be systematically confronted with the specifications of the independent factor of war; that is, degree of war involvement (active, marginal, and neutral) and prewar stratum of development (upper, middle, and lower). As findings arise, they will be categorized by their confirmation of one or another of the basic theoretical possibilities; that is, by the productive, destructive, unpredictable, and irrelevant hypotheses. At the very least, presumably, the findings will add in some significant way to the degree of confidence one may store in these hypotheses as alternative explanations of war and development. At the most, the findings might contribute to a first statement on a theory of world inequality in a century of total war.

4 Order

*The eyes of chaos shining through
the veil of order.*
French, unknown

Order in the development hierarchy refers to the relative rank stability of rich nations and poor over time. The hierarchy exhibits order in the degree to which nations sorted in it collectively maintain or strengthen their positions. The application of world culture by each nation is the foundation of the order specification in the development hierarchy.

World culture refers to sets of instrumental ideas and principles, beliefs and values to the effect to control the environment. It is unevenly arranged, available to the interested, capable of swaying the uninformed, cumulative, and extraterritorial. Because it transcends specific nations, nations are able to use it to maintain or strengthen their positions. They all draw from it, and, at different times, contribute to it.

A number of authors have found the concept of world culture to be significant to an understanding of history. Thus: "A world culture affecting all advanced societies has been developing for the past four centuries or so; hence there is a *common* history that is important for all advanced societies."[1] Another author uses the concept more boldly.

This world culture is of course the essence of what we think of as modern life. It is based on a scientific and rational outlook and the application in all phases of life of ever higher levels of technology. It is a reflection of urban and industrial society in which relations are premised on secular rather than sacred considerations. It embraces the spirit of enlightenment, at least a formal acknowledgment of humane values, and the acceptance of rational-legal norms for . . . behavior.[2]

Ideas count in the control of the environment. An idea about a new type of disease-resistant seed, an improved method of plowing, a better layout in a workshop, more roads to take goods to market, a new supply of energy behind each pair of hands, can help all nations to produce more with the same amount of work; that is, once an idea is converted into practice it is available as a pattern for development anywhere. It has often been pointed out that a less developed nation can borrow an idea or technology instead of having to invent it anew; that is, because communication occurs on a vast scale, ideas need not be discovered twice. In fact as far back as the invention of writing, ideas have been storable for future use. It should go without saying that since recorded history, mankind has always lived on everybody else.[3]

More is known today than yesterday and still more will be known tomorrow. The issue of whether growth occurs because one new idea suggests another or because ideas are responses to problems that demand solving need not detain us.[4] The aim here is to identify the simple reality of growth of useful ideas. However evenly or unevenly, culture cumulates and proliferates over time. Independent increases in world culture from science and technology are snowballing. And one of the most optimistic signs of a better material future is the continued growth of invention in chemistry, electrical goods, transportation, and other fields, which will add to the development of any nation.[5]

The notion that instrumental culture affects development is taken so much for granted that present-day investigators no longer bother to debate its merits. Kerr and associates, for example, maintain that "at one moment of time there may be several best economic and social arrangements, but only one best technology. The technology can be up to date or antiquated, but there is no question which is which, and the modern is constantly replacing the ancient."[6] Furthermore, the products of instrumental culture are urged upon less developed nations nowadays as a matter of policy by concerned observers. "Now automatic production, with its relatively low capital and labor requirements per unit of output, radically changes their prospects. Instead of trying to lift the whole economy by the slow, painful methods of the past, an industrially backward country may take the dramatic short cut of building a few large up-to-date automatic plants. Towering up in the primitive economy like copses of tall trees on a grassy plain, they would propagate a new economic order."[7]

The Problem

Into the process of culture comes war with all of its destructive fury and constructive potentialities. For war to affect the stability of rich nations and poor in the development hierarchy, it must increase or decrease the amount of instrumental knowledge stored and disseminated within each nation as well as affect patterns of recruiting and applying such knowledge. Universities, for example, cradles of culture, empty themselves of their personnel, shift research to applied projects, and give remaining students accelerated or substandard educations, depending on the severity of national involvement in war. The issue in its broadest scope was recognized and stated late in the nineteenth century by Marshall.

Ideas, whether those of art and science, or those embodied in practical appliances, are the most "real" of the gifts that each generation receives from its predecessors. The world's material wealth would quickly be replaced if it were destroyed, but the ideas by which it was made were retained. If however the ideas were lost, but not the material wealth, then that would dwindle and the world would go back to poverty. And most of our knowledge of mere facts could quickly be recovered if it were lost, but the constructive ideas of thought remained; while, if the ideas perished, the world would enter again on the Dark Ages.[8]

On the one hand, it has been noted that war can destroy instrumental knowledge and its products. The following quotation clearly describes such destruction. "When the Mongols invaded Iraq in the 12th century they destroyed the essential parts of the system of irrigating which had been built up gradually during the preceding three thousand years; and the country has not recovered to this day, as its cultivated area is less extensive now than it was in the days of Babylon."[9] On the other hand, it has been noted that world war need not significantly affect twentieth century culture. "It is highly improbable that European culture will have to retreat . . . to find a basis for its reorganization. Even under the worst conditions enough of modern science and technology will survive to provide economic resources far above those of the Dark Ages."[10]

From these several quotations, it is uncertain whether or not war affects culture, and if so, whether war slows or quickens growth in world culture. To the extent that war does affect culture, positively or negatively, so it might be expected to affect order in the development hierarchy. It is relevant therefore to ask whether order is increased, decreased, both, or unaffected by war. The fit of each of these hypotheses will be determined as the findings emerge and subjected to interpretation in the last section of this chapter.

The appropriate method of analyzing order is by product-moment correlation of the development hierarchy through history. Nations are located in the hierarchy at various points in time and the resulting arrays for these various points in time are intercorrelated. This method permits comparison of those arrays of nations and thus a determination of the extent to which the development hierarchy remains stable through war.

The following are the implications for the four basic hypotheses about the relationship between world war and order in the development hierarchy. If the correlations in the forthcoming tables go up through war, then order has increased and the productive hypothesis will be taken to have been confirmed; if the correlations go down, then order has decreased and the destructive hypothesis will be taken to have been confirmed; if the correlations go up for one war and down for another, then order has both increased and decreased and the unpredictable hypothesis will be taken to have been confirmed; and, if the correlations do not vary significantly, then order has not varied and the irrelevant hypothesis will be taken to have been demonstrated.

Findings

The correlation of the development hierarchy, as indicated by telephones per thousand, for 1913 with that for 1952 is 0.93. This high correlation indicates that the hierarchy remained remarkably stable for a rather long period of time. Put differently, the positions of nations in 1913 fairly accurately predict their positions in 1952. Of course, many individual changes of position in the hierarchy occurred within that period but apparently not enough to change in any important way the hierarchy which persisted in the face of two world wars. This capacity of nations in the development hierarchy to maintain their positions demonstrates the existence of order in development.

The development hierarchy is thus much more stable than might have been supposed. To the extent that a given civilization may be defined by the current configuration of rich nations and poor, civilization has not been significantly affected by the two world wars of this century. Statistical methods do not show war affecting civilization, and therefore Toynbee's conclusion, that war breaks it, can only be demonstrated when actual instability in the rank order of nations results from war.[11]

Over shorted time intervals, the hierarchy changes very little, if at all. We see this in Table 4-1, where the product-moment correlations approach unity for arrays fairly close to each other in time. The correlations reveal the difficulty of overcoming an established lead in development. While the less developed nations progress along with the more developed nations, the poor still lag behind the rich. This finding, that the rank stability of nations is about the same at the end of the time span as it was at the beginning, demonstrates the irrelevant hypothesis: order in development does not associate with war.

Table 4-1
Correlations of Arrays of Nations,[a] at Selected Dates

| Year | Base[b] | | | | | |
| | The First World War | | | The Second World War | | |
	Telephones	Income	Steel	Telephones	Income	Steel
Second[c]	0.9891	0.8582	0.9919	0.9863	0.9017	0.9968
Seventh[c]	0.9850	0.8585	0.9992	0.9876	0.8996	0.9989

[a]These correlations are based on per capita data located in Appendix Tables A-3, A-6, and A-9, respectively.

[b]The year immediately prior to world war; that is, 1913 and 1938.

[c]Refers to those years after world war: the second year applies to 1920 and 1947; the seventh year applies to 1925 and 1952.

Level of Development

What is true for the world as a whole may not be true for the most developed or more powerful nations. Consider this assessment of the effects of the First World War on finance and credit:

The world emerged from this gigantic struggle very much impoverished, and the economic system reared during the preceding fifty years was in a state of utter disorganization. These consequences were not manifested immediately after hostilities ceased in a manner striking enough to impress public opinion. Privation has been great among neutrals as well as belligerents and many articles necessary to life, or at least to well-being, were exhausted. It was, therefore, urgent to renew supplies at once. There was in this exigency the opportunity for a temporary resumption of business. The fact that the resulting boom was artificial was disregarded, and then succeeded a period of reckless speculation favored in great part everywhere by financial policy thrown out of balance by the needs of the war. For two years fortune seemed to be smiling on everyone, but then came a crisis formidable in its extent and its intensity which made men fully realize the ruin and wreckage caused by the war. Great empires lie collapsed in a state of confusion out of which it seems impossible that they should rise for many years; wealthy nations have suddenly lost their political and economic supremacy, the work of years undone.[12]

It seems obvious that war has an effect at least on the order within parts of the development hierarchy. If war causes differential order among various parts of the hierarchy, then the introduction of an intervening variable, development stratum, may reveal its extent and intensity. It is possible to have a degree of instability within a development stratum that would remain undetected in a correlation of all nations over time. The possible hypotheses about the relationship between war and order, taking into account this intervening variable of development strata, are as follows. If rank stability associates positively with development stratum through war, that is, the highest stratum of nations exhibits the greatest stability, then this confirms the productive hypothesis; if it associates inversely, this confirms the destructive hypothesis; if it associates variably, this confirms the unpredictable hypothesis; and if it remains unaffected, this signifies a lack of relationship. To test these hypotheses, arrays of nations in each development stratum were correlated over the same time span. The result can be seen in Table 4-2.

Despite the attrition in the number of nations caused by sorting them into categories, the correlations are quite high. The lowest correlation in Table 4-2 occurs among the nations in the lower stratum and then only since the Second World War. Why these nations should exhibit less order, or rank stability, is implicit in the definition of development. They are in far less control of their

Table 4-2
Correlations of Arrays of Nations, at Selected Dates, by Stratum of Development[a]

Year	Base Year 1913: The First World War	Base Year 1938: The Second World War
	Upper	
Second	0.9839	0.9754
Seventh	0.9800	0.9759
	Middle	
Second	0.9642	0.8612
Seventh	0.9330	0.7349
	Lower	
Second	0.9784	0.3783
Seventh	0.9136	0.6441

[a]Stratification of nations as of 1952 (see Table 2-3) and correlations are of data in Appendix Table A-3.

environment and are thus more prone to be victimized by it. Why the instability should be greater after the Second than after the First World War is also clear. The scope of the Second World War was greater and so was its impact. But, strikingly, the most developed nations were least affected by world war; the highest correlation in the table occurs among these nations. Therefore, to the extent that the last sentence of the foregoing quotation assesses postwar rank stability for nations in the upper stratum of development, that assessment can be considered as untrue. Such a statement seriously minimizes the enormous recuperative resources of nations on the whole and their capacity to maintain their positions over time and through crises. All of this can be shown even more pointedly. Comparing the strata over the longer term, that is, the correlations of the arrays of nations of 1913 with those of 1952, the figures are: 0.91, 0.75, and 0.70, for the upper, middle, and lower strata, respectively.

The finding of Table 4-2 confirms the productive hypothesis, even though the correlation variations among strata resulting from the Second World War are larger than those resulting from the First World War. Rank stability associates positively with development stratum through war: nations of the upper stratum tend to stay relatively more stable in rank than nations of the lower stratum. In other words, the richer a nation, the more secure its position in the development hierarchy over time.

"The accumulation of knowledge, and the methods of rational explanation by which it was achieved, is no doubt the most generally recognized aspect of modernization, and as an attitude of mind it lies at the center of this process."[13] War apparently does not significantly affect the amount of knowledge stored in a nation or accumulated under the skin of man. Rich nations apply more of the instrumental culture of the world than poor nations and this pattern is maintained before, during, and after war in noticeable degree. Therefore, greater rank stability or order in the development hierarchy should be anticipated among upper stratum than among lower stratum nations through history and war.

Degree of War Participation

At this juncture, degree of war participation will be advanced as an independent factor to consider in the study of order in the development hierarchy or rank stability. Involvement in total war implies an escalation of inventions which have included metallurgy and rocketry. Thus culture is stimulated. At the same time, however, war consumes. It consumes men, minds, materials, and money. The world wars of this century were so far-reaching and costly as to stagger the imagination. So the question arises: Is a nation at war so boosted by its inventions or by those of others as to more than compensate for war destruction, so that it actually strengthens its position on the development hierarchy more than would be the case for a neutral, or is the reverse true? On the one hand, it has been said that "certain neutrals, such as Sweden, Switzerland and Argentina, profited by war markets, and that fact should be taken into an account in any attempt to draw up a war balance sheet."[14] And it has been said that none escape the costs of war. One author asserts this after arraying the economic costs of war by size, the smallest costs first: "Direct costs of actual participation in a war; physical loss and destruction, waste of labor power and physical resources. Costs that follow in the train of war; industrial dislocation and disorganization, making for wasteful use of resources and aggravated depressions. Costs of insecurity; the effect on economic life of the menace of the next war. . . . Only the first of these costs is wholly spared to a neutral, and it is the least."[15]

The effect of war involvement on order in the development hierarchy can be determined. It requires only that nations be sorted by degree of war participation (active, marginal, and neutral). If war causes differential rank stability, then the introduction of the intervening variable, degree of participation, may reveal its extent and intensity. The familiar hypotheses about the relationship between war and order in the development hierarchy will again be tested, this time taking into account this intervening variable of participation. If rank stability associates positively with degree of participation through war, that is, if the more war-involved nations exhibit greater stability, then this confirms the productive hypothesis; if it associates inversely, this confirms the destructive hypothesis; if it associates variably, this confirms the unpredictable hypothesis; and if it remains unaffected, this demonstrates the irrelevant hypothesis.

Both world wars are combined to form a single event or what will be called the Thirty-One Years War (1914-45) and nations differentiated according to their degree of participation, in that long war, to determine the exact magnitude of influence participation may have had on rank stability. The result of correlating arrays of nations, so classified in 1952 with arrays as of the base year of 1913, can be seen in Table 4-3.

Throughout the Thirty-One Years War, three out of the four classifications remained quite stable in rank. The magnitude of the correlations demonstrates the remarkable persistence of world inequality through a costly and dreadfully long conflict. These data, moreover, would seem to challenge the cycle thesis as propounded by Ibn Khaldoun and Giambattista Vico.[16] For these three classifications, then, rank stability does not associate with degree of participation through war. In whatever way war involves these nations, therefore, it does not significantly affect the strength of their position in the development hierarchy over the long term.

Because nations sorted into the minimum category appear out-of-line, rank stability must be considered to associate variably with degree of participation through the Thirty-One Years War. The finding tends to confirm the unpredictable hypothesis about the relationship between war and order in the development hierarchy.

So much for the long term. Will there be more rank stability over the short term or nearly the same amount and will the data demonstrate the irrelevant or the unpredictable alternative in the relationship between war and order in the development hierarchy? Prior findings create no expectation that rank stability will be any less. To prove it out, arrays of nations in each category of participation were correlated over the same time span; that is, before and after each world war. The results can be seen in Table 4-4.

The magnitudes of correlations in Table 4-4 might be considered extraordinary in the context of common-sense perception of the consequences of general wars for rank stability or order in the development hierarchy. While these high correlations could have been predicted from earlier tables, this reconfirmation encourages a view of the stability of inequality among nations

Table 4-3
Correlations of Arrays of Nations at Selected Dates, by Degree of War Participation[a]

| | The Thirty-One Years War: 1914-45 | | | |
Year	Maximum	Medium	Minimum	Neutral
1913 and 1952	0.9438	0.9722	0.7575	0.9768

[a]Maximum means officially in war for six or more years; medium means officially in war from three to six years; minimum means officially in war for less than three years; and neutral means absence of official war participation in both the First and the Second World Wars. Nations sorted as in Table 3-3 and correlations are of data in Appendix Table A-3.

Table 4-4
Correlations of Arrays of Nations at Selected Dates, by Degree of War
Participation[a]

Year	Base Year 1913: The First World War			Base Year 1938: The Second World War		
	Active	Marginal	Neutral	Active	Marginal	Neutral
Second	0.9909	0.9996	0.9947	0.9851	0.9699	0.9983
Seventh	0.9902	0.9985	0.9935	0.9858	0.9681	0.9981

[a]Active means officially in war for three years or more; marginal means officially in war for less than three years; and neutral means absence of official war participation. Nations sorted as in Table 3-2 and correlations are of data in Appendix Table A-3.

that can only be considered as remarkable. Similarly remarkable is the following uncanny prediction of the results of the Second World War:

Everything considered, a European debacle of the H.G. Wells type seems highly improbable. This war may be a little more destructive than the last, if it continues long enough, and all the nations are entering it poorer, but the chances are that they will emerge from it much as they emerge from the last one. The only difference will be the deeper poverty and increased confusion of the survivors. Great and widespread civilizations do not end in the splendor of flame and battle. They die bit by bit through centuries. It is exceedingly improbable that the student of a thousand years hence will consider this war as even a turning point in history. He is more likely to see it as a minor event which made certain pre-existing difficulties more acute and accelerated the working out of trends already present.[17]

The uniformly high correlations between the several hierarchies in Table 4-4 shows that degree of participation makes absolutely no difference in rank stability over time. Rank stability does not associate with degree of participation through war and this is entirely consistent with the irrelevant hypothesis. In whatever way war involves a nation, therefore, it does not affect the security of its location in the development hierarchy through history.

As I mentioned before, war does not importantly affect the amount of knowledge stored, disseminated, recruited, or applied by a nation. To achieve victory and to compensate for war costs, nations maximally involved in war patently demonstrate neither more nor less resistance to science and technology than either minimally involved or neutral nations. Hence no greater rank stability should be anticipated among the actively involved than by the marginally involved in war.

Active Nations and the Second World War

Because warring nations occupy different positions in the development hierarchy, a common speculation has been that the edge in being able to maintain rank resides with the more developed warring nation over the less developed nation. "In modern war," says Adam Smith in 1776, "the great expense of fire-arms gives an evident advantage to the nation which can best afford that expense; and consequently, to an opulent and civilized, over a poor and barbarous nation. In ancient times the opulent and civilized found it difficult to defend themselves against the poor and barbarous nations. In modern times the poor and barbarous find it difficult to defend themselves against the opulent and civilized. The invention of fire-arms, an invention which at first sight appears to be so pernicious, is certainly favourable both to the permanency and to the extension of civilization."[18]

Degree of participation and level of development are obviously not mutually exclusive. These factors inevitably overlap. They have not been a problem heretofore because the task has been to appreciate the separate influence that each had on rank stability. Now that those findings are in, it becomes necessary to learn something about the combined relative influence of these factors on order in the development hierarchy or on rank stability.

To test the relative influence on rank stability of participation degree and development level, the forty-three nations active during the Second World War are selected for close examination. These active nations occupy positions in every stratum of the development hierarchy. By holding the active category of participation constant, the influence of each development stratum can be measured. The result of this method should allow for a clear understanding of the combined relative influence of these factors, as previously specified, on postwar stability.

On the basis of the finding in Table 4-2, that the more developed nations have a more stable rank order than less developed nations, the following prediction of the productive hypothesis seems reasonable: the more developed active nations will exhibit the greatest rank stability through war. The information contained in Table 4-5, designed to provide support for the prediction, does so almost perfectly.

Table 4-5
Correlations of Arrays of *Active* Nations at Selected Dates, by Stratum of Development

Year	Base Year 1938: The Second World War		
	Upper Active	Middle Active	Lower Active
Second	0.9729	0.7639	0.2648
Seventh	0.9716	0.5769	0.7757

[a]Stratification of nations as of 1952 (see Table 2-3) sorted as in Table 3-5 and correlations are of data in Appendix Table A-3.

Military Occupation during the
Second World War

Occupation by a foreign force occurred during the Second World War on a grand scale. Out of the forty-three active nations reviewed in Table 4-5, twenty-seven were occupied. The event of occupation is an overwhelmingly coercive status, and it naturally suggests the question of its impact on postwar stability. Would a clear advantage lie with the conquering nation? According to Bryce, neither the loser nor the winner gain as a result of war because the direct losses appear so great. "Against these losses there may be set, in the case of a conquering country, what it acquires by seizure of property, annexation of territory, levying of contributions and of indemnities, although these forcibly gotten gains do not always prosper. There may also be new openings to foreign trade, and victory may evoke an enterprising spirit which will push that trade with new vigor. But such possible direct benefits are usually far outweighed by the direct loss."[19]

To test for the effect on order in the development hierarchy that the status of occupation might have, active nations during the Second World War were sorted in terms of whether or not they were occupied. In each category, the nations were arranged in several arrays according to development, one array for each point in time. The points in time are the same as those used in previous tables for the Second World War. In each category, correlations were made of these arrays. The result can be seen in Table 4-6.

From Table 4-6 it can be seen that nonoccupied active nations were no more rank stable than occupied active nations through the Second World War. The really remarkable fact, apart from the striking similarities in the magnitudes of the correlations, is that occupied nations resisted instability in the development hierarchy through war, though one might have reasonably predicted instability as a result of occupation. The relatively high and almost equal degree of rank stability of nonoccupied and occupied nations invites discussion as to why occupied nations retain their positions in the development hierarchy.

The general object of an invading occupation force seems to be to secure the

Table 4-6
Correlations of Arrays of *Active* Nations at Selected Dates, by Whether Occupied or Not[a]

Year	Base Year 1938: The Second World War	
	Occupied	Nonoccupied
Second	0.9912	0.9831
Seventh	0.9867	0.9866

[a]Nations sorted as in Table 3-4 and correlations are of data in Appendix Table A-3.

territory, to continue institutional patterns and to gain the allegiance of the population. To hold an occupied nation in line, to seal permeable national borders, and to compensate for drained-off output, the control exercised by the occupying force must be very thorough indeed. Stability of rank in the case of occupied nations, then, may perhaps be accounted for by the dramatic and new overlay of centralization. New men of decision emerge to issue hourly communiques, to make daily reports, to write fresh laws from hastily renovated offices, all to one purpose: to maintain internal discipline.

But the control exercised by the occupying force must not be so thorough as to alienate the inhabitants of the occupied land. The care that must be exercised to avoid alienating the inhabitants politically can be illustrated by the following quotations:

It is in the nature of military occupations that military governors and administrators are faced essentially with short-run problems. An important requirement of wise military government is to plan in such a manner as to insure continuity of policy and to make the change from the military occupation to permanent stability in as smooth a manner as possible.[20]

Occupation forces normally seek to maintain or reestablish legitimate authority. Thus:

Their task is usually enormously more difficult than the guerrillas' because the latter have only to smash an intricate and delicate web of economic installations and social relations while the [occupation forces] must not only defeat the guerrillas but do so in such a way as to preserve the system which is under attack.[21]

Continuity of policy and the maintenance of public discipline within an occupied land are usually promoted by the preservation of the operations of previously existing judicial agencies and the retention of native officials in office. "The courts ... continue to operate under the same laws and with substantially the same personnel as in the days preceding the invasion. ... [And importantly], the retention of large numbers of local and regional officials by occupying authorities has been a basic policy followed in almost all military occupations during recent wars."[22]

The characteristics of the occupying force, then, would seem to make for less difference in postwar stability than whether the occupied nations stand high or low in the development hierarchy. Previous findings suggest the view that occupation provides a necessary but not a sufficient explanation for variation in rank stability. Thus the following prediction seems reasonable: occupied nations in the upper stratum of development will exhibit greater rank stability than occupied nations in the lower stratum of development. To test the prediction of the productive hypothesis, occupied nations will be sorted by level of development. Whatever differences result, therefore, will redound from development

Table 4-7

Correlations of Arrays of *Occupied* Nations, at Selected Dates, by Stratum of Development[a]

Year	Base Year 1938: The Second World War		
	Upper	Middle	Lower
Second	0.9815	0.8719	0.0631
Seventh	0.9774	0.7087	0.6801

[a]Nations sorted as in Table 3-6 and correlations are of data in Appendix Table A-3.

level and not from whether occupied or not. The result of correlating these three hierarchies with themselves at the same point in time as used heretofore can be seen in Table 4-7.

These correlations show that occupied nations of the upper stratum are more rank stable than occupied nations of the middle and the lower stratum through the Second World War. It is evident that development level makes a difference in rank stability. These correlations, then, confirm the prediction of a positive relationship which was made above: rank stability does associate directly with the level of development of occupied nations through war; occupied nations in the upper field of development have more stability than occupied nations in the lower field of development. Therefore, the higher the development level of an occupied nation, the greater its capacity to maintain its position in the development hierarchy over time.

Interpretation

World culture functions to promote rank stability. The application of ideas and principles, values and beliefs, to the effort to control the environment enables nations to maintain or secure their positions over time. This proposition has been stated in many ways by many different authors from many fields of inquiry.[23] Since the Wars of Coalition against France, it has become less and less conceivable that a basis of mass ignorance can ever be laid again in light of the notable increases to world culture no matter what intervenes short of cosmic disaster or thermonuclear holocaust.

The rise of literacy, the spread of mass communication, the decline of mortality, the enlargement of cities, the growth of industry, and the expansion of trade indicate an increasing world culture increasingly diffused. It also indicates fundamental change that results in higher levels of living. But sheer additions to world culture will not automatically lift a nation. World culture has to be applied: ideas have to be converted into practice, science into technology.

Granting that increases in culture lead to greater mastery over the environment, application of culture remains uneven, leaving nations unequal in their ability to cope or succeed with the environment. In any nation, mastery depends on the stream of invention, the capacity to innovate, the propensity to invest, and the willingness of society to accept innovation.[24] In all these respects, nations may well differ from one another. The advancement of world culture is obviously an indispensable basis for mastery of the environment over the longer run, and the results of instrumental knowledge are accessible to all nations able to make use of them. This holds true, however, to a far lesser extent for the sources of such knowledge.[25] The step from the bare scientific ideas to technical invention encompasses a creative process requiring ingenuity, imagination, and perseverance. Although the process of invention has become increasingly organized and made less haphazard than it used to be, there are marked differences between nations in the rate at which scientific ideas are exploited for practical application. It is a familiar observation that the United Kingdom and France, although highly productive in science, have been less distinguished than Germany, Switzerland, and the United States in utilizing the findings of science for inventing new techniques and products.[26] The proportionate number of scientists is no smaller in France and Britain than in Germany, Switzerland, or the United States. The difference seems to be rather that German, Swiss, and American scientists are more "application-minded" than their French and British counterparts,[27] and they operate in a far more conducive setting which stimulates higher rates of productivity; that is, one of interuniversity competition.[28]

Among highly developed nations, then, there are observable differences not only in the rate at which scientific ideas are exploited for practical application, but also in the rate of adaptation of existing technologies such as computers, nuclear energy, aerospace, and telecommunications. Such differences relate directly with the development hierarchy; as nations ascend that hierarchy, they apply more of the instrumental culture of the world than nations below them.

When such differences exist among developed nations, one need only imagine the even greater differences existing between them and the underdeveloped nations. The knowledge of an average man in an underdeveloped nation of how material things work is still very limited. He is insufficiently schooled in experiment to explore all the ways in which matter can be manipulated. There are few ways known of making better seeds; not very much has been tried in the way of constructing better plows; better plows have to wait on more refined techniques for dealing with iron ore; and experiments with iron ore have in turn to wait on finding a substitute for charcoal. In short, the heat of wood, the energy of wind and water, the speed of a horse, the skill of the hand still represent the outer limits of what can be applied. This represents a very restricted technology.[29]

To the extent that history consists of a shared written meaning which becomes part of the biographies of millions of people, helping to shape those biographies and to give them a common purpose, it must be said that much of the less developed world had no history. "It is only today that it has become possible for the first time even to imagine a whole world consisting of peoples who have in the fullest sense entered history and become the concern no longer of the colonial administrator or the anthropologist, but of the historian."[30] An oral culture depends for its preservation upon a series of interlocking conversations; only in social situations does the individual come in contact with such a culture. Furthermore, such a society cannot store up portions of its tradition for later retrieval; whatever goes out of current use, whatever drops out of those interlocking conversations, is gone for good. This not only limits the complexity of a given oral culture, it also permits the unconscious operation of a self-regulating process called "structural amnesia." The people preserve only that part of their past which they modify as needed in order to keep it socially useful.[31] In contrast to these underdeveloped peoples or from the perspective of the more developed nations who have a written culture, "the age of nationalism represents the first period of universal history."[32]

World culture serves to maintain rank stability among nations because it is differentially applied. "It is the races that know how to think . . . that have led the world. Thought, in the form of invention and inquiry, has given us those improvements in the arts of life and in the knowledge of nature by which material progress and comfort have been obtained."[33] The differential use of world culture reinforces the hierarchy because the more developed nations are the ones that use this culture more. If the less developed nations were the ones, the differential use of world culture would result in the destruction of the hierarchy, to wit, instability, or the reversal of ranks within it. Such differential application of world culture by nations causes continuing inequality in development among them.

This explanation of order in the development hierarchy may be put more formally. Rank stability is a function of differential success in coping with the environment. Coping with the environment varies inversely with resistance to advances in science and technology. Therefore, rank stability depends on the differential application of the instrumental aspects of world culture.

For very great changes in relative positions to come about over the short term, important discontinuities in world culture or in the pattern of differentially applying the culture would have to occur to enable the less developed nations to catch up or even overtake the more developed. But such discontinuities are not observable in this century of total war.[34]

No idea or principle about environmental mastery was lost even temporarily or significantly eroded as a result of either world war. World culture exists, grows, and is diffused despite war. "The remarkable collection of new inventions and scientific discoveries, which the postwar population inherit and which make these years more notable than others, results from the part the war played in developing science and invention in certain lines. Ordinarily this decade would

5 Integration

Natura non facit saltum.
Latin proverb

Integration in the development hierarchy refers to the diminishing of relative spread between rich nations and poor throughout history. The hierarchy exhibits integration in the degree to which nations sorted in it conserve or decrease the gaps between their positions. The utilization of global communication by each nation is the foundation of the integration specification in the development hierarchy.

Everything considered relevant to development matches national boundaries almost perfectly and therefore they count. They count politically both in war and in peace. They count socially as points of separation between "we" and "they." And they count developmentally as differentiating the material and psychic quality of human life. The relative impermeability of boundaries is a comparatively recent phenomenon. Its thrust arose most energetically sometime during the late nineteenth century. "In no previous period of modern history have frontiers been so rigidly demarcated, or their character as barriers so ruthlessly enforced, as to-day."[1] The rise of protectionist bills, the height of tariffs, the usage of passports, and the difficulty of migration all reflect a growing impermeability of national boundaries. Moreover, all operating units of communication, production, transportation, health, education, and welfare systems halt at the border of the nation; and they are all authorized solely by the nation through its governing arm, which registers voluntary associations and charters corporations. As edges harden, the populations within form into one vast endogamous unit. At times, even the recording of ordinary births and deaths takes on imperial meaning in a world fraught with international rivalries for the allegiance of men.

But nations are not immune to the process of global communications or its effects.[2] In this era, nations are in absolutely if not relatively greater communication with each other than ever before and this heightened contact yields an ever greater exchange of useful principles, practices, and products. As no man steps into the same river twice, both having changed, so with nations and development. As to the rare nation that seems to stand still, this static condition most likely will have resulted rather from its own barriers and isolation from the effects of international interaction than from anything else. Additions to world culture and global communication tend to affect all nations and thus "the distinctive character of social change in the new countries today is that it is occurring largely in response to the diffusion of what we may call a world culture based upon modern science and technology, modern practices of organization, and modern standards of governmental performance."[3] So even as edges harden, national boundaries remain permeable. In varying degree, global communication overcomes barriers to contact by penetrating all boundaries.

Diffusion of world culture causes nations to move closer together, as all move upward in absolute development. Bryce observes that "the thought of any people is most active when it is brought into contact with the thought of another, because each is apt to lose its variety and freedom of play when it has worked too long upon familiar lines and flowed too long in the channels it has deepened. Hence, isolation retards progress, while intercourse quickens it."[4] The consequence of contact between nations unequal in development is taken to be predictable by a number of observers. "Higher cultural forms tend to dominate and replace lower, and the range of dominance is proportionate to the degree of progress. So modern . . . culture tends to spread around the globe. :. ."[5] A more graphic description is depicted by Levy. "We are confronted—whether for good or for bad—with a universal social solvent. The patterns of the relatively modernized societies, once developed, have shown a universal tendency to penetrate any social context whose participants have come in contact with them. . . . The patterns always penetrate; once the penetration has begun, the previous indigenous patterns always change; and they always change in the direction of some of the patterns of the relatively modernized societies."[6]

Global communications of the twentieth century have diffused the products of world culture so effectively that nations, once at very different developmental levels now, through cultural diffusion, share to one degree or another a jet-age level of development, and, will not subsequently tend to draw apart. In the Arctic Circle, the Himalayas, the Andes, the Amazon, the jungles of Pacific Islands, and tropical Africa, people who never used wheeled vehicles now live with airplanes. A plane can land almost anywhere, and in a short time it can bring all the accessories of an efficient airfield to a selected site at a crossing of caravan trails, on a tiny island, or in an oasis surrounded by bare desert. A country too rugged and too poor to build railroads and highways can have a network of airfields. The radio penetrates the wilderness ahead of the telephone and telegraph, indeed ahead of the elementary school. Hence, the facility with which the products of world culture can be transferred characterizes contemporary civilization. World culture spreads as widely as gaseous matter released from a container.

Global communication has become more institutionalized and frequent than ever before. A vast system of communication now girdles the globe. Flows of travelers, mail, telegrams, money, trade, and migrants are part of this system. So are the various occupational, industrial, financial, educational, and charitable international organizations. This century has witnessed the emergence of the first general purpose organizations—the League of Nations and the United Nations. And the century has also witnessed a proliferation of single purpose international organizations. Over 5,000 governmental and nongovernmental organizations now connect 126 nations, and there exist about 4,200 bilateral and multilateral international exchange agreements between them.[7]

Some of these systems of communication seem more urgent or more interesting than others. But regardless of the type and aim and size, they all convey aspects of world instrumental culture, and by their means its impact is felt virtually everywhere to some degree. Because nations are in greater communication with each other than ever before, the heightened contact between them yields not only a greater exchange of useful products of world culture, but additions to it as well. Development has proceeded at a fairly rapid rate for the last twenty-five years. Since the Wars of Coalition against France, each succeeding generation has witnessed a steady increase in material improvements, and while there are fits and starts in development, the long term trend is upward.

The Problem

Into the process of global communication comes war. And war obviously rattles these world systems of cultural diffusion. For war to affect the spread of rich nations and poor, or integration in the development hierarchy, it must increase or decrease the degree of border impermeability as well as facilitate or frustrate any of the well-known means of global communication and contact.

"Nowadays an important curtailment of exchanges between nations would seriously jeopardize the well-being of their citizens, would unbalance their economic system, and would endanger their political stability. The economic and financial interests of all nations are so closely bound together that a crisis of any importance breaking out in one of them has almost immediately its repercussion in the others. Our world now lives an economic life that flows over the political frontiers; and this economic integration that has developed since the beginning of the second half of the nineteenth century with ever increasing speed is one of the principal causes of the great social betterment that has come to the world as a whole."[8]

As war attenuates some of the international exchange of goods and services, people and messages, so it accelerates other exchanges. War itself is clearly a form of communication if only because opponents are in continuous contact throughout. War quite naturally intensifies some forms of communication, for example, intelligence about the enemy is eagerly sought and usually gotten (the spurt in anthropological writing on the Japanese during World War II is merely one illustration of academic interest provoked by the American government's interest). Moreover, ties between allies and neutrals, so-called, which do not exist are created, and existing ties are strengthened through increased activity among them as in exchanges of mail and trade and as in shorter term survival arrangements. "In the case of the Allies, shortages of food were so great that they did much to effect interallied economic cooperation. Early in the war England and France learned that in their anxiety to buy food abroad they were bidding up prices to their mutual disadvantage; later they realized that with shipping in such short supply they would have to pool their tonnages if they were to feed their people. Accordingly combined Anglo-French boards were created for making joint purchases, an Interallied Wheat Executive was set up in November, 1916, and the all-important Allied Maritime Transport Council for the allocation of tonnnage to meet the most urgent needs was established (November, 1917). Here was a form of international economic cooperation which was to be extended to almost all of Western culture in the economic reconstruction after World War II."[9]

Global communication as a process affects the development of nations and world inequality. The greater the contact between unequals, the less their inequality over time. Any barrier to exchange between rich nations and poor, the graver the consequence for the less developed nation. Blockades, as a form of barrier, may alter or warp cultural diffusion because some transnational ties are loosened while others are tightened. If barriers erected during war are successful, then nations in the lower stratum would have to be affected most; but if they are unsuccessful, the reverse might obtain. Because the effects of war on the great network of global communication, and hence their efforts on integration in the development hierarchy, are not clear, this chapter will explore and attempt to clarify them.

There are basically four hypotheses about the relationship between war and integration. Integration either strengthens, or weakens, does both, or remains unaffected by war; that is, as a result of war, the gaps between nations in the development hierarchy either narrow, or widen, do both, or remain about the same. The fit of these hypotheses—productive, destructive, unpredictable, or irrelevant—will be tested and the findings will be interpreted in this chapter.

Although the development hierarchy proves, as we saw in the preceding chapter, to be remarkably stable, this implies nothing about the gaps between nations. While it is true that all nations are collectively marching upward in fairly stable single file, it remains to be discovered how closely and how evenly they march. Are the leaders maintaining their lead, are the others catching up, or lagging behind?

To measure the gaps between rich nations and poor requires a statistic not previously utilized. The task involves comparing the spread of nations around the mean. The standard deviation would ordinarily do to describe how widely nations are spread. The larger the standard deviation, the greater the spread of nations; but this is a figure applicable only to absolute units (a single distribution around a single mean). It is necessary here to compare arrays of nations according to development at six points in time, each with its own mean and standard deviation. To determine whether nations in one array are more dispersed than nations in another obviously requires a relative measure. Such a measure exists; it is known as the coefficient of variation. It is derived by dividing the mean into the standard deviation. It is a very simple statistic, really, and by it an important idea can be illuminated.

Because the coefficient of variation is a relative measure, it will indicate whether nations in one array are more or less spread out around the mean than nations in another array. The various hypotheses about war and integration will be supported by the results as follows. If the coefficients of variation decrease through war, then integration has strengthened and the productive hypothesis will be taken to have been confirmed. In other words, the mean has outpaced the standard deviation, and hence there is less relative spread; that is, the gaps between nations in the development hierarchy have narrowed over time. If the coefficients increase through war, then integration has weakened and the destructive hypothesis will be taken to have been confirmed. In other words, the standard deviation has grown more rapidly than the mean, and hence there is more relative spread; that is, the gaps between nations in the development hierarchy have widened over time. If the coefficients fluctuate impressively through war, then integration has both weakened and strengthened and the unpredictable hypothesis will be taken to have been confirmed. And if the coefficients do not vary significantly through war, then integration has not varied and no relationship will be evident; thus the irrelevant hypothesis. In this last situation, the relationship between the mean and the standard deviation has remained constant; that is, the gaps between nations in the development hierarchy have neither narrowed nor widened over time.

Findings

Both capitalist and Communist commentators, when they address themselves to the question of integration in the development hierarchy, stress an historic widening of gaps between nations and suggest the need to close them fast or face the brutal consequences. Raul Prebisch claims that the gaps between rich nations and poor are a "growing source of internal and world-wide tension" and Aurelio Peccei says that "no headway can be made to relieve appreciably the immense tensions mounting in the world" unless these gaps are closed.[10] The values these commentators hold are admirable however untrue and partial their facts. Nations are not moving away from one another. That can be seen plainly in Table 5-1. The problem of tension—its cause and consequence—will be fully discussed in Chapter 7.

From the coefficients of variation in Table 5-1, it can be seen that over the long term, nations slightly decreased the gap between their positions from 1913

Table 5-1
Coefficients of Variation of Arrays of Nations,[a] at Selected Dates

Year	The First World War			The Second World War		
	Telephones	Income	Steel	Telephones	Income	Steel
Base[b]	200	50	338	159	58	352
Second[c]	188	46	267	166	66	370
Seventh[d]	179	50	372	164	59	373

[a]The coefficients are based on per capita data located in Appendix Tables A-3, A-6, and A-9, respectively.
[b]Refers to the year immediately prior to world war, or 1913 and 1938.
[c]Refers to the second year after world war, or 1920 and 1947.
[d]Refers to the seventh year after world war, or 1925 and 1952.

through 1952 in number of telephones and slightly increased the distance in real income and steel production. At the beginning of the time span, the standard deviation of the telephone data was 200 percent of the mean and at the end it stood at 164 percent. Although the dispersion of rich nations and poor has been reduced by 36 percent, the world is hardly on an equalization course. The reduction is modest, and the standard deviation is still much greater than the mean. The finding demonstrates the irrelevant hypothesis. Integration does not associate with war; the spread of nations on the development hierarchy remains about the same at the end as it was at the beginning of the time span. The conservation and modest decrease and increase of gaps between nations, however, reveals the existence of integration in the development hierarchy.

Level of Development

If war causes differential integration among the various parts of the development hierarchy, then the introduction of an intervening variable, like development stratum, may reveal its profile. It is not unreasonable to expect variations in integration by development stratum that would remain undetected in coefficients of variation of all nations over time. The four hypotheses about the relationship between war and integration will now be tested, taking into account this intervening variable of development stratum. If integration associates positively with development stratum through war, that is, if the highest stratum exhibits the greatest narrowing of gaps, then this confirms the productive hypothesis; if it associates inversely, this confirms the destructive hypothesis; if it associates variably, this confirms the unpredictable hypothesis; and, if it remains unaffected, this is indicative of a lack of relationship. To determine the fit of these hypotheses, the national arrays according to development in each development stratum will be observed over the same time span. The result can be seen in Table 5-2.

Table 5-2
Coefficients of Variation of Arrays of Nations, at Selected Dates, by Stratum of Development[a]

Year	The First World War			The Second World War		
	Upper	Middle	Lower	Upper	Middle	Lower
Base	110	105	155	71	64	127
Second	104	111	148	79	55	107
Seventh	96	117	151	74	46	74

[a]Stratification of nations as of 1952 (see Table 2-3) and coefficients are of data in Appendix Table A-3.

The general findings of Table 5-2 for the long-term corroborates the destructive possibility, even though the coefficients vary variably as a result of the First World War. Without exception, nations in each stratum have decreased the gaps between their positions from 1913 through 1952. Not only have the gaps narrowed, the amount of reduction associates inversely with development stratum. By subtracting the coefficients of 1952 from those of 1913, the array of categories becomes lower (81), middle (59), and upper (36). To see how this operates, take the upper stratum of nations as an example. In the base year to the First World War, the upper stratum coefficient was 110 percent of the mean; in the seventh year after the Second World War, the upper stratum coefficient was 74 percent of the mean. The difference of 36 percent in reduced spread about the mean among the nations in the upper stratum thus appears as less than the amount of integration exhibited by nations in either the middle or lower stratum. Therefore, integration associates inversely with development stratum through war; nations in the lower stratum exhibit a greater narrowing of the gaps between them than nations of the upper stratum, even though the dispersion of the latter also reduces over time.

That integration associates inversely with development stratum might seem odd if it were previously assumed that upper stratum nations would integrate most. Upper stratum nations simply cannot be credited with a monopoly of science and technology or their products, much less credited with a monopoly of global communication ties. "To put this in technical terms, the diffusion of European technology and science to the rest of the world has robbed Europe of its advantage."[11] Other nations are on the move obviously and possibly possess an equal urge to develop and redress existing gaps.

War does not significantly affect the results of transnational contact even though it may alter or warp such contact. Upper stratum nations are tied into the network of communications more than are lower stratum nations. Therefore, upper stratum nations cluster more than lower stratum nations through war and history. However, the data show that even though upper stratum nations are and remain relatively closer together than lower stratum nations in the development hierarchy, that is, show a higher *existing level* of integration, lower stratum nations have been reducing the gaps between their positions at a faster rate since 1913; that is, they exhibit a greater *rate* of integration. A direct relationship exists between development rank and transnational contact. The inability of rich nations to reduce the gaps between them any farther may be explained by the fact that they have already moved so close together; the same inability among poor nations is due to their greater distance from one another. In either case, differential utilization of the network of global communications promotes inequality among nations, or rank spread in the development hierarchy over time.

Degree of War Participation

But perhaps the development level is not the only factor determining the degree of integration in development through war. War participation may have an effect. As stated at the beginning of this chapter, war may interrupt global communication; blockades and international polarization could create barriers to exchange which might tend to slow the diffusion of principles, practices, and products of world culture. But some ties between cooperating nations strengthen during war since contact between them increases. Therefore the interruption can only be partial, and it is possible that some nations are more affected than others. The question, then, is: will nations at war be so helped by emergency contacts as to offset the effects of interruptions of ordinary contacts? In other words, do nations at war conserve or decrease the gaps between their positions in the development hierarchy more than do neutrals, or is the reverse true?

On the one hand, observers have pointed to instances where neutrals have gained more than warring nations as a result of war.

The rapid expansion of our trade both with the Allies and with neutral countries [especially those outside Europe, which had formerly depended on the belligerents for their manufactured goods] necessitated a sharp increase in our industrial capacity. This was reflected in record activity in the capital goods industries supplying the new machinery and tools. Domestic business was stimulated by the unprecedented outpouring of Allied funds, business activity rising almost 50 percent from the end of 1914 to the early part of 1916.[12]

On the other hand, neutrals have felt some of the costs of war. For example: "twenty-one vessels with cargoes for Switzerland were held up at Gibraltar after the fall of France, and for the next two months, while the [British] Ministry waited to see how Switzerland would behave, ships were released very sparingly." The other belligerent, Germany, controlled the export of coal to Switzerland, her mail was routed through Germany via Stuttgart, and some of the Swiss trading and financial arrangements with other nations were under the control of the Germans. Nevertheless, Switzerland remained important through-out the war as a communication link between these opposing forces.[13]

The effect of war involvement on integration in the development hierarchy can be determined. It requires only that nations be sorted by degree of war participation. If war causes differential integration, then the introduction of an intervening variable, degree of participation, may reveal its extent and intensity. The familiar hypotheses about the relationship between war and integration in development will again be tested but with the new specification of participation. If integration associates positively with degree of participation through war, that is, if the more involved nations exhibiting a greater move to the mean, then this confirms the productive hypothesis; if it associates inversely, this confirms the destructive hypothesis; if it associates variably, this confirms the unpredictable hypothesis; and if it remains unaffected, this confirms the irrelevant hypothesis.

Again, both world wars can be considered as a single event or what is here called the Thirty-One Years War: 1914-45. Nations are distinguished by the number of years they have participated as combatants in that long war. National arrays according to development in each category of participation were manipulated over the same time span as in previous tables. The result can be seen in Table 5-3.

From Table 5-3, it can be seen that the amount of total reduction in spread, or integration in the development hierarchy, varies by degrees of war participation. Subtracting the bottom from the top, the differences in coefficents of variation diminish from left to right; that is, maximum participants exhibited the greatest reduction in spread (37), medium participants the next greatest (33), minimum participants the least (4), and the neutrals increased the spread (−8). This finding tends to confirm the productive hypothesis about the relationship between war and integration in the development hierarchy. Integration associates positively with degree of war participation through war; nations in the maximum category tend to reduce the spread between them more than nations in the minimum category. The more war involves a nation, therefore, the greater its capacity to move toward the mean of its category over time.

Table 5-3
Coefficients of Variations of Arrays of Nations, at Selected Dates, by Degree of War Participation[a]

	The Thirty-One Years War: 1914-45			
Year	Maximum	Medium	Minimum	Neutral
1913	160	203	121	136
1952	123	170	117	144

[a]Maximum means officially in war for six or more years; medium means officially in war from three to six years; minimum means officially in war for less than three years; and neutral means absence of official war participation in both the First and Second World Wars. Nations sorted as in Table 3-3 and coefficients are of data in Appendix Table A-3.

It can be concluded that, over the long term, emergency contacts established between nations do offset the general barriers to exchanges; and nations, in war, actually decrease the gaps between their positions in the development hierarchy.

Turning now to shorter units of time, the findings in the relationship between degree of war participation and integration in development should not be significantly different from those over the long term. After each world war, the gaps between nations in various participation categories should narrow. What cannot be predicted is the magnitude of reduction and the arraying of categories. The results of manipulating arrays of nations according to development, with their degree of participation in the First and Second World Wars, can be viewed in Table 5-4.

In these time segments no consistent set of results obtains. Only from the marginal nations do we see a similarity; they lead in closing the distances between themselves, statistically speaking, in both wars. The other two categories of nations, however, switch positions in array from one war to the next. This finding confirms the unpredictable hypothesis about the relationship between war and integration in the development hierarchy; integration associates variably with degree of participation through war. It is clear, however, that the First World War reduced the gaps between nations to a much greater degree than did the Second World War. Because of the peculiarity of results of the Second World War, it merits special analysis.

Active Nations and the Second World War

Heretofore we have not controlled the observations for participation variability; now we will. To test the relative effects of development level and degree of war participation on integration, the forty-three active nations during the Second World War were sorted by their level of development. In Table 5-5, the

Table 5-4
Coefficients of Variation of Arrays of Nations, at Selected Dates, by Degree of War Participation[a]

Year	The First World War			The Second World War		
	Active	Marginal	Neutral	Active	Marginal	Neutral
Base	156	378	139	136	113	157
Second	154	363	147	147	110	166
Seventh	145	346	142	142	104	161

[a]Active means officially in war for three years or more; marginal means officially in war for less than three years; and neutral means absence of official war participation. Nations sorted as in Table 3-2 and coefficients are of data in Appendix Table A-3.

Table 5-5
Coefficients of Variation of Arrays of *Active* Nations, at Selected Dates, by Stratum of Development[a]

Year	The Second World War		
	Upper Active	Middle Active	Lower Active
Base	64	57	125
Second	73	42	130
Seventh	68	39	82

[a]Nations sorted as in Table 3-5 and coefficients are of data in Appendix Table A-3.

coefficients of variation tell the story of integration before and after the Second World War for active nations classified by stratum of development.

From Table 5-5 it can be seen that, among active nations, integration varies with stratum of development. Integration associates inversely with development levels; active nations in the lower stratum narrow the gaps between themselves faster than active nations in the middle stratum, while active nations in the upper stratum tended to widen the gaps between their positions through the Second World War. When degree of war participation is controlled, therefore, level of development bears a continuing and considerable effect on integration in development.

Military Occupation during the
Second World War

Still another factor, that of foreign occupation, may have contributed to the peculiar pattern of integration through the Second World War. The world wars were apparently dominated by a strategy of attrition. Decisions centered upon the "gradual wearing down of the enemy's mobilizable potential" and decisions on surrender were considered strategic. "Strategic surrender is both the terminal act of a war and the initiating act of the new postwar relationship between the belligerents. The military act of surrender strips the losing sovereign of his war-making capability. It is followed by a political act that provides for the belligerents' postwar status and relationship on the basis of this one-sided military outcome."[14]

In occupation the occupant not only commands the inhabitants of the occupied nation but also commands their prior external relations; for example, their embassies abroad and their trading contacts. This latter aspect of communication, the control over the global communications of an occupied nation, has not been discussed sufficiently in the literature. Such control should bear directly on postwar integration in the development hierarchy of occupied nations. To the extent that control becomes a barrier to prior contacts, occupied nations should exhibit a decrease in their integration. If such control does not constitute a barrier, occupation will matter little in terms of integration in the development hierarchy.

Out of the forty-three nations considered active during the Second World War, twenty-seven were occupied. Both the occupied and nonoccupied active nations in arrays according to development will be compared over the same time span. The impact of occupation on the integration of these nations can be viewed in Table 5-6.

From Table 5-6 it can be seen that the spread of nations in the development hierarchy, among those active in the Second World War, varies by whether or not they were occupied. The gaps between occupied nations narrowed slightly while the gaps between nonoccupied nations increased slightly. So the phenomenon of occupation affects the capacity of nations to decrease the gaps somewhat between their positions in the development hierarchy over time. The intervening factor of occupation seems interesting in itself and invites consideration in conjunction with level of development.

As a nation may be helped by occupation, so it may be hindered as well. Consider only the level of development of the occupied nation and that of the occupying nation to imagine the possibility of an occupied nation absolutely gaining in socioeconomic progress as a result of occupation. A less developed nation could acquire, as a result of its occupation by a more developed one, a variety of new ideas and principles by means of which it could rise above its prewar level. Of course, the more developed occupying force probably neither intends nor plans to be helpful but the less developed occupied nation could nevertheless become the unintended and unplanned beneficiary of newly diffused ideas and principles (and possibly even of materials like factory buildings and machinery) which it would not have otherwise obtained as quickly. The reverse situation of a less developed nation occupying a more developed nation might be helpful to the occupying nation through the acquisition of new ideas and principles via such contact, but it probably would not hinder the recovery of the more developed occupied nation.

Table 5-6
Coefficients of Variation of Arrays of *Active* Nations, at Selected Dates, by Whether Occupied or Not[a]

Year	The Second World War	
	Occupied	Nonoccupied
Base	136	130
Second	139	144
Seventh	133	141

[a]Nations sorted as in Table 3-4 and coefficients are of data in Appendix Table A-3.

When two nations are about equal in development, the result of one occupying the other should produce little postwar change in the degree of their integration.

From Table 5-7 it can be seen that occupied nations of both the upper stratum and the lower tended to conserve their existing degree of integration through the second year after the war. These nations differ in their clustering only in the seventh postwar year; that is, the gaps narrowed by (8) among the former and by (15) among the latter. The nations of the middle stratum, however, acted differently; they markedly narrowed the distances between their positions. This finding clearly confirms the unpredictable hypothesis about the relationship between war and integration in the development hierarchy. So the proposition that a more developed occupying nation can upgrade or at least not downgrade a less developed occupied nation proves true for both the nations of the West and the East.[15]

Interpretation

Global communication functions to promote integration. The utilization of travelers, mail, telegrams, money, trade, and migrants to diffuse the principles and products of world culture enables nations to conserve or decrease the gaps between their positions through history. The unequal utilization of international contact by each nation is the foundation of the level of integration specification in the development hierarchy. The greater the communication utilized by a nation, the less its social distance from other nations.

The process of global communication is at least as old as the transasian trade route mentioned by Herodotus,[16] which the Persians controlled and which Alexander the Great sought to bring under his dominion, on which Marco Polo later traveled, and which was, during Roman times, quite busy all along its 6,250 miles with commerce between the East and West. "Up to twelve caravans yearly, with a hundred men and a corresponding number of pack animals apiece, left

Table 5-7

Coefficients of Variation of Arrays of *Occupied* Nations, at Selected Dates, by Stratum of Development[a]

	The Second World War		
Year	Upper	Middle	Lower
Base	59	75	76
Second	58	41	76
Seventh	51	30	61

[a]Nations sorted as in Table 3-6 and coefficients are of data in Appendix Table A-3.

China for the West." At the same time, around 100 B.C., some twenty Roman freighters a year sailed from Aden to India. "When Egypt was conquered by the Romans in *circa* 30 B.C., this number suddenly soared. A hundred ships were now dispatched to India yearly, and they were not only freighters and tramp ships that sailed when they had enough cargo; there was a proper liner service with passengers on board and fixed times of sailing." Then by stages the Romans sailed around India to Burma, up the coast of Vietnam to Haiphong and finally to Canton.[17]

Diffusion of world instrumental culture causes nations to move closer together in the development hierarchy. Integration increases when nations increase the permeability of their borders, and it declines when barriers arise. Accordingly, an improvement in the means of global communication, or in the opportunities for transnational contact, furthers integration. Nations move ahead by a combination of invention and of borrowing from each other. It is this ease of borrowing which permits generalization about the the development of nations formerly at lower levels of development.[18] Diffusion goes on whenever two nations are brought into contact. Today, world culture is being diffused all over the world and the speed with which it spreads will be realized by anyone who travels around the world: all factories and nightclubs look alike; all government bureaus and brothels are organized along the same lines; all hospitals and ball games have invariant rosters; and so forth. In fact, since the Second World War, nations have become indistinguishable due to world culture as a common heritage and are as different from one another as the hardware stores of New York City; that is, they differ only in wealth and size and location.

By the turn of the century, for the first time in all time, the greater part of the world was in the position where, though the absolute inequalities among different nations were enormous, the relative movement toward greater development was shared in some degree by all. The organization which made possible that situation was the institutionalization of the great network of global communication and contact.[19] The denser that network, the stronger the transmission of information and artifacts, and thus the more mastery nations exhibit over the environment.

The interruption of global communication in war is a deliberate policy of warring powers, but fortunately this interruption is never complete. The modern world would fall apart if it were. An interruption of the great network is far more significant than (say) an interruption of a steady addition to world culture. Even if, temporarily, all research bureaus shifted to projects specific to war and all universities emptied themselves of their personnel, useful ideas and principles, beliefs and values, would still remain under the skin of man. But without contact, no diffusion of instrumental culture is possible, no matter what brilliant innovations are independently added to the body of it. Although additions to world culture may be less frequent in wartime and the activity of the great network may alter and warp, the world remains integrated nevertheless; the thrust of global communication appears to be uncontainable and these interruptions are only partial.[20]

According to Dean Acheson, there are two aims of economic warfare. One is "to cut the enemy's supplies, information, and funds from foreign territory and prevent his communication with it." The other is "to control overland trade between neutrals and the enemy within the continent he dominated."[21] The blockade is the favored or most suited mechanism with which to gain these aims. Blockades are somewhat effective but never as effective as intended. If they were more effective, then a losing nation would capitulate much sooner and its postwar integration might be seriously hampered to the extent that it cannot easily reknit its ties to other nations. Dean Acheson goes on to discuss the most thorough blockade of a nation ever contemplated. Yet the evidence at hand of the circumvention of restrictions on contact proves how permeable that blockade became. During the Second World War, for example, Germany received goods from the United States, Brazil, Soviet Union, Japan, Manchukuo, China, Afghanistan, and Iran, via Soviet Union from September 1939 through June 1941; and directly from Sweden, Turkey, Spain, and Portugal, from 1939 through 1944.[22] In any case whenever a nation becomes the subject of a blockade it will immediately respond by devising methods to circumvent the restriction on contacts with other nations for the duration of the emergency. The following five examples of contact *during* war demonstrates the permeability of blockades.

1. In the 1740s, during the War of the Austrian Succession, English marine insurance companies insured French vessels against capture at sea by the British navy, and Parliament, after protracted debate, refused to make the practice illegal.[23]
2. During the Wars of Coalition against France, 1805-15, many instances of trade between opponents have been recorded. For example, England sold army uniforms to its enemy France despite the Continental System imposed by Napoleon.[24] At the same time, France sold wheat to its enemy England, even in a bad harvest year, despite a naval blockade.[25]
3. During the Crimean War, 1854-56, "the British board of trade ruled that an English merchant might legally import Russian goods if he purchased them in a neutral country. A prize court decision allowed a subject of the British Protectorate of the Ionian Isles to trade with the enemy. British orders in council allowed Russian ships six weeks of grace in which to load at any British or colonial port and return to Russia immune from capture. A Russian loan, to pay interest on Russian bonds was floated on the London market during the progress of the war with the permission of the English government. There were also friendly gestures in the relations of Russia and France. When diplomatic relations were broken, the Tsar gave the French minister, Castelbajac, a decoration as a parting gift. While the

war was going on, the French government invited Russia to participate in the Exposition of Industry and the Arts."[26]

4. If blockades were so permeable between belligerents, then it may be imagined how they were when neutrals were involved. Prior to the First World War, "rules of law were recognized in which it was considered entirely legal and normal that a nonparticipating state should permit passage through its territories or might render support to a belligerent in the form of soldiers, provisioning, or loans. This was not considered as incompatible with its status as a neutral. Thus, neutral governments frequently lent or hired out numbers of their troops for payment. On the other hand, belligerent states often paid subsidies to other states to keep them neutral. It was at times a purely business arrangement, in which the highest bidder was successful.[27]

5. During the last quarter of 1940 Russia had imported some 28,000 tons of cotton from the United States, although her own cotton harvest was supposedly an extra large one and although there was no reason to believe that her normal imports of cotton from adjacent Asiatic nations had been reduced. Due to this information the following letter was sent by Lord Halifax to Mr. Sumner Wells about the lack of U.S. aid in blockading supplies to Germany:

My government have definite evidence of actual shipments from Russia to Germany of over 60,000 tons of cotton in the first ten months of 1940. Russia has committed herself to supply Germany with 90,000 tons of cotton per annum and recent reports have indicated that this figure has been increased to 120,000 tons. The Soviet Government are also exporting cotton to other various European destinations, such as 8,000 tons to Slovakia and at least 6,000 tons to Hungary. It seems evident, therefore, that the Soviet Government imports have been made in order to enable them to replace the domestic cotton which they are supplying to Central Europe.

In the covering letter Lord Halifax shows the same concern over the actions of other neutral nations by noting that "Germany had bought $3 millions worth of rubber in Brazil, and $1 million worth of this rubber had already reached Japan on its way to Germany, after being carried in Japanese ships via the Panama Canal."[28]

Global communication, and its attendant notion of interdependence, appears ageless rather than novel. Teggart, for example, has shown that troubles in China in the period from 58 B.C. to A.D. 107 were diffused all along the way to Rome and vice versa. He says that "every barbarian uprising in Europe followed the outbreak of war either on the Eastern frontiers of the Roman Empire or in the 'Western Regions' of the Chinese. Moreover, the correspondence in events was discovered to be so precise that, whereas wars in the Roman East were followed uniformly and always by outbreaks on the lower Danube and the Rhine, wars in the Eastern T'ien Shan were followed uniformly and always by outbreaks on the Danube between Vienna and Budapest." What is the linkage of such seemingly quite distant phenomena? Teggart's answer is that "the correspondence of wars in the East and invasions in the West was due to *interruptions* of trade."[29] Such a hypothesis assumes that all the peoples of the heartland depended upon this "international commerce" and that any interruption of the trade (due to assassinations and shift in allegiances along the routes) between the Chinese West and Europe affected all the tribes in the regions in between to such an extent that they either revolted or invaded or migrated. This unplanned, unintended, and unanticipated barrier between the Great Empires, however, was largely circumvented. The interruption of the transasian trade by land caravans encouraged increasing sea contact as I described it earlier in this interpretative section.

Global communication sways all nations and affects nearly all inhabited places: it exists and grows. Agents of contact continuously diffuse the principles and products of the phenomenon called world culture despite the growing impermeability of national boundaries, the rise of intended and unintended barriers, both in peace and war. In this way, global communication promotes integration in the development hierarchy. But the instrumentalities of global communication or transnational contact are not applied equally by nations. A direct relationship exists between development rank and ties to the great network that services the world: the higher a nation stands in the hierarchy, the closer and stronger its ties to that network.

Development proceeds by a combination of new ideas and diffusion. An idea on how to further control the environment is an addition to the stock of knowledge or world culture. World culture is universal, transnational, and extraterritorial. It may be added to and drawn from indiscriminately but for various reasons it is not. Between a new idea and its diffusion and later application, there is a time and space lag from one nation to another. The following quotation discusses this fact.

The lag may be prolonged by indifference to new ideas as such or to the discovery itself: by habits of mind hostile to scientific thinking or unable to come to terms with it: by incapacity to grasp the relevance of the new discovery: by inability to adapt it to a different set of circumstances: or by powerlessness to take advantage of it. All these influences are at work in the under-developed countries to delay the transmission to them of advances in science and technology occurring elsewhere and to delay still further the dissemination within them of what is known and applied at their points of contact with other countries. Their stock of unabsorbed technology is therefore far larger than in the countries where innovations most commonly originate or where the process of diffusion is made more rapid and effective by better education, wider experience and a keener sense of commercial advantage.[30]

The presumed effects of global communication do not become instantly incorporated into the life of every needy nation. Various resistances present themselves on the road from diffusion of technological information to its application. "Technological information is not an ordinary commodity, and ordinary markets will not transfer it efficiently from developed to poor countries. The uncertain value of information not yet owned, the difficulty of owning information exclusively, and its inexhaustibility in use, have led to a complex and still imperfect network for its international diffusion. . . ."[31]

Incapacity to absorb new technology and resistance in various forms to new ideas impede advancement. These difficulties vary from nation to nation in inverse relation to their level of development. Differential utilization of the network of global communications, then, serves to maintain the existing inequalities among rich nations and poor or rank spread in the development hierarchy over time.

This explanation of integration in the development hierarchy may be cast in stricter terms. Rank spread is a function of degree of border impermeability. Border impermeability varies with interest in global communication. Therefore, rank spread depends on differential communication between nations in the development hierarchy.

The differential use of global communication reinforces the hierarchy because the more developed nations are the ones that use communication and contact more. If the less developed nations were the ones, the differential use of global communication would result in the destruction of the hierarchy, to wit, equality, or the abolition of the social distances between rich nations and poor within it. For equality to come about, or very great change in relative spread, over the short term, important barriers to global communication among the more developed nations would have to have arisen to enable the less developed nations to close the gaps between themselves and the more developed nations. But such barriers are not observable in history. No important contact invention for relaying either information or artifacts between nations has been lost or eroded permanently without a more efficient replacement, not even, as I have shown, as a result of war. And certainly most barriers designed to cut existing contacts and communications among the enemy during the First and Second World War have proven to be permeable.

6 Progress

Progress refers to the relative speed of material improvement of rich nations and poor in the development hierarchy over time. The hierarchy exhibits socioeconomic progress in the degree to which the average of its members results in increasing mastery over the environment. The mobilization of cohesion by each nation is the foundation of its progress.

Science when disseminated and used leads to greater productivity. The application of science reinforces the working of a nation's hand and brain so that the final output is much greater than would otherwise be possible. The possibilities of adding to the body of science, diffusing it, and absorbing technological information to further mastery over the environment are all greatly enlarged by the mechanism of the nation. Put differently, the link between world culture, global communication, and development is the organized nation.

Around 1850, Friedrich List claimed that an enterprising nation anywhere could make another nation's head start in development short-lived. He was probably the first to associate nationhood and social mobilization with material improvement, and he spent a considerable amount of time attempting to persuade the German people of it. Here is a characteristic example of his argument:

Between each individual and entire humanity ... stands The Nation ... as the individual chiefly obtains by means of the nation and in the nation mental culture, power of production, security, and prosperity, so is the civilisation of the human race conceivable and possible by means of the civilisation and development of the individual nations.[1]

That argument was unusual in the early part of the nineteenth century because nations, as currently understood, hardly existed. Nowadays the argument that nationhood conditions material progress is taken for granted. Here is a contemporary exposition of the view:

It was the rise of the nation state which gave the impulse to the conception of economic development as a desirable objective reality. Under the Roman Empire the area of administration was so vast, under feudalism the concentration of power so feeble, that the idea of policies deliberately adopted to bring about or facilitate economic change cannot readily have suggested itself to the speculative intelligence.[2]

The more developed a nation, the greater its cohesion. Cohesion is an important idea because of its direct bearing on material improvement. The more cohesive a nation, the more progress it will exhibit over time. If progress is defined empirically by the per capita increase in the number of telephones, the same point will be reached by various nations at different dates as long as they are able to mobilize their cohesion accordingly. All nations are seen as taking part in the same race; some were early starters, others late starters; their speed is measured by their rate of growth, and all of them will, eventually, reach the same goal. Such a definition serves as a basis for evaluation. Nations constantly evaluate themselves and others in terms of their relative mastery of the environment. Because they are under a constant state of competition or rivalry, nations rely on objective measures to rate their relative standing in development.

Rivalry among nations is not an episodic or unique event which comes and goes periodically but rather a normal and perennial condition. The clear result of it is firm boundaries. Without rivalry, the structure and function of the nation would alter, cohesion would slacken, and boundary interests would crumble. There is on the horizon, then, quite obviously a context of rivalry among nations. While this context of rivalry impinges differentially on nations, any nation is overwhelmingly shaped by its exposure to it. This happens regardless of any singularity of its political or economic system, its history or its culture.[3] Any ideology pretending to be universalistic, therefore, can never effectively succeed in its pure form primarily because of its inability to abrade sufficiently this context of rivalry. Djilas is quite emphatic about this in so far as devotees of Communism may have thought that it could have exercised universal dominion. "Communism no longer exists. Only national communisms exist, each different in doctrine and in policies practiced and in the actual state of affairs they have created."[4]

Because grievances between nations can never be fully redressed, the expectation of violence is ever present. During peace the expectation of violence will remain high even if only borders stay at issue. During "the autumn of 1965 there were 49 active border disputes—one for every two significant sovereignties in the world."[5] Perhaps because border questions do not always make newspaper headlines or engage universal sentiment or, due to their insolvable nature, sustain interest, "the number of active and incipient boundary disputes in various parts of the world in times of peace is greater than might be suspected.[6] Moreover, as the number of nations increases, so should the number of disputes increase proportionately. "The 100,000 or more miles of boundaries in the world occasion frequent altercations among the nations that live along them."[7] Accordingly, "the alternative to world war, it seems, is not world peace. It is a world full of small wars and rumors of wars."[8] Lest it be assumed that border wars occur only between nations, it should be noted that preliterates have exactly the same problem and to the same degree. A study of 298 primitive peoples found 8 peoples who did not know war at all; 4 among the lower hunters, 2 among the higher, and 2 among the lower agricultural peoples.[9]

During peace one nation may pursue a policy aimed at either helping or hindering—when not actually ignoring—another nation. This aspect of diplomacy may involve extending influence without directly fighting another nation, or intervening into the civil disturbances of another nation without appearing to do so. After all, there are many forms of violence besides war, and more prevalent than war, which require the services of armies, navies, and police: insurrection, terrorism, and civil war are obvious examples.[10] From this perspective, then, it became altogether understandable for some observers to categorize the period between the two world wars as the twenty-year crisis, when there was no peace.[11] And since the Second World War, internal violence was notably common to a number of nations: Greece, Malaya, the Philippines, Kenya, Cyprus, Algeria, Cuba, the Congo, Laos, Colombia, Korea, Turkey, the Dominican Republic, Ethiopia, Indonesia, and Vietnam; and in some of these nations internal disturbances occurred more than once.

During peace, nations engage one another for economic mastery. The prevalence of protectionist bills, the height of tariffs, and the differential access to markets reveal the impermeability of borders and the competition of national interests. While the drive for impermeability may vary over time and from nation to nation due to a variety of factors, it proceeds at least as much from competitive interests as from any other cause. For Czechoslovakia to sell steel to Saudi Arabia in exchange for oil means mutual gain; but when French steel begins displacing Czechoslovakian in the Saudi Arabian market, then we have a glimmer of the ceaseless contest. The competition of nations (feudalistic, capitalistic, or socialistic) for markets and for fields of investment must be recognized as a struggle for existence. On its success in this competition depends a nation's ability to feed and employ its people, to maintain and increase its population, wealth, prestige, and power. This conflict is nonetheless real because bloodless. Defeat could spell decline in comparative development and produce a motive for more fatal engagements.

The elements constituting a context of rivalry among nations are clear and now may be summarized. During peace, expectations of violence remain high, border conflicts are rarely resolved, internal disturbances loom here and there ceaselessly, and externally nations are in an inescapable struggle for existence everywhere and always.

The Problem

Into this context of rivalry among nations comes war. War exacerbates some of the existing rivalries and attenuates others. The difference between rivalry and war lies not in the goals nations pursue (security, autonomy, territory, wealth, power, prestige, allies, trade, ideology, and development), but rather in the means employed: threat and intimidation as opposed to actual violence. In war, the structure and function and boundary interests of nations remain nearly the same. What differs is the degree of cohesion mobilized by each nation for war purposes. How much mobilization varies, depending in part on the perceived amount of menace to its integrity and in part on what is at stake. For war to affect the speed of material improvement of nations in the development hierarchy, it must increase or decrease cohesion.

Nations vary by their cohesiveness and thus their socioeconomic progress. The more cohesive a nation, the more flexible it can be "in devising institutions to accomplish its purposes under changing conditions."[12] In war, there is a diversion of man power into the military, the unemployed secure jobs, extensive retraining of labor takes place, and longer hours are worked. Population movements occur on a grand scale, for example, growth of defense or munitions towns. Some industries are expanded (for example, armaments), while others using vital raw materials and labor tend to be retarded (for example, refrigerators and automobiles). To overcome shortages, new products are developed and ersatz materials tend to supplement or replace natural products, for example, artificial rubber. Various luxury items are curtailed, products become simplified, and the main consideration becomes the functional use of a good rather than its ornamentation. The production of war goods must be increased tremendously, and, since resources are limited, part of this expansion must be at the expense of civilian supplies. If the war effort is of sufficient intensity and long enough duration, the result might include a decline in the standard of living, which is one of the sacrifices that tends to accompany modern war. It is achieved through either a rise in prices or an increase in taxes that is not offset by an expansion of income. The impact upon living standards is not the same for all groups, and hence a redistribution of income and wealth could take place. With restrictions placed upon profits and with the institution of heavier progressive income and estate taxes, there tends to be a more equal distribution of income and wealth.[13] Trade relations with foreign nations are disrupted, and this in turn also has its effects domestically.[14]

The enormous stimulus war gives to national cohesion and thus to production is perhaps the most ironic fact of war. But while the nation works harder to raise its production, the costs of war in men, minds, material, and money are also rising. Hence, war consumes much of the product it stimulates. So at this point, it is not clear how the scale would look once gains and costs are placed on it. It will be the purpose of this chapter to find out which outweighs the other, under various circumstances.

The appropriate method for testing hypotheses about progress is by regression coefficients. The regression coefficient is represented by the slope of the line which travels best through the scores at various points in time of nations, in number of telephones per thousand. The regression coefficient expresses growth over an entire time span. Put differently, time is taken as the independent variable affecting the number of telephones. Thus, on the average, each succeeding year will be accompanied by an increase of so much of a telephone instrument for every thousand people.

Findings

From Table 6-1, it can be seen that the world bore straight on a course of material improvement. On the average, each succeeding year in the time span is accompanied by an increase of 0.83 of a telephone instrument (or nearly one) for every thousand people, a growth in real income of 2.89 international units (or 1929 dollars) per capita, and an addition of three metric tons of steel per one hundred people. Because neither of the two world wars substantially affected the overall trend, the finding confirms the irrelevant hypothesis about the relationship between war and progress. Progress does not associate with war; the collective speed of material improvement was about the same at the end as it was at the beginning of the time span.

Apparently nations have benefited from steady world progress; though socioeconomic development facilitates greater war destruction, it also facilitates greater postwar recovery. Under twentieth-century conditions, war neither accelerates nor interrupts the underlying trend of sustained per capita growth when nations are viewed collectively. But are all nations benefiting equally in this world progress?

Table 6-1
Regression Coefficients of Time and Scores of Nations[a]

	All Nations	Telephones	Income	Steel
	Slope[b]	0.83	2.89	0.03
	Intercept[c]	7.50	266.75	3.18
	Correlation[d]	0.98	0.86	0.35

[a]The regressions are based on per capita data located in Appendix Tables A-3, A-6, and A-9, respectively.
[b]The slope expresses the annual amount of growth through the time span which extends from 1913 through 1952.
[c]The intercept refers to the value of the data at the start of the line.
[d]The correlation indicates the distance of the plot entries from the line.

Level of Development

If war causes differential progress among the various parts of the development hierarchy, then the introduction of an intervening variable, such as development stratum, may reveal its profile. It is not unreasonable to expect variations in progress by development stratum that would remain undetected in a regression coefficient of time and the scores of all nations. The four hypotheses about the relationship between war and progress will be tested, taking into account this intervening variable of development stratum. If progress associates positively with development stratum through war, that is, if the upper stratum exhibits the greatest amount of material improvement, then this confirms the productive hypothesis; if it associates inversely, this confirms the destructive hypothesis; if it associates variably, this confirms the unpredictable hypothesis; and, if it remains unaffected, this indicates no relationship or the irrelevant hypothesis. To determine the fit of these hypotheses, time and scores of nations sorted by development stratum will be observed over the same time span. The result can be seen in Table 6-2.

The general finding of Table 6-2 corroborates the previous finding of overall continuity in material improvement. Without exception, nations in each stratum exhibit a steady annual increase in their mastery of the environment from 1913 through 1952. But it is clear that the strata did not move upwardly evenly; that is, speed of improvement varied. This information confirms the productive hypothesis about the relationship between war and progress among nations sorted by development stratum. Progress associates positively with achieved level of development through war; upper stratum nations improve their situation faster than lower stratum nations, even though lower stratum nations have improved their material situation in absolute terms. The more developed a nation, therefore, the greater its capacity to increase its mastery of the environment through history.

War does not significantly affect the distribution of the internal cohesion of nations when they are sorted by achieved level of development. Its effect across the board of rich nations and poor appears to be equal. Upper stratum nations consistently exhibit greater cohesion before and after war than lower stratum

Table 6-2
Regression Coefficients of Time and Scores of Nations, by Stratum of Development[a]

	Upper	Middle	Lower
	2.16	0.24	0.03

[a]Stratification of nations as of 1952 (see Table 2-3) and regressions are of data in Appendix Table A-3.

nations. Therefore, greater speed of material improvement should be anticipated among upper stratum than among lower stratum nations through war.

Nations exhibiting low, but desiring higher, rates of progress, then, necessarily must make more effective the key social processes described earlier in Chapter 3. They need for one thing to become more centralized for the obvious reason that not a single decision is assured compliance throughout the nation.[15] "A power to amalgamate men is the more needed that the combative and self-regarding instincts are more energetic than those which prompt us to union. This is the part of that cohesive force in society, everywhere called government, the business of which is at once to combine and to direct."[16]

Combative and self-regarding "instincts" is an important indicator of low consociation or communication in a nation. Former President Nasser had to contend with this problem throughout his political career.

Before July 23rd I had imagined that the whole nation was ready and prepared, waiting for nothing but a vanguard to lead the charge. . . . I thought this role would never take more than a few hours . . . —but how different is the reality from the dream! The masses that came were disunited, divided groups of stragglers. . . . There was a confirmed individual egotism. The word "I" was on every tongue. It was the solution to every difficulty, the cure for every ill.[17]

Low consociation can be generalized as a product of a nonunified communication system, having the effect of limiting the rate of progress. With low consociation, mass media, for example, reach only the urban population while the rural population, the vast majority, still communicate by word of mouth. Low consociation appears endemic among nations exhibiting a low rate of material improvement.

As low centralization and consociation impede national cohesion, and thus progress, so does low cooperation or consensus. Gunnar Myrdal calls it "voluntariness" and claims that

there is little hope in South Asia for rapid development without greater social discipline. To begin with, in the absence of more discipline—which will not appear without regulations backed by compulsion—all measures for rural uplift will be largely ineffective. In principle, discipline can be effected within the framework of whatever degree of political democracy a country can achieve; in the end nothing is more dangerous for democracy than lack of discipline.[18]

Among the social aspects of development, in which there appears to be a large area of agreement, Lerner includes "a measure of public participation in the polity—or at least democratic representation in defining and choosing policy alternatives."[19] This is precisely the impediment to progress in Latin American nations that Gino Germani focuses attention on; that is, the general absence of national identification and acceptance of political authority.[20]

Time leading in socioeconomic progress seems best explained by time leading in national cohesion. The earlier and more complete the cohesion, the earlier and more sustained the nation's progress. Nations in the upper stratum of development tended to achieve nationhood and greater cohesion before nations in other strata. For nations of the middle or lower strata, any acceleration of cohesion to effect material improvement is unfortunately overmatched by the acceleration that nations in the upper stratum constantly exhibit. Under no conditions will one nation willingly wait for other nations to catch up, even though a handful of lead nations might be willing to give limited help to latecomers on the time trail of development. In this sense the development hierarchy is essentially conservative in operation.

Degree of War Participation

Degree of war participation may also have an effect on progress. Will nations at war be so helped by an acceleration of their key social processes as to be able to offset the general costs and actually increase their control of the environment more than can neutrals, or will the reverse be true? Wright argues for the first possibility:

In the past half-century, the economic and propaganda aspects of war technique have so gained in importance that the diplomatic and military advantage of highly centralized and militarized states appears to have increased.[21]

Linton presents a view of the second possibility:

It seems safe to predict that Europe will emerge from the struggle [of the Second World War] impoverished in fairly direct ratio to the length of the war. The victor will be little better off than the vanquished since he will have slight chance of recouping his losses on the outside. The spread of the machine and the theft of world markets by neutral powers will see to that.[22]

A third possibility is presented by Condliffe who argues against gains from war by either participants or neutrals.

When the war ends, however, all the peoples—belligerents and neutrals, victors and vanquished—become involved in the ultimate costs inherent in the destruction of trade, the demoralization of moneys, the dissipation of reserves, and the accumulation of debts. There is no victor in a modern war, nor any real gain to the neutrals. All the nations are involved in the collapse of their common economic welfare. Neutrality and isolation may avoid military casualties, but there can be no neutrality or isolation from the economic wreckage that is the inevitable aftermath of a great modern war.[23]

The effect of war involvement on progress in the development hierarchy can be determined. It requires only that nations be sorted by degree of war participation. The familiar hypotheses about the relationship between war and progress in development will again be tested but with the new specification of participation. If progress associates positively with degree of participation through war, that is, if the more involved nations exhibit greater amounts of growth, then this confirms the productive hypothesis; if it associates inversely, this confirms the destructive hypothesis; if it associates variably, this confirms the unpredictable hypothesis; and, if it remains unaffected, this confirms the irrelevant hypothesis.

As in the preceding chapter, both world wars can be considered as a single event called the Thirty-One Years War: 1914-45. Nations are distinguished by the number of years they have participated as combatants in that long war. Time and scores of nations in each category of participation are observed over the period extending from 1913 through 1952. The result can be seen in Table 6-3.

Judging from the regression coefficients in Table 6-3, war costs must be slight in proportion to the total resources of a nation in the twentieth century. World wars apparently neither thwart nor retard socioeconomic progress. For whatever the category of war participation, nations moved ahead. It is a fact from this table that any interruption in material improvement which may be due to war involvement is normally made up within a decade without any apparent effect on the underlying trend.

General continuity in progress, however, should not be taken as a signal that war can be waged with impunity. There are costs even though gains may compensate partially for them, and both vary. Although nations in all four categories of participation in the Thirty-One Years War exhibit an increasing mastery of the environment, this increase is not uniform. There is indeed a relationship between speed of progress as measured by regression coefficients, and degree of war participation. Comparing the regression coefficients, it can be seen that nations in the maximum participation category had the greatest amount of growth, followed by those in the medium category, and the minimum category. The only deviation from this pattern is that nations which were neutral in this long war had a greater amount of growth than nations in these other

Table 6-3
Regression Coefficients of Time and Scores of Nations, by Degree of War Participation[a]

The Thirty-One Years War: 1914-45			
Maximum	Medium	Minimum	Neutral
1.20	0.88	0.12	1.38

[a]Maximum means officially in war for six or more years; medium means officially in war from three to six years; minimum means officially in war for less than three years; and neutral means absence of official war participation in both the First and Second World Wars. Nations sorted as in Table 3-3 and regressions are of data in Appendix Table A-3.

categories. This finding tends to confirm the productive hypothesis about the relationship between war and progress. Progress associates positively with degree of war participation through war; nations of the maximum category improve their situation faster than nations of the minimum category, even though minimally involved nations have improved their material situation in absolute terms. The more war involves a nation, therefore, the greater its capacity to increase its mastery of the environment through history.

Nations at war tend to experience the acceleration of their key social process and this seems to account for their greater amounts of material improvement. They tend obviously to become more centralized. Out of a need to coordinate and rationalize collective action, the governing arm is strengthened and its influence extended. This can be seen in the regulation of industry, for example, when government controls the kind of products manufactured, the quality and amount of output, the prices, and the supply of credit.[24] Secondly, warring nations tend to achieve greater consociation or internal communication and interaction within their boundaries. This has the effect of reducing or at least putting off internal conflicts which tend to fragment nations. At first consociation increases as a result of the common threat. The external threat alone, however, is not enough to counter internal problems like slacking, strikes, blackmarketeering, minority discrimination, class conflict, and the rest. So government acts to reduce the costs of such practices: slackers are ridiculed, strikes are banned, blackmarketeers are supposedly prosecuted, minorities are promised fairer treatment, and issues between classes are coopted. And thirdly, in war, nations tend to gain in cooperation. It may be assumed that in total war there will be a willingness on the part of almost every person to make some positive effort to support his government at such a time. But the rise in cooperation occurs neither accidentally nor automatically; the decision to resort to war depends on an elaborate preparation of climate. Total war requires general willingness. Because the government ultimately controls all the mass media within its borders, it can effectively mobilize consensus, supposedly, in direct proportion to the threat presented by an opponent's stance.[25] As a consequence of these accelerating processes, output completion also escalates.[26] As borders become firmer with the polarization resulting from war, the nation realizes a new discipline or power, a new solidarity or pulse, a new sentiment or passion, and, therefore, a new output or pride. Hence nations at war should sustain if not increase their prewar rate of growth through the postwar years.

Turning now to shorter time spans, the finding in the relationship between degree of war participation and progress should not be significantly different from that over the long term. After each world war, the slopes for various categories of nations should still increase. What cannot be predicted is the magnitude of increases and the arraying of categories. The results of manipulating time and scores of nations with their degree of participation in the First and Second World Wars can be viewed in Table 6-4.

Table 6-4
Regression Coefficients of Time and Scores of Nations, by Degree of War Participation[a]

| | The First World War | | | The Second World War | |
Active	Marginal	Neutral	Active	Marginal	Neutral
0.93	0.30	0.77	1.61	0.16	1.91

[a]Active means officially in war for three years or more; marginal means officially in war for less than three years; and neutral means absence of official war participation. The time span for the First World War is from 1913 through 1925; for the Second World War from 1938 through 1952. Nations sorted as in Table 3-2 and regressions are of data in Appendix Table A-3.

Despite a global momentum upward, speed of progress varies by degree of war participation as indicated by Table 6-4. Through each world war, the array of war categories in rate of material growth is the same: active and marginal. It seems reasonable to reassert that the faster rate of subsequent improvement among active nations is because the key social processes of centralization, consociation, and cooperation are accelerated more within them than within nations marginally involved in war. While war exacts a cost, it is clear that this cost is more easily absorbed under conditions of greater than of lesser involvement. Neutral nations tend to bear fewer direct costs in men, minds, money, and material relative to nations at war and so may find war, at best, an opportunity to obtain new business and allies or, at worst, an interruption in prewar dealings. The only difference between the two world wars, then, is in rate of growth. Both active and neutral nations exhibited greater amounts of growth through the Second than through the First World War. In the main, these findings confirm the productive hypothesis about the relationship between war and progress. Progress associates positively with degree of war participation through world wars; nations of the active category improve their material situation faster than nations of the marginal category, even though these latter nations have improved their material situation in absolute terms. The more war involves a nation, therefore, the greater its capacity to increase its mastery over the environment through time.

Active Nations and the Second World War

At this juncture two findings will be reviewed. In Table 6-2 it was found that level of development and progress associate positively; that is, richer nations improve their material situation quicker than poorer ones. In Tables 6-3 and 6-4 it was found that degree of war participation and progress associate positively; that is, the most involved nations exhibited the greatest growth. So both level of development and degree of war participation associate positively with progress.

Inasmuch as these two variables—level of development and degree of war participation—have similar effects on progress, it becomes necessary to determine, if when degree of war participation is held constant, whether or not level of development still has an effect. Heretofore we have not controlled the observations for participation variability; now we will. To test the relative effects of development level and degree of war participation on progress, the forty-three active nations during the Second World War were sorted by their level of development. In Table 6-5 the regression coefficients tell the story.

From Table 6-5 it can be seen that progress among active nations varies with development stratum. The finding confirms the productive hypothesis about the relationship between war and progress when prewar level of development is introduced. Progress associates positively with achieved level of development through war; active nations in the upper stratum improve their material situation very much faster than active nations in other strata. So when degree of war participation is controlled, prewar level of development bears a considerable effect on the postwar progress of nations in the development hierarchy. Moreover, Table 6-5 shows that active nations in the lower stratum actually exhibited a retardation of progress. The more war involves a more developed nation, therefore, the greater its capacity to increase its mastery over the environment through history.

Military Occupation during the
Second World War

Foreign occupation may also affect progress. One of the outstanding phenomena of the Second World War was the fact of military occupation of wide stretches of territory over long periods of time by both Allied and Axis armies. According to Article 42 of the 1907 Hague Convention on Laws and Customs of War on Land, a territory is considered occupied only when it is actually placed under the authority of the occupying army. Out of the forty-three nations considered active during the Second World War, twenty-seven were occupied according to this definition.

Table 6-5
Regression Coefficients of Time and Scores of *Active* Nations, by Stratum of Development[a]

| | The Second World War | |
Upper Active	Middle Active	Lower Active
3.63	0.31	−0.01

[a]Stratification of nations as of 1952 (see Table 2-3), sorted as in Table 3-5 and regressions are of data in Appendix Table A-3.

The policy of an occupying force consists in extracting more work time and thus more output from an occupied nation than might otherwise be required. The increase in output, or surplus value, goes, of course, to the occupying force. For example,

after its victories over Denmark, Holland, France, Belgium, and others . . . Germany obtained large stores of equipment and food supplies as well as factories to use in its war efforts. Similarly, the conquest of Czechoslovakia . . . placed in Germany's possession one of the leading munitions works in the world. The high occupation costs levied on France after its downfall should also be mentioned in this connection. In addition to these materials and equipment, a large labor supply was obtained, and where voluntary measures were not successful, measures were taken to force this labor to work.[27]

An extraordinarily simple and interesting series of methods was devised by the German high command to conserve or increase the productivity of occupied nations.

A small group of engineers was given almost unlimited powers to carry rationalization to the limit, an elaborate system of "efficiency" competition has been instituted between firms, and bonuses have been given for suggestions leading to increased output. The exchange of inventions and patented processes has been made compulsory. All these devices had one aim, to increase output, or at least to maintain it at the old level.[28]

The policy of an occupying force in extracting more work time and thus more output from an occupied nation should bear directly on the latter's postwar progress. To the extent that occupation policy affects cohesion negatively, occupied nations should exhibit low postwar rates of material improvement. If such a policy does not affect cohesion, occupation will matter little.

Time and scores of both the occupied and nonoccupied active nations were observed over the same time span. The impact of occupation on the progress of these nations can be viewed in Table 6-6.

From Table 6-6 it can be seen that the progress of nations in the development hierarchy varies by whether or not they were occupied. Nonoccupied active nations improve their material situation after war faster than occupied nations.

Table 6-6
Regression Coefficients of Time and Scores of *Active* Nations, by Whether Occupied or Not[a]

The Second World War	
Occupied	Nonoccupied
1.16	2.13

[a]Nations sorted as in Table 3-4 and regressions are of data in Appendix Table A-3.

Even though foreign occupation makes a difference in material improvement among active nations through war, the finding should not obscure the actual progress made by occupied nations. The annual addition of over one telephone instrument for every thousand people occupied during the Second World War is more than might have been expected from the commentary preceding Table 6-6. On the basis of that foregoing commentary, we merely expected no diminution in rate of improvement among occupied nations; this was because occupation involves some standard procedures; that is, maintenance of the occupied nation's processes of centralization, consociation, and cooperation. This makes good sense for it is easier for all concerned to live under a single coordinated system of control, communication, and compliance, although circumstances alter cases.

Military occupation necessarily involves coercion. In the economic field, coercion manifests itself by the establishment of control mechanisms. In order to coordinate the economic life of a region with the military requirements of the occupying army and with considerations of welfare of the local population these controls will have to be centralized in the occupation authority. For this reason the occupation authority will exercise the greatest influence in those fields which are habitually subjected to extensive governmental interference—currency, taxation, control of the money market, price control, and rationing. Because of the disruption of normal relationships of production and the requirements of a war economy, also the control of physical output of commodities, of the labor market, and of the distribution apparatus will be of immense importance under military occupation.[29]

The reason occupied nations did as well as they did then is obvious; it lies in the nature of the modern nation. The two world wars of the twentieth century, for example, can be visualized as terminal situations,

essentially representing the last stage of a siege. The main feature of that pattern was the unimpaired cohesive structure of the loser's residual forces (and, in World War II, even of his political and social fabric), together with the drying up of sources of supplies and reinforcements. . . . In such a situation, the loser [can] offer "surrender" in the shape of handing to the winner control over cohesive residual capabilities and over a society that is still a going concern."[30]

As nations go under occupation with some degree of cohesion, so they emerge after occupation with some degree of cohesion. If, in the transition, the form of government or economy or any other particular item has changed, this is of no import; what matters is the cohesiveness of the nation. The regression coefficient in Table 6-6 proves this idea dramatically. The intervening factor of occupation seems interesting in itself and invites consideration in conjunction with level of development.

Occupied nations can be sorted into upper, middle, and lower strata of development. What can be predicted from prior findings about nations stratified in various ways? It was shown that progress associates positively with development stratum, with degree of war participation, and, among active nations, with stratum of development. It would seem reasonable, therefore, to predict that occupied nations in the upper development stratum will be found to have fared better than occupied nations in the middle and lower strata of development through the Second World War. That prediction, the productive hypothesis, is entirely borne out by the information in Table 6-7. Progress associates positively with achieved level of development through war; occupied nations in the upper stratum of development improve their material situation faster than occupied nations in the lower stratum of development, even though these latter nations have improved their material situation in absolute terms. The more developed an occupied nation, therefore, the greater its capacity to increase its mastery over the environment through time.

Interpretation

National cohesion functions to promote socioeconomic progress. The mobilization of centralization, consociation, and cooperation within each nation enables nations to strengthen or increase their national cohesion. The greater the cohesion mobilized by a nation, the greater its progress; that is, the more smoothly its complex organizations work, the greater its improvement speed and environmental mastery.

It would be difficult indeed to grasp the idea of progress without paying some attention to the formation of the nation. As a matter of fact, until very recent times, war was almost the only kind of collective action undertaken on a truly large scale. There were armies of hundreds of thousands when empires and city republics were states not coextensive with their societies and when production was carried on in the main only in small farms and workshops. Only during the last century did large complex organizations come into existence. The nation is a relatively new form of social organization representing a coincidence of state and society; it supersedes empires and city republics but may not last as long; the Byzantine Empire and the Republic of Venice, for example, each lasted nearly a thousand years.[31]

The modern nation cannot be dated prior to 1800. The nation we all know

Table 6-7
Regression Coefficients of Time and Scores of *Occupied* Nations, by Stratum of Development[a]

	The Second World War	
Upper	Middle	Lower
2.88	0.21	0.02

[a]Nations sorted as in Table 3-6 and regressions are of data in Appendix Table A-3.

today was created, in a manner of speaking, through social forces unleashed about 150 years ago. Most nations that are today in the upper stratum were directly or indirectly involved in the Wars of Coalition against France, followed the policies of economic protectionism, and were caught up by the principles and practices of nationalism. These conjoined nineteenth-century circumstances contributed decisively to the formation of the modern nation and thus constituted for those nations affected an earlier start on the time trail of development and progress.

One great cause contributing to the formation of the nation as a type of social organization is mercantilism. It refers to a cumulative doctrine which guided the foreign policy of most European nations in a context of rivalry from the sixteenth through the eighteenth centuries. Its sole objective consisted not in progress (or material welfare in per capita terms) but in competitive power or plenty. Mercantilism,

in its innermost kernel . . . is nothing but state-making—not state-making in a narrow sense, but state-making and national-economy making at the same time; state-making in the modern sense, which creates out of the political community an economic community, and so gives it a heightened meaning. The essence of the system lies not in some doctrine of money, or of the balance of trade, not in tariff barriers, protective duties or navigation laws; but in something far greater: namely, in the total transformation of society and its organisation, as well as of the state and its institutions, in the replacing of a local and territorial economic policy by that of the national state.[32]

As the idea of mercentilism in the sixteenth century amounts to "a system of economic nationalism," which had its origin in "the relentless pressure of war and the fear of war," so too the idea of neomercantilism in the nineteenth. "In the protectionist view, there is a reciprocal action between the economic and war: industrialization facilitates the conduct of war, and military victories increase the possibilities of industrialization and economic prosperity. This point of view recalls that of the mercentilists: wealth increases power, and power augments wealth."[33]

The other great cause associated with the formation of the nations is the fervor of nationalism. By its principles and practices, the Great Revolution in France accelerated the worldwide trend toward seeing in the nation a model of effective power. Its objective consisted not of progress but of extending political and social rights to the formerly disfranchised. In August 1789 the National Assembly enunciated, in its Declaration of the Rights of Man and the Citizen, the principle that "all sovereignty rests essentially in the nation" thus making state and society legally coextensive. The new levee en masse, which defeated the dynastic armies, represented the coincidence of state and society in practice. Most groups, first in Europe and then elsewhere, developed a new stake in their nations, as newly responsive states abolished serfdom, granted the right to land ownership, sponsored wage earning through national insurance, changed a man's status from subject to citizen, and rewarded military service with government allocations in health, education, and welfare facilities. The attractiveness of these general ideas appears limited neither by time nor space. Ito Hirobumi, one of the architects of the Meiji Restoration, said in 1880:

The European concept of revolution, which were carried out for the first time in France about one hundred years ago, have gradually spread to the various nations. By combining and complementing each other, they have become a general trend. Sooner or later, every nation will undergo changes as a result. . . . In this period of changes from old to new, revolution often broke out. In fact, revolution continues at present. It has not yet stopped. Elsewhere enlightened rulers, with the help of wise ministers, led and controlled these changes, thus solidifying their nations. In brief, all have had to discard absolutist ways and share political power with the people. . . . Now, European ideas and things are coming into our country like a tidal flow; moreover, new opinions concerning the form of government have become popular among the ex-samurai. . . . However, if we take a general view of causes, it appears that this experience is common to the whole world, Like the rain falling and the grass growing, it is no wonder that we, too, have been affected.[34]

Notable among the objectives of mercantilism and nationalism is the conspicuous absence of the material welfare of persons. The primary concern of any nation, subject to an unavoidable context of rivalry, is how to best opposing nations. (This is the meaning of politics; it is a normal and perennial condition in the life of nations.) In the race to achieve more power, plenty, and prestige, the winners unwittingly achieved progress through their achievement of nationhood. Patently, then, a competitive international setting counts for something.

The nation as currently known existed hardly anywhere before the nineteenth century as mentioned earlier. But wherever it did emerge, it emerged with formidable speed; and national progress has increased in the same manner over the same period. Because of different circumstances, nations did not come into nationhood together or evenly. They emerged at different times and grew at different speeds. The importance of a head start in nationhood lies in rapid progress. It may be considered as an unplanned, unintended, and unanticipated consequence of competitive actions between conflicting political units. In itself, however, nationhood is insufficient to account for progress; what does is the cohesiveness of the nation. The earlier and tighter the cohesion, the earlier and more sustained the nation's material improvement.

Granting that cohesion promotes progress, what promotes cohesion? The answer has been discussed in several places already. Cohesion is promoted by the key social processes that operate within any nation; that is, its centralization, consociation, and cooperation. The magnitudes of these processes determine a nation's degree of cohesion and influences its rate of output completion or speed of material improvement.

Interest in centralization might well begin with Niccolo Machiavelli. In the *Discorsi* he says: "There cannot be good laws where there are not good arms, and where there are good arms there must be good laws."[35] Several centuries later in 1776 Adam Smith makes a very similar statement.

It is only by means of a standing army . . . that the civilization of any country can be perpetuated, or even preserved for any considerable time. A standing army establishes with an irresistible force, the law of the sovereign through the remotest provinces of the empire, and maintains some degree of regular government in countries which could not otherwise admit of any.[36]

When groups within a nation are in continuous contact with one another and able to communicate their grievances under common rules of behavior, then their conflicts over principles, procedures, and policies are much more susceptible to management than if they were not normatively in accord. In any case, the level of consociation in a nation bears directly on the capacity of a nation to get things done. Consociation as a key social process has been identified by Spengler who sees it as a problematic factor in the life of any nation.

The inner constitution of a nation aims at being *"in condition"* for outer fight (diplomatic, military, or economic) and anyone who treats a nation's constitution as an aim and ideal in itself is merely ruining the nation's body. But, from the other point of view, it falls to the inner-political pulse-sense of a ruling stratum (whether belonging to the First or Fourth Estate) so to manage the internal class-oppositions that the focus and ideas of the nation are not tied up in party conflict, nor treason to the country thought of as an ace of trumps.[37]

A government backed by cooperation from the people has far more authority to accomplish its purposes and set new directions than one without such backing. Talleyrand knew this, as he discussed the need for political legitimacy in sufficient detail, as did many before him, for example, Confucius.

Tzu Kung asked about governing, and the Master said, "Adequate supplies for food, adequate stores of munitions, and the confidence of the people." Tzu Kung said, "Suppose you unavoidably had to dispense with one of these, which would you forgo?" The Master said, "Munitions." Thereat Tzu Kung asked if of the remaining two he had to dispense with one, which he would forgo. The Master said, "Food; for all down history death has come to all men (and yet society survives); but the people who have no confidence (in their rulers) are undone."[38]

Nations may be evaluated by social scientists in terms of any or all of the key social processes. But generally nations tend to evaluate themselves and each other instead in terms of output completion, or progress, rather than in terms of centralization, consociation, and cooperation. This makes good sense because completion implies relative mastery of the environment, a crucial determinant of military and diplomatic might, and nations require an objective indicator of their relative standing in this regard. After all, a wrong evaluation here means something in the context of rivalry where decisions carry heavy weight and create irrevocable impact.

Obviously, nations differ in the amount of cohesion they are able to mobilize. Such differential mobilization of cohesion causes differential speeds of material improvement which results in perpetuating the inequalities among nations. National progress may be explained by the theory of differential application as follows. Speed of material improvement is a function of centralization, consociation, and cooperation. The combined magnitude of these processes determine the degree of cohesion that any nation experiences. Therefore, speed of material improvement, or progress, varies with a nation's existing degree of cohesion.

The differential mobilization of cohesion reinforces the development hierarchy because the more developed nations are the ones that mobilize cohesion more.[39] If the less developed nations were the ones, the differential mobilization of cohesion would result in the destruction of the hierarchy, to wit, equalization; that is, upper stratum nations slowing down and lower stratum nations speeding up. For equality to come about, or more uniform progress, over the short term, important internal breakdowns in the key social processes promoting cohesion among the more developed nations must have had to arisen to enable the less developed nations to match their rates of growth. But such internal breakdowns are not observable in history. No key social process contributing to national cohesion has broken down or departure from it been unadjusted to as a result of war. Neither have propaganda techniques of fifth-columnist activities initiated in war to reduce the effectiveness of the enemy's cohesion proven to be sufficient.

Even the extermination of some little nation of antiquity, announced again and again by conquerors, was nearly always followed by the re-emergence of the same nation, usually stronger than before and always thirsting for the blood of its exterminators. Nations, when they are genuine cultural and ethnic entities conscious of their own existence, seem to possess an amazing vitality. It is almost impossible to exterminate a modern European one with a population running into millions.[40]

7 Satisfaction

Our life is what our thoughts make it.

Marcus Aurelius

Satisfaction refers to the reduction of relative stress felt by rich nations and poor in the development hierarchy through history. The hierarchy exhibits satisfaction in the degree to which its members gain internal agreement and external acceptance about their positions. The varying achievement of domestic and foreign consensus about positions is the foundation of the specification of satisfaction in the development hierarchy.

The development hierarchy may be called just, or legitimate, or satisfactory, when its arrangement is consented to by the nations that compose it. In this strict sense, satisfaction appears more of a value or goal to be realized than an imperfect and ever-modifying process. For at any time in history some nations wish to conserve, while others wish to change, the hierarchy: some accept, and others reject, their own positions; and some ignore, while others work for or against, the positions of other nations. From this it follows that satisfaction can never be completely actualized and that dissatisfaction must be considered as an inevitable phenomenon among nations operating in a context of constant rivalry.

At any moment in history, every nation has an unequivocal position in the hierarchy. Given less than complete consensus about the hierarchy raises the issue about the rightness of unequal positions in it. The reason for the questioning attitude is clear. A nation's rank in the hierarchy is a relative ability to master the environment and this means a relative ability to be satisfied. The problem of any nation in the hierarchy is in articulating its rank with satisfaction. It is a problem because of the many difficulties which attend the process.

Feelings and attitudes about position are particularly strong under circumstances of change. The task faced by any nation exhibiting any kind of change in rank is adapting to the stress that change produces, that is, adjusting its values to its perception of the material situation and vice versa. Since adjustment requires effort on all parts, it follows that the more adjustment necessary, the more dissatisfaction. The less change, or the less adjustment required, the more satisfaction with position. The more perfect the match between the felt material situation and the values and definitions of the nation, the greater will be the satisfaction in the development hierarchy.

103

A rank loss evokes powerful and perduring feelings.[1] Because of the nature of hierarchy, what one nation gains another must lose. Any change, therefore, will influence the satisfaction of nations and so conditions the feelings of millions of people about position. A rank loss, however, need not imply a corresponding loss in relative satisfaction if a falling nation can point to another that has fallen even farther. Quincy Wright, in the following quotation, ignores this alternative possibility.

Economic decline may not cause great anxiety if slow, as has often been the case in India and China, because the energy of the population may be reduced more rapidly than their consciousness of deteriorating conditions. Rapid economic decline, however, may arouse the awareness of people while they still have energy and induce them to accept propagandas of violence and revolution.[2]

Decline, whether slow or rapid, will under some circumstances be accompanied by satisfaction. An absolute decline in development rank need not evoke dissatisfaction when the average man in one nation knows that his counterpart in another has declined even farther.

Because peoples consider their achievements both absolutely and relatively, an improvement in their material situation may be accompanied by a decline in psychic situation, and, conversely, a material decline may be accompanied by psychic improvement. The relationship between the material and psychic situations is neither direct nor linear. Other nations, changing as well, inevitably serve as referents.[3]

But apart from that limiting condition, no nation accepts falling behind or being outpaced by another nation. It is certainly not taken with equanimity. Any nation resents a loss in its rank, envies a gain in another's, and gloats over the losses of a more developed nation. Each of these feelings may be illustrated.

Any Nation Resents a Loss in Its Rank. The most popular representation of this feeling is undoubtedly to be found in Adolf Hitler's MEIN KAMPF. Thus it requires only mentioning. Less wellknown, perhaps, is present-day feeling in China on this matter. In the 1930s Mao Tse-tung called attention to areas controlled by China under the Manchu Empire but since removed from Chinese control: Korea, Taiwan, the Ryukyus, The Pescadores, Burma, Bhutan, Nepal, Annam, and Outer Mongolia. In more recent years, Chinese leaders have added to the list part of Soviet Central Asia, eastern Siberia, and Tibet. I think we can take this as valid evidence of Peking's historic sense of loss if not its Asian ambitions. As Oliver Edmund Clubb says, "the urge to revolutionary empire is fortified by the feeling drilled into all Chinese since the beginning of the Republic that all territory ever included in the vast Manchu Empire rightfully belongs to China."[4]

Any Nation Envies a Gain in Another Nation. This may be objectified in Lord Balfour's summary of the feelings of Heinrich von Treitschke to an English audience.

While Germany was in the throes of the Thirty Years' War or slowly recovering from its effects, England, the detested rival, was laying the foundations of the English-speaking communities beyond the seas. . . . What Britain secured must be worth having. If there was something worth having and Germany had it not, this must be due to the bad luck which sometimes pursues even the most deserving. If Germany had it not and England had it, this must be due to the good luck which sometimes befalls even the most incompetent. But such inequalities are not to be tolerated. They must be redressed, if need be, by force.[5]

Any Nation Gloats Over the Losses of a More Developed Nation. After remarking how rapidly the British colonial empire crumbled before the advancing Japanese armies, Nehru, writing in prison toward the end of the war, asked:

Was this proud structure then just a house of cards with no foundations or inner strength? Inevitably, comparisons were made with China's long resistance to Japanese aggression in spite of her lack of almost everything required for modern war. China went up in people's estimation, and though Japan was not liked, there was a feeling of satisfaction at the collapse of old-established European colonial powers before the armed strength of an Asiatic power. That racial, Oriental-Asiatic, feeling was evident on the British side also. Defeat and disaster were bitter enough but the fact that an Oriental and Asiatic power had triumphed over them added to the bitterness and humiliation. An Englishman occupying a high position said that he would have preferred it if the *Prince of Wales* and the *Repulse* had been sunk by the Germans instead of the yellow Japanese.[6]

Just as nations find rank loss insufferable, so they find rank gain difficult to bear. Because this statement might raise doubt or unnecessarily abrade common sense, I will single out three reasons why a gain in rank need not imply a corresponding gain in relative satisfaction.

First, a nation gaining in rank will tend to reject or not accept its own gain. This is a result of the phenomenon of rising expectations; that is, the more a nation has, the more it wants. Thanks to a rising tide of world development (as indicated by proportionate increases in the consumption of meat or paper or toothpaste or automobiles or energy, longer vacations farther away, and shorter working hours) all nations are exhibiting increasing mastery of the environment. This improvement has set off expectations which normally outpace the possibilities of achievement. The resulting dilemma ensnares every nation caught up in it. This suggests that where the material situation has undergone the most rapid improvement, and it has among the rank-gainers by definition, there the most dissatisfaction will likely be found because of the difficulty of adjusting to that improvement. As an example, de Tocqueville observes,

it was precisely in those parts of France where there had been most improvement that popular discontent ran highest. . . . Patiently endured so long as it seemed beyond redress, a grievance comes to appear intolerable once the possibility of removing it crosses men's minds. For the mere fact that certain abuses have been remedied draws attention to the others and they now appear more galling; people may suffer less, but their sensibility is exacerbated.[7]

Second, other nations observing a rank-gainer will also tend to reject or not accept its gain. Their feelings will differ according to the perspective afforded them by different positions and interests in the development hierarchy: nations superior in rank will feel threatened; nations losing rank will feel resentment; and nations inferior in rank will feel envy. Any one of these reactions from other nations means the withholding of external or foreign consensus and therefore further adds to the difficulty of the rank-gainer's adjustment to change. Each of these reactions may be illustrated.

Nations Superior in Rank Will Feel Threatened. Throughout the period extending from 1871 to just after the Second World War, England apparently felt threatened by the rise of Germany and so blocked German expansion at every turn. Not in Europe, not in the colonies, not in the world market, not even on the high seas, could England tolerate Germany as a near-equal competitor or accept its claim for higher reputation; a new claim of greater prestige based on recent rank gains. There were, in fact,

a great deal of articles published in the English press at the end of the nineteenth century and more especially the beginning of the twentieth century—articles fulminating against the expansion of Germany, which was described as a deadly threat to Britain, and suggesting a resort to arms as the only means of saving Old Albion's prosperity.[8]

Former Prime Minister Winston Churchill, speaking in the House of Commons on February 27, 1945, had the following to say on the matter:

I have been through the whole story since 1911, when I was sent to the Admiralty to prepare the fleet for the impending German War. In its main essentials it seems to be one story of a thirty years war in which the British, Russians, Americans and French have struggled to their utmost to resist German aggression.[9]

Nations Losing Rank Will Feel Resentment. Perhaps the first to see the improvement of one nation as a source of resentment to another was Thucydides in his discussion of the first general war on record.

The real cause I consider to be the one which was formally most kept out of sight. The growth of the power of Athens, and the alarm which this inspired in Lacedaemon, made war inevitable.[10]

As with Athens and Sparta, so with the mighty houses of Hapsburg and Bourbon, or Spain and France. Heavy taxation was introduced and war justified in France by the "unceasing purpose to stay the progress of Spain."[11]

Nations Inferior in Rank Will Feel Envy. As one nation rejects or even tends to wage war against an improving nation, so an improving nation, as it begins to achieve parity with a superior nation, might think in terms of waging war against it. Thus,

it is possible that as peoples outside Western culture acquire and perhaps improve upon Western culture's methods of producing goods and of waging war, these peoples will become embroiled with the West in war. . . . Cultures with inferior civilization but with growing economic power have always attacked the most civilized cultures during the latters' economic decline. The chance that this may happen again is so great that enormous amounts of human resources will undoubtedly be dissipated during the coming years in preparation for war.[12]

But as Robbins notes, this is not an automatic reflex. A considerable amount of pressure—in the form of trade restrictions, market closures, immigration quotas—must build up as a precondition.

Whatever we may think of the justice of the Japanese attack on China, there can be no doubt of its connection with the restriction of the Japanese market. In 1929, with the advent of the Great Depression, the market for Japanese silk in the United States and elsewhere collapsed. Now silk was the chief item of Japanese export. The collapse was a major catastrophe. It was only to be expected, therefore, that the Japanese would turn as rapidly as possible to other forms of export. This they did; and immediately the markets elsewhere were effectively closed against them. In Ceylon, for instance, in one year the import of a certain kind of Japanese cloth was reduced to one-tenth of its former dimensions. The connection between such events and the invasion of China is so obvious as to need no elaboration.[13]

And more pointedly, Rostow contends:

to the extent that the great struggles for power of the twentieth century have an economic basis, that basis does not lie in imperialism or in compulsions arising from an alleged monopoly stage of capitalism; nor does that basis lie even in an automatic oligopolistic competition over colonies: it lies in the contours of the Eurasian arena of power, as determined by relative stage-of-growth and of military potential. And quite particularly it lies in the temptations and fears of certain new mature powers with respect to the transitional societies that lay close by, in Eastern Europe and in China, societies that were by-passed in the series of take-offs that got under way in, roughly, the third quarter of the nineteenth century, which destroyed the world of 1815 and after.[14]

Third, a nation gaining in rank might find it difficult to accept and bear especially when that gain is comparatively viewed with like nations. To inform the average man in a nation that he is now more educated, healthier, more productive and better clothed than he was a generation ago will not abrade his dissatisfaction upon learning, as he must, under the conditions of expanding international awareness, that the material situation of his counterpart in a nation formerly inferior to his own has improved to an even greater degree. This is the familiar idea of relative deprivation applied to international appraisals.[15] Failure to consider the circumstances under which a rank gain will produce not satisfaction in the nation that has experienced the gain but dissatisfaction will unfortunately lead to false confidence. In this light of failure to consider the circumstances, consider the following statement:

Among nations the agricultural states are relatively poor compared to the industrialized ones; and, when a nation whose occupations are largely farming and handicraft becomes possessed of power-driven factories that turn out products in profusion, the leadership, industrial and political, is likely to be optimistic. . . . The optimistic attitude is frequently correlated with the spirit of confidence, for optimism is often a result of achievement. A ruler or a political party claims credit for good times, though they be due to the forces of the business cycle or to the weather. Newly industrialized nations, like new cities, tend to have confidence.[16]

Satisfaction varies with stress and stress varies with change, whether it is for better or for worse. A sense of satisfaction cannot be expected to result from any rank change, however, and satisfaction may therefore be most profitably viewed as problematic under twentieth-century conditions of expanded international awareness. In this context, dissatisfaction among nations might well be considered the paramount concern of this age if only because of the awareness of change.

The Problem

Into the process of accepting and rejecting changes comes war. War means even more change: change in the positions of nations in the development hierarchy, and resulting changes in feelings about those positions. Some nations will exhibit gains while others will exhibit losses, some of small magnitude and others of large, but any such change may be presumed to affect directly or indirectly the satisfaction of nations. For war to affect the satisfaction of nations, it must increase or decrease the amount of stress through rank changes and substantially affect the conditions of domestic and foreign consensus about position.

The development hierarchy can be presented as an ordinal hierarchy by merely converting raw scores into ranks. The result may be viewed in Appendix Table A-4. The rank of a nation at various points in time can be compared by eye: its rank in 1913 with its rank in 1925; its rank in 1938 with its rank in 1952; and, for the long term, its rank in 1913 with its rank in 1952.

Once viewed, it is quite clear that the development hierarchy was not made in heaven and positions in it are not eternal. Rank changes, or increases and decreases in comparative advantage, can be plotted for almost every nation from century to century and from generation to generation. No nation appears thoroughly ensconced in its position in the hierarchy, and even the threat of change excites feelings.

In previous chapters, the development hierarchy has proven to be remarkably stable, rich nations and poor within it have exhibited a modest reduction in relative spread, and a healthy rise in speed of material improvement. But none of these general findings implies anything about satisfaction or stress. What is the trend in rank satisfaction in this century of total war, what is the amount of rank change: its intensity and history?

There are basically four possible hypotheses about the relationship between war and satisfaction. Satisfaction either increases, decreases, does both, or remains unaffected by war. The fit of these hypotheses—productive, destructive, unpredictable, and irrelevant—will be determined and the findings will be interpreted in this chapter.

The appropriate method of testing change is by rank analysis. This method allows for comparison of national arrays over time, and by such comparison a rather convincing answer can be given to the question of the extent to which nations in the development hierarchy change positions and thus experience stress. A more perfect method of indicating stress, however, would be to measure it more directly; that is, by well-done surveys of attitudes of representative men in most nations toward rank changes and world inequality. But such surveys have never been done and are unlikely ever to be done. So, one is always limited by what exists and should appreciate even that much in this imperfect world. Hence, given the limitation, one must accept a certain margin of improvisation: in this instance, in order to accomplish the task of measuring stress, I shall leap from an objective fact, rank changes, to a subjective state, stress. At best, therefore, an analysis of rank change will provide clues as to what a dominant subjective state might be.

In what follows, I shall assume that satisfaction varies with the extent of change; regardless of whether this consists of gains or losses in rank and regardless of the appraisals of relative deprivation. It has been sufficiently demonstrated, hopefully, that a gain in rank is neither more nor less difficult to adapt to than the combination of a gain-loss. A nation's rank is not fixed, for change is constant. Furthermore, no single nation undergoes a change of rank without affecting the rank of another nation, and usually that of a third. Any change in rank, then, will presumably have ramifications for the material and, especially, for the psychic situation of millions upon millions of people.

All the figures in the following tables are ratios. They show the relative magnitude of change; that is, the number of ranks involved in change (for example, a nation traveled two, or three, ranks up or down) to the number of nations that have changed ranks. To derive these ratios, the number of ranks affected by change is divided by the number of nations which have changed rank. These figures therefore purport to indicate the intensity of stress.

Because ratios are standardized figures, they are capable of showing whether or not nations in one array have undergone more change and thus subject to more stress than nations in another array. The following are the possible hypotheses about the relationship between war and satisfaction in the development hierarchy. If the ratios decrease through war, then satisfaction has increased and the productive hypothesis will be taken to have been confirmed; if the ratios increase through war, then satisfaction has decreased and the destructive hypothesis will be taken to have been confirmed; if the ratios vary irregularly through war, then satisfaction has both increased and decreased and the unpredictable hypothesis will be taken to have been confirmed; and, if the ratios do not vary significantly through war, then satisfaction has not varied and the irrelevant hypothesis will be taken to have been confirmed.

Findings

Change of any sort requires adjustment. Remembering the stipulation that satisfaction decreases as the need for adjustment increases, it can be seen in Table 7-1 that the average magnitudes of affected ranks to nations changing have varied somewhat from war to war. This finding confirms the unpredictable hypothesis in the relationship between war and satisfaction in the development hierarchy: satisfaction or stress does associate with war. But were the steel series held aside, then the finding would more readily confirm the irrelevant hypothesis. As is its nature, steel production is far more cyclical and vulnerable to events than most any other series I can think of. Over the long term, however, nations in the steel series have experienced far less alteration of their positions than in the other two series.

Level of Development

What is true for the world, however, may not be true for nations in a given stratum of the development hierarchy. If war causes differential stress among various parts of the hierarchy, then the introduction of an intervening variable, development stratum, may reveal its extent and intensity. It is possible to have a

Table 7-1
Ratios of Affected Ranks to Nations Changing, at Selected Dates, by Arrays of Nations[a]

Year	Telephones	Income	Steel
First World War[b]	3.4	2.9	3.5
Second World War[b]	3.8	3.3	2.3
Thirty-One Years War[b]	5.7	3.6	2.6

[a]The ratios are based on the ordinal hierarchies located in Appendix Tables A-4, A-7, and A-10, respectively.

[b]Refers to a comparison of the base and seventh years: for the First World War, 1913 is compared with 1925; for the Second World War, 1938 with 1952; and for the Thirty-One Years War, 1913 with a special 1952 ranking which is identified in the tables as 1952y.

degree of stress within a development stratum that would remain undetected in a rank analysis of all nations over time. The four hypotheses about the relationship between war and satisfaction, taking into account this intervening variable of development stratum follow. If satisfaction associates positively with development stratum through war, that is if the highest stratum exhibits the least change and therefore by definition the least need to adjust, then this confirms the productive hypothesis; if it associates inversely, this confirms the destructive hypothesis; if it associates variably, this confirms the unpredictable hypothesis; and, if it remains unaffected, this confirms the irrelevant hypothesis. To test these hypotheses, the change over time in arrays of nations in each development stratum was analyzed. The result can be seen in Table 7-2.

Location in the development hierarchy was defined as expressing the extent to which rich nations and poor are able to master the environment. Table 7-2 reveals that intensity of stress tends to associate with development stratum: nations in the upper stratum move up or down through fewer ranks proportionately than nations in other strata. While it is true that these nations gain and lose less rank through war than nations in other strata, it is also true that they require less adjustment to stress. These figures tend to confirm the productive hypothesis about the relationship between war and satisfaction in the development hierarchy. Satisfaction associates positively with level of development through war; fewer upper stratum nations change, and they change less than nations in other strata. The more developed a nation, therefore, the greater its satisfaction with its position over time.[17]

The more volatile character of middle and lower stratum nations invites further comment. These nations move in greater numbers and through more ranks in the development hierarchy than upper stratum nations. The magnitude of rank change exhibited by these nations indicates that they experience greater stress and hence must adjust more. The fact of change and stress is emphasized at this point because authors as different from one another as Aristotle and Karl Marx have tended to equate absolute and relative impoverishment with internal

Table 7-2
Ratios of Affected Ranks to Nations Changing, at Selected Dates, by Stratum of Development[a]

Stratum	The First World War	The Second World War	The Thirty-One Years War
Upper	2.3	2.3	3.3
Middle	4.6	4.1	6.2
Lower	2.8	4.9	6.9

[a]For the First World War time segment, nations are stratified as of 1925; for the Second World War, nations stratified as of 1952 (see Table 2-3) and ratios are of data in Appendix Table A-4.

disturbances and ideologies of violence. It is not mere location in the development hierarchy alone which causes unrest but the actual amount of change and stress to which these nations are subject. The new phenomenon in the world today is not poverty but expanded awareness and heightened contact among formerly isolated nations, awareness of their inclusion in a system of inequality which insistently and forcefully embraces the world. It is this greater awareness and contact among these nations below the upper stratum, and the fact that the changes they experience are of large magnitude, that causes unrest among them.[18]

Degree of War Participation

Another factor, war participation, may also affect the intensity of rank change and stress. In war the world becomes polarized and borders become firmer. Hostility toward opponents escalates and even neutrals begin to feel uncomfortable, especially during a world war, if they are not in fact already intimidated by one of the contending powers. Hostility can affect satisfaction. An increase in hostility means, for one thing, increasing denials of claims of injustice made by opponents and often increasing postponements of the claims made by neutrals. But obviously the situation reverses itself within an allied camp. To maintain solidarity, allies seem constantly ready to grant almost any claim. And many an ally has been seduced into war on precisely such a promise. To what extent, however, the denial of claims between opponents in war balances the readiness to grant claims among allies is undetermined. In any event, the making of claims is constant.

The effect of war involvement on change in the development hierarchy can be observed. It requires only that nations be sorted by degree of war participation. If war causes further differentials in rank change among nations, then the introduction of an intervening variable, degree of war participation, may reveal its extent and intensity. The familiar hypotheses about the relationship between war and satisfaction in the development hierarchy, taking degree of participation into account, are as follows. If satisfaction associates positively with degree of participation through war, that is, if the more involved nations exhibit the least change and therefore, the least need to adapt to change, then this confirms the productive hypothesis; if it associates inversely, this confirms the destructive hypothesis; if it associates variably, this confirms the unpredictable hypothesis; and, if it remains unaffected, this confirms the irrelevant hypothesis. To test these hypotheses, the arrays of nations in each category of participation in the Thirty-One Years War were analyzed. The result can be seen in Table 7-3.

It is quite apparent from Table 7-3 that magnitude of average rank change associates curvilinearly with degree of participation when all categories are taken into account. Were the neutral category of nations to be excluded, then the data

Table 7-3

Ratios of Affected Ranks to Nations Changing, at Selected Dates, by Degree of War Participation[a]

| Year | The Thirty-One Years War: 1914-45 | | | |
	Maximum	Medium	Minimum	Neutral
1913 and 1952y	4.6	6.8	7.0	4.7

[a]Maximum means officially in war for six or more years; medium means officially in war from three to six years; minimum means officially in war for less than three years; and neutral means absence of official war participation in both the First and Second World Wars. Nations sorted as in Table 3-3 and ratios are of data in Appendix Table A-4.

suggest a rough positive relationship between involvement in a long war and a subsequent need to adapt to change. In any case, Table 7-3 shows that stress is least both when nations are very involved in a long war and officially uninvolved. Will the situation differ when nations are viewed over shorter spans of time? The answer lies in Table 7-4.

As Table 7-4 shows, the ratios of the number of affected ranks to the number of nations changing does not depend consistently on degree of participation in war. The findings from each war differ: as a result of the First World War, the magnitude of average change associates positively in that the active nations moved through fewer ranks and so required less adaptation to change than the marginal and neutral nations. As a result of the Second World War, the magnitude of average change associates inversely. Intensity of stress varies therefore irregularly. The contrary nature of these findings invites further analysis, for at this point no general conclusions can be drawn from them other than the confirmation of the unpredictable hypothesis about the relationship between war and satisfaction in the development hierarchy.

Table 7-4

Ratios of Affected Ranks to Nations Changing, at Selected Dates, by Degree of War Participation[a]

Category	1913 and 1925: The First World War	1938 and 1952: The Second World War
Active	2.3	4.3
Marginal	4.1	4.0
Neutral	3.8	2.6

[a]Active means officially in war for three years or more; marginal means officially in war for less than three years; and neutral means absence of official war participation. Nations sorted as in Table 3-2 and ratios are of data in Appendix Table A-4.

Active Nations and the Second World War

Let us start by reviewing two findings with regard to the Second World War. First: in Table 7-2, it was found that intensity of stress associates positively with stratum of development; that is, nations in the upper stratum affected and moved through fewer ranks than nations in other strata (2.3, 4.1, 4.9). Second: in Table 7-4, it was found that intensity of stress associates inversely with degree of war participation; that is, nations in the most involved category affected and moved through more ranks than nations in other categories (4.3, 4.0, 2.6). Inasmuch as these two factors, level of development and degree of participation, have contrary effects on rank change and thus satisfaction following Second World War, it becomes necessary to determine their relative influence.

A procedure used in previous chapters is applicable here. To test the relative influence on satisfaction of degree of participation and level of development, the forty-three nations active in the Second World War are selected for closer examination. These active nations occupy positions in every stratum of the development hierarchy. By holding the active category of participation constant, the influence of each development stratum can be measured. This procedure should produce a clear understanding of the combined relative influence of these variables on rank change.

On the basis of an earlier finding, that rank change varies positively with level of development (Table 7-2), the following prediction of the productive hypothesis seems reasonable: the more developed active nations will exhibit the least amount of change through the Second World War. Table 7-5, designed to provide support for this prediction, does so perfectly.

It is quite apparent from the ratios in Table 7-5 that the socioeconomic location of an active nation makes a difference in the magnitude of its average rank change through the Second World War. Although active participation costs, apparently it costs far less in rank change for rich nations than for poor ones. Table 7-5 clearly reveals the situational weakness in stability of rank among lower stratum active nations. The finding confirms the prediction of the productive hypothesis about the relationship between war and satisfaction in the

Table 7-5
Ratios of Affected Ranks to *Active* Nations Changing, at Selected Dates, by Stratum of Development[a]

Time	The Second World War		
	Upper	Middle	Lower
1938-52	2.4	4.1	6.5

[a]Stratification of nations as of 1952 (see Table 2-3) and sorted as in Table 3-5 and ratios are of data in Appendix Table A-4.

development hierarchy. Satisfaction associates positively with development among active nations through war; upper stratum active nations change less and thus require less adaptation to change than lower stratum active nations. In other words, the more developed an active nation, the greater its satisfaction with its position over time.

Military Occupation during the Second World War

Another specification, military occupation, can be introduced to understand further why active nations during the Second World War exhibit more rank changes than active nations during the First World War. Occupation by a foreign force occurred during the Second World War on a grand scale. Of the forty-three active nations included in Table 7-5, twenty-seven were occupied. Although the status of occupation is an overwhelmingly coercive one, national identity is not lost by it primarily because the nation while coming to terms with it cannot be subjugated.

Subjugation of a people was possible in former times when, frequently, the conquered were inarticulate because in such circumstances empires and feudal houses expected little or no assimilation of the vanquished. Whenever there is a clear-status schism, it generally does not really matter to the ruled if one set of rulers is replaced by another because the lot of the many remains the same: all it means is that they will have to pay taxes to a different sovereign. But this is not so in a world where nationalism predominates. The capacity of the conquerors to subjugate the vanquished in war has been very severely limited since the French Revolution, which brought nationalism in its train. Once nationalism has rooted in a land, the population tends to resist subjugation or assimilation after a defeat because change in the power structure matters very much to the articulate many who now have a stake in rulers and ruling. Nowadays the nation can be defeated, humiliated, and forced to bear the costs of war, but it will probably resist any attempt at subjugation or assimilation. Thus, under an occupier's rule, people retain their identity while they willingly or unwillingly adjust to the situation.

The real life of the peoples of occupied Europe lay between the two extremes of collaboration and resistance. In each occupied country the great majority of the population came to terms with the reality of the occupation. This applies not only to Western Europe but also to Eastern Europe and the Balkans, where the Third Reich pursued an even more barbaric policy than in the West. The real history of occupied Europe therefore has been less heroic than many observers supposed during and sometimes even after the war. Most people, against their wills, were caught in a social system which of necessity continued to function under the occupation, to some extent to the advantage of the German war economy. Unwilling adjustment was the rule—intentional resistance the exception.[19]

What then is the effect on rank change of military occupation? To test for the effect by status of occupation, the forty-three nations active during the Second World War were sorted according to whether or not they were occupied. If nonoccupied nations change less than occupied nations through the Second World War, then this confirms the productive hypothesis; if they exhibit more stress, this confirms the destructive hypothesis; and, if no differences obtain, this confirms the irrelevant hypothesis. In each category, the array of nations was analyzed over the same time span. The result can be seen in Table 7-6.

The finding of Table 7-6 leads to a clear confirmation of the productive hypothesis in the relationship between war and satisfaction in the development hierarchy: nonoccupied nations change less and thus require less adaptation to change than occupied nations. The more autonomous an active nation in war, therefore, the greater its satisfaction with its position over time.

So the status of military occupation does make a difference in postwar intensity of stress. But to be occupied by a foreign force might make for less difference in rank change than whether a nation stands high or low in the development hierarchy. All that has been learned up to this point constrains the view that occupation provides a necessary but not a sufficient explanation for variation in rank change. Thus the following prediction seems reasonable. Occupied nations in the upper stratum of development will exhibit less change than occupied nations in the lower stratum of development. To test the prediction, occupied nations will be sorted by level of development; that is, occupation will be held constant. Whatever differences obtain will then redound from development level and not from occupation. The result of analyzing these three hierarchies over time can be seen in Table 7-7.

Table 7-6
Ratios of Affected Ranks to *Active* Nations Changing, at Selected Dates, by Whether Occupied or Not[a]

Time	The Second World War	
	Nonoccupied	Occupied
1938-52	3.6	5.5

[a]Nations sorted as in Table 3-4 and ratios are of data in Appendix Table A-4.

Table 7-7
Ratios of Affected Ranks to *Occupied* Nations Changing, at Selected Dates, by Stratum of Development[a]

Time	The Second World War		
	Upper	Middle	Lower
1938-52	2.0	4.8	3.8

[a]Nations sorted as in Table 3-6 and ratios are of data in Appendix Table A-4.

Magnitude of average rank change tends to vary by stratum of development of occupied nations. That upper stratum occupied nations affected and traveled through far fewer ranks than middle and lower strata occupied nations shows that location in the development hierarchy matters. The findings of Table 7-7 roughly confirms the productive hypothesis about the relationship between war and satisfaction in the development hierarchy. Satisfaction associates positively with the development stratum among occupied nations through war, in that upper stratum occupied nations change less and thus require less adaptation to change than middle and lower stratum occupied nations. In other words, the upper occupied nations have greater satisfaction with their position over time.

Interpretation

The ability to achieve consensus enables nations to adjust or cope with the stresses that change provokes. The unequal achievement of consensus is the foundation of the satisfaction specification in the development hierarchy. The greater the consensus effected by a nation, the greater its relative satisfaction. But the more effort this requires, the more dissatisfaction will be experienced. On the assumption that adapting to change creates a turmoil in which people become newly critical and question the justice of any rank, superior or inferior, to which the nation has moved, it was expected that any nation exhibiting the greatest amount of change in rank would also experience, as a result, the greatest amount of stress.[20]

Any nation feels a need to adjust not only to its own rank change but to the rank changes of other nations as well. A rank change anywhere in the hierarchy demands adjustment to the stresses it creates. Domestic consensus means that a nation accepts its position in the hierarchy, foreign consensus means that other nations also accept that nation's position; and both are required to produce satisfaction within the nation.

But domestic and foreign consensus to rank position and toward change of position is neither given nor automatic. Consensus is variable and therefore subject to conditions. These conditions are identifiable and are of considerable interest because, as stated, they limit adjustment to the perceived material situation and held values in any nation. The conditions of consensus will be discussed first from the standpoint of an individual nation and then from the standpoint of another nation observing it.

Since satisfaction is imperfect, the development hierarchy will always be subject to the actions of nations that wish to maintain their ranks and nations that wish to modify their ranks. Thus the following question arises: when does a nation accept or reject its own rank in the hierarchy?

Each nation uses another nation in evaluating its own situation; when a nation feels advantaged by comparison with a second nation, then its satisfaction with its own situation is promoted. In such circumstance, domestic consensus or internal acceptance of a nation's own rank is at a high level. Contrariwise, when a nation feels disadvantaged by comparison with a second nation, its dissatisfaction rises because of the probability that it rejects its own rank increases. For instance, two nations occupied during the Second World War might evaluate each other in terms of relative magnitude of war costs. The nation which incurred fewer costs as a result of wartime occupation would feel clearly advantaged by comparison with the other which incurred more war costs (and which might thereby feel clearly disadvantaged).

The closer two nations are to one another in rank or situation, the less satisfaction each is likely to derive as they mutually compare themselves. This is because among near-equals comparative advantage and disadvantage from small gains or losses are magnified all out of proportion. In this connection consider the general situation during the Age of Imperialism. In no period since the Mongol invasions, according to several authors, were nations so successfully aggressive and competitive over colonies. The imperialist powers were situated close together in the development hierarchy, and each viewed the advance of the other as a clear disadvantage.[21]

At any time the development hierarchy can be known and objectified; through its social scientists each nation knows its relative place and, significantly, other nations know it too. When a nation dissatisfied with its rank attempts by some action to improve it, observing nations may respond by acting either to obstruct the improving nation or to aid it. In so doing they work to maintain their own sense of justice. To the extent that observing nations control an improving nation by, for instance, practices of exclusion—trade restriction, market closure, immigration quotas—to that extent a dynamic nation might be held in line and suffer substantial damage as a result of its efforts to improve itself. It is precisely the desire of nations to maintain and strengthen the existing satisfaction with their own positions that causes them to reject or accept the efforts and claims of other nations in the development hierarchy. Thus the question about consensus has necessarily also to be put from the standpoint of an observing nation: when will it accept or reject another nation's claim of injustice?

Each nation uses its own situation to evaluate another nation's claim of injustice; when a nation feels advantaged by comparison with another, it will accept that nation's claim more readily than will a third nation which feels clearly disadvantaged. The more distant two nations are from one another in rank or situation, the more is foreign consensus or external acceptance accorded to the claims of the less advantaged nation by the more advantaged nation. This kind of calculation may be irrelevant when two nations close to one another enjoy a special relationship; for example, a heavy economic interdependence.

The closer two nations are to one another in rank or situation, the more likely one nation will reject the material improvement of the other nation. The association of intensity of rivalry with similarity of rank or situation has already been identified in the first section of this chapter. I am thinking of the cases of Athens and Sparta, of Spain and France, and of Germany and England.

Even though the idea of consensus as a mechanism facilitating satisfaction was presented from the standpoints of both the individual nation and the observer nations, it is still only one idea. It refers to the acceptance of rank, and I have tried to show when, or under what conditions, it would be most likely to occur. No nation's rank is totally unaffected by change occurring somewhere in the hierarchy, and most nations must constantly adapt. All nations attempt to achieve a modicum of satisfaction with position through an adjustment to the stress that change provokes. Unfortunately for most, adjustment is imperfect on the twin assumption that change and evaluation is constant. In any case, satisfaction with position has more of a chance of being achieved and sustained when both domestic and foreign consensus function to promote it.

Domestic and foreign consensus serve to reduce the discomfort of stress felt by nations in the development hierarchy through history. The relationship between satisfaction and the amount of consensus needed, however, is inverse. The less additional consensus required for the attainment of satisfaction, the more satisfaction will be experienced. Upper stratum nations tend to expend less effort in the achievement of consensus, because they exhibit less rank change. If lower stratum nations needed less consensus, greater rank changes among the upper stratum nations would have to appear to enable the lower stratum nations to increase their amount of satisfaction in the development hierarchy. But such equilibrations in rank change are not observable in history. Rank changes at the top of a hierarchy are small compared with those at the bottom. These magnitudes of change persist over time and, as I have shown through war. And certainly the need to adapt internally and to elicite external acceptance has not diminished as a result of either world war.

8 Conflict

War is the father of all things.
Heraclitus

The world wars of this century were the most costly in all history. These wars, like all wars, have inescapable costs in men, minds, money, and material; for example, the First World War had over sixteen million casualties and the Second had fifty million.[1] These wars could have been far more costly than they were had not political and normative restraints entered upon the scene. But as high as the actual costs were, apparently, they were not high enough, even collectively assessed, to stay the course of material progress in this century. For as the various data reveal, development has proceeded without significant interruption or alteration due to war.

My conclusion, then, is that the two total wars of this century have neither helped nor hindered development or noticeably affected the inequalities between rich nations and poor. This broad finding lends substantial support to the irrelevant hypothesis about the relationship between war and development. These wars have proven to be unrelated to socioeconomic development and world inequality: nations continue their normal rate of material improvement whether or not wars occur.

War

This conclusion suggests that perhaps past wars were not as costly as stories told about them would indicate. According to the careful researches of Hans Delbruck and Ferdinand Lot, no reliable evidence exists on the size of armies of more than 10,000 combatants from the eleventh through the fifteenth century.[2] Chroniclers of the Middle Ages, for example, count 120,000 Burgundians at the battle of Grandson; Delbruck (I, pp. 8-9) reduces the number to 14,000 at most. Now into the seventeenth century with its advances in population size and military technology (or in the years since the fifteenth century when firearms had become the decisive weapons in war and democratized it), the size of armies doubled and tripled. But this enlargement of combatants and the development of unskilled weapons does not mean that the costs of war have also increased disproportionately. As a matter of fact, there exist several reports that question the all destructive fury in Germany of the Thirty Years War that we all grew up to learn about in school.[3]

121

Given the broad finding, that rich nations and poor in our time continue their normal rate of material improvement whether or not wars occur, why, then, have the various authors reviewed in Chapter 1 and elsewhere presented diverse possibilities on the matter of war and development? One reason is that some authors see what they want to see and thus fit data to the procrustean bed of a certain point of view. This argument by illustration means the selection of given bits of true evidence in order to demonstrate one and only one theoretical possibility which inheres in the relationship between war and development. To guard against the urgency of a preconception in this matter, a researcher must follow a methodology which adheres to the accepted canons of measurement testing, presentation of deviant cases, and above-board analysis.[4]

Another reason is that some authors are so politically oriented that when they observe the "disintegration" or the formation of an empire, the circulation of political and economic elites, the rise and fall of social classes, even victory and defeat, through, by, and as a result of war, they unwarrantedly infer something about development. Such authors are particularly susceptible when examining one nation; while the single case is terribly important to the inhabitants of a region and may even be equally important to history, it hardly bears emphasizing that whatever the finding, it lacks the authority of generalization beyond that case. For instance, no one can speak of the postwar recovery of such dispersed peoples as the Trojans or the Carthaginians or the Mayans. But to go from that datum to a generalization about war and development which speaks to the averages and broad tendencies in the experiences of many, many nations is to proceed boldly but all too blindly to the facts of history.

Other reasons why authors present disparate views on the matter of war and development have already been presented and are so obvious as not to require spelling out: they have not selected the same wars or talked of the same nations or considered the same units of time before and after war or used the same kind of data as measures or even agreed on the meaning of development. Under these circumstances, the emergence of four inherently possible theoretical alternatives in the relationship between war and development would seem inevitable. In this research, I tested the four possibilities and found support for only one; that is, a nonexisting relationship between war and development in this century was revealed as the dominant finding of this study.

Attempts at Explaining War

War can be dissected, examined, and described; but in a scientific sense, it cannot be explained, for it does not systematically depend on any other yet known factor which may be considered independent. No one can tell for example at what date a war will come about or explain any or all past wars in terms of either their frequency or their intensity or their ferocity (the extent to which armies are restrained by norms). Until an independent factor is success-fully identified, therefore, no explanation of war exists.[5]

Wars are occasionally provoked, supposedly, by a perception of justice denied. In such a case one nation makes a claim that is unmet by another. For instance, "A country will fight when it believes that its prestige in diplomacy is not equivalent to its real strength." The author of that line goes on to observe that wars also occur "when each of the two countries believes itself to be stronger than the other."[6] While that might be true once or twice in all history, surely the decision to wage war is more complicated than that proposition would make it out to be.

Wars are occasionally provoked, supposedly, by a perception of rank loss. Long after the din of the decisive battle, the heart-rending cries of "unre-deemed" people now politically separated and "bleeding wounds" of lost territory and "fallen" prestige in the power or development hierarchy can still be heard. These cries ring with more resonance in the twentieth century, though not with more validity, because the historical outlook of all people has broadened through mass literacy, and nations and their fortunes have become more visible through the effects of global communications. So while a nation may be reconciled to defeat in war, its reconciliation to a loss of rank in war seems doubtful. No settlement can expunge the humiliation of rank loss incurred in war enough to erase the desire of the losing nation for revenge. Note well, however, I said revenge and not war. It is easy to reason from a desire for revenge to war, and so I will categorically deny that loss may serve as a necessary, let alone a sufficient, condition for war.[7]

And wars are occasionally provoked, supposedly, by a universal desire for rank gain. Nations may have feelings of dissatisfaction about their positions in the development hierarchy, obviously. But whether a nation uses or is used by these feelings to move at the expense of another nation or not is subject to considerable debate. According to Frederick of Prussia, there is no problem: nations are universally stimulated to move for gain even at the expense of other nations.[8] This assertion can be regarded as only partly correct because it is partly wrong. In the history of Europe, for example, since even before Frederick it has been possible at almost any moment to distinguish between those nations interested in revision of boundaries and those devoted to the maintenance of the status quo.[9]

Although war can be considered as an independent factor affecting the course of development, even though it has not done so, it cannot be considered as a dependent factor of development, even though it could be so considered logically, because the various attempts to do so have yielded contradictory or unconvincing findings. Some scholars have claimed that the frequency of war varies by degree of development. Two irreconcilable views have been advanced on this matter. One of these views, stemming from a linear conception of history, sees steady increases in development as reducing the chances of war; this view is expressed in the writings of Auguste Comte, Herbert Spencer, and Karl Marx. The other view, stemming from a cyclical conception of history, sees steady increases in development as promoting the chances of war; this view is found in the works of Friedrich Nietzsche, Jacob Burckhardt, and Oswald Spengler.[10] The failure of scholars to explain the frequency of war, causally or even functionally, in terms of an easily demonstrated increase in development, is apparently not from want of trying, then, but from their failure to demonstrate such a relationship empirically or even logically. I am not so presumptuous as to dismiss such celebrated authors out-of-hand, there is a factual basis for all this; it may be considered in Table 8-1.

The following classification of 278 wars shows that the frequency of war has not varied significantly by increases in development or by any other yet known factor over a span of 461 years.

This classification of war frequency suggests further that during the intervals between wars the expectation of violence must have been ever present because of unredressed grievances and especially because of war preparations. Put differently, if the expectation of peace remains low, then nations could take the shape of garrisons and subject themselves to "the domination of specialists on violence"[11] not because of any variability in war but because of its nonvariability as an available means to the settlement of a conflict. There is no first war or last war because conflict is an unbegun and unending process in the life of nations that operate in an unavoidable context of rivalry. It is hardly surprising then that different authors find it difficult to disentangle the dual themes of peace and war in world history.[12] Plato, for one, regarded conflict as the natural state of all existence—individual against himself, man against man, family against

Table 8-1

The Amount of International War, by Fifty-Year Periods: 1480-1941

Period	Wars Fought	Average Duration of Wars
1480-1550	32	3.8
1550-1600	31	4.9
1600-1650	34	7.6
1650-1700	30	5.2
1700-1750	18	4.9
1750-1800	20	3.4
1800-1850	41	4.2
1850-1900	48	2.7
1900-1941	24	3.6

Source: Quincy Wright, A STUDY OF WAR (Chicago: University of Chicago Press, 1942), Vol. 1, p. 651, Table 45.

family, village against village, and nation against nation—not discrete episodes proclaimed by heralds, but a continuous perpetual condition.[13]

In the dream of peace, the arguments against war have been heard along every step of mankind's bloody and belligerent course. And yet war, not peace, has been mankind's most faithful and, unfortunately, unexplained companion. In thirty-five centuries of recorded history, only one year out of fifteen has not been drenched by the blood of the battlefield. The record of most nations, woebegone or not, contains many wars: in Spain, in 67 percent of the years of her history there were wars; in Poland and Lithuania, 58; in Britain, 56; in France, 50; in Germany, 46; in Russia, 46; in the Netherlands, 44; in Austria, 40; and in Italy, 36.[14] Today, a world that presumably cherishes peace as fervently as ever nevertheless keeps many millions of men under arms—many of them, here and there, actively engaged in combat. Yet nations actively do try to make peace, even though they will now attempt to achieve their ends through diplomatic might instead of military force. The study of peace settlements from this perspective should further illuminate the inherent tension which characteristically exists between idealism and realism in world politics.[15]

Development

It is no longer possible to speak of the presence or absence of development anywhere in the world; it is, in the view of a number of authors, a process continuous in time at least since the last century.[16] The essential reason why development arose noticeably in this period can be accounted for, as discussed individually in Chapters 4, 5, and 6, by the relatively more effective operation of three mechanisms: culture, communication, and cohesion. I shall review these mechanisms in terms of their continuing contribution to the process of development.

World Culture

It is the application of ideas and principles, values and beliefs, which enables rich nations and poor to gain further mastery over the environment. A sudden growth in instrumental knowledge allows possessing nations to move ahead. The preeminence of the nineteenth century in this connection can be derived from some of the figures on inventions. The number of important industrial inventions was greater during the nineteenth century than in any two previous centuries together. The count is 50, 15, 17, 43, and 108, in the 15th, 16th, 17th, 18th, and 19th centuries.[17] Even without such precise details on hand, most observers are likely to agree with Bury's summary:

The most striking advance has been in the technical conveniences of life—that is, in the control over natural forces. It would be superfluous to enumerate the discoveries and inventions since 1850 which abridged space, economised time, eased bodily suffering, and reduced in some ways the friction of life, though they have increased it in others. This uninterrupted series of technical inventions, proceeding concurrently with immense enlargements of all branches of knowledge, has gradually accustomed the least speculative mind to the conception that civilization is naturally progressive, and that continuous improvement is part of the order of things.[18]

Indeed, the "invention of the method of invention" was perhaps the greatest innovation, if not the hallmark, of the nineteenth century.[19] The advance of science and technology will increase in scope and implication. It is now a truism to say that most of the scientists and technicians who ever lived are alive today. The number of currently published scientific periodicals in the world was about 100,000 in 1850 and will probably be 1 million by the year 2000.[20]

Global Communication

The utilization of tourists, mail, telegrams, money, trade, and migrants to diffuse the principles and products of instrumental knowledge describes global communication. Its application enables nations to conserve or decrease the gaps between their positions over time. In fact, the history of nations can be meaningfully written in terms of the spread and restriction of world culture in competition with national culture. Some of the aspects of this mechanism gained wide institutionalization sometime late in the nineteenth century. A case in point is the structure and function of the international economy.

By 1900 the organization of economic activities throughout the world had so changed that anyone with sufficient money, in any of a multitude of different currencies or in the form of uncoined precious metal, could command the resources of the whole earth. He could order the delivery at a specified time and place of any commodity the production of which was known to be technically possible, however rare and scattered were the knowledge and materials involved, and could reasonably expect his order to be accepted and fulfilled. That was new, and it was a condition of things created by the changes of the previous half century or less.[21]

Since 1900, moreover, elements of world culture have been diffused to every nook and cranny of the earth's surface. Achille Viallate specifically relates much of the great worldwide material improvement exhibited in the first quarter of this century directly to the diffusion of the many contact inventions of the nineteenth century: telephone and telegraph, and railways and steamships.[22] Now, it should go without saying, all peoples are "absorbing the instrumentalities of urban-industrial civilization at a rapid rate. The instrumentalities embracing technology, economic organization, and political forms are in fact so universal that they are ... regarded simply as the well-known means by which any nation, whatever its background, can enhance its national power and level of living."[23]

National Cohesion

Because of different histories and circumstances, nations did not come into nationhood together or evenly. They emerged at different times and grew at different speeds. The importance of a head start in nationhood lies in furthering environmental mastery. In itself, however, nationhood is insufficient to account for furthering mastery; what does is the cohesiveness of the nation. The earlier and tighter the cohesion, the earlier and more sustained the nation's progress.

The process of building nations found its inspiration and momentum in mercantilism and nationalism. Mercantilism is a policy aimed at fusing state and society by replacing the medieval combination of religious universalism and political localism for the territorially bounded nation in order to promote thereby its power over all other political units both domestic and foreign in a context of rather intense rivalry.[24] What gave it its cohesive thrust is nationalism, a nineteenth-century phenomenon. The newness of all this can be gauged in a circular letter the Austrian foreign ministry sent in 1855 to Habsburg diplomats abroad; it claims that

the pretension of forming new States, according to the limits of nationalism, is the most dangerous of all utopian schemes. To put forward such a pretension is to break with history; and to carry it into execution in any part of Europe is to shake to its foundations the firmly organized order of States, and to threaten the continent with subversion and chaos.[25]

The nation appears in the nineteenth century as a new form of social organization; it appeared because of peculiar and compelling events. Since then the idea of nationhood has been diffused around the world under the influence, however inadvertently the intention, of colonialism.[26] Just as nature abhors a vacuum, so the number of nations increased as colonialism retreated. "By 1950 about 8 percent of the world's population lived in officially dependent areas; in 1913 the figure was around 30 percent. ... Once created, the new nations have been forced to find ways of maintaining their independence and their integrity as nations in a highly competitive world."[27]

If war is to positively or negatively affect world development, then it must alter or warp these mechanisms of development. That it does has been argued by many. I shall condense the entire argument as follows. If no war, then instrumental knowledge or science and technology would not move by fits and starts; that is, the nation would not need to seek out the most advanced ideas and gadgetry to increase productivity and create new principles and artifacts for the emergency: research bureaus would not shift away from projects unrelated to war, and schools and universities would not shorten a student's training time nor be relieved of younger faculty. If no war, then global communication would not be distorted; that is, the nation would not suffer the consequences of an immediate growth in border impermeability; a slowing-down of the flow across the borders of useful ideas and principles through the agency of travelers, mail, telegrams, money, trade, and migrants; reduced participation in the activities of governmental and nongovernmental international organizations; and a deceleration of political exchange between nations because of the severing of diplomatic contacts. And if no war, then the cohesion of the nation would not quicken; that is, the nation would not exhibit an increase in its key social processes of centralization, consociation, cooperation, and completion (of output): men, minds, money, and material would not be mobilized and the nation would not increase its use of resources or exhibit greater rationality or efficiency in their use.

But from the evidence reviewed, in previous chapters, war cannot be credited with helping nor discredited with hindering development. War does not affect world development because it has neither sufficiently stimulated nor stalled the work of these mechanisms. As a result of war, no important piece of information on how to master the environment was lost, no important method of diffusing that information failed to penetrate national borders, and no important organizational technique for administering that information faltered. This is not to argue that war has been incapable of affecting development in this century for better or worse. The possibility existed and it could have happened. But, importantly, it did not. The lack of affect by war on the long run of world development can be clearly seen in the following table which shows four important indicators of development before and after the First and the Second World Wars.

In spite of world wars, then, and limited wars, Fascist and Communist take-overs, colonial successions, revolutions or civil wars, Great Depressions or local economic crises, natural disasters, and other upheavals, the rising tide of twentieth-century development lifts all nations: rich and poor. This achievement is even more remarkable in the face of a corresponding growth in population. In comparing the specific figures of number of telephones per thousand of national populations of 1913 with those of 1952, it is interesting to note that not one of the nations in this study registered a decline. On the contrary, most nations exhibited substantial increases over this forty-year period.

Development is the ascending arrow of the three great mechanisms. In this century, the arrow is pointing upward in a dramatic direction. Not only has man begun to unlock these three fundamental contributing factors, he is now learning to manipulate and alter them. For example, he is working against such things as ignorance, isolation, and (anarchic) individualism—diseases which make for

Table 8-2
World Means of Development Indicators at Selected Dates

Year	Telephones	Income	Steel	Energy
1913	8.8	256	3.2	6.5
1920	13.4	316	1.8	6.9
1925	16.9	302	4.4	7.1
1938	23.5	301	2.5	7.3
1947	32.9	347	3.0	8.7
1952	40.0	406	4.9	9.9

Source: The population figures used to compute these per capita world means are located in Appendix Table A-1. Gross figures on energy are from the source listed in Chapter 1, Table 1-1; as mentioned there, these figures do not reveal the great and steadily increasing efficiency in either production or use of energy over this time period. Gross figures on telephones, income, and steel are located in Appendix Tables A-2, A-5, and A-8, respectively.

victimization by the environment. For the first time in all time, man understands the bases of development and can undertake to design his future. He will do this presumably by recruiting and applying ideas, by encouraging and widening diffusion of those ideas through increasing interaction, and by articulating the goals and channeling the energies of diverse interest groups.

9 Inequality

*In rivers, the water that you
touch is the last of what has
passed and the first of that
which comes: so with time
present.*
Leonardo da Vinci

Since the Second World War, several authors have insisted that the present world inequalities in development appear to have a common point of departure early in the last century.[1] Inequalities in development among nations of course did not make their first appearance in the middle of the nineteenth century. Nations have always varied by their relative command of the environment, as stories of former civilizations indicate. Indeed, the comparative researches of Herodotus, Tacitus, Marco Polo, and Ibn Batuta clearly reveal the differences in relative development between peoples in the past.

But let us assume for a moment that the present world inequalities have a common point of departure in the nineteenth century and ask how that idea came to be. The answer was adumbrated in the preceding chapter. It lies in the spurt of science and technological activity, the significant application of contact inventions, and the relatively sudden emergence of nations. The combined effect of these facts gave development an enormous boost and provided the speculative mind with yet another process with which to contend. Indeed, some authors contend that world inequalities are increasing;[2] other authors contend that differences among nations will persist only until the plateau of full development has been reached, that is, the effect of the initial time differences in development among nations will eventually diminish (though not necessarily to the point of equalization) in the achievement of a common goal;[3] and still other authors contend that world inequalities will persist variably, that is, only so long as certain concomitant conditions which produced the initial differences continue to remain influential—such a cause as possessing a monopoly over certain technologies is suggested.[4]

Although every nation is developing in this century, and rapidly, too, there is no real prospect of international equalization. As the White Queen told Alice, it takes a lot of running just to keep in place. It is easy to locate and enter upon the historical trail of development; no nation has failed to do so. But it is difficult to pass another nation which has gotten onto it earlier. In 1959, former Premier Khrushchev predicted from comparative annual increases in gross industrial product that the Soviet Union would pass the United States by 1972 in "production per head of population."[5] The allotted time has passed and the inequality between these nations remains about the same now as it was before.

A head start counts, and for one nation to surpass another requires extraordinary efforts. For example, a thousand telephone instruments added to the Burmese exchange would indicate a quick step forward in development, and it would increase the ease of communication in Burma, say, for argument, to that of Japan in 1913. By the time the Burmese cover the remaining distance, the Japanese, assuming that their existing rate of growth continues, will have moved far ahead again.

Although the development hierarchy has proven to be remarkably stable, it is not fixed; rich nations and poor are not locked in place. Small changes occur even though nations are roughly in the same positions. The hierarchy is stable because though nations change, both up and down, such change is small and occurs over a short span of time. Some authors, however, have contended that latecomers on the historical trail of development have an advantage or that they can turn an initial disadvantage around. The most cited cases are Germany, Japan, and Soviet Russia. While anything is possible, large changes in the short run are highly improbable. Oddly enough these authors do not provide any evidence for the proposition. What evidence does exist is to the contrary. The relative position of each nation just prior to the First World War, for instance, is nearly the same as its position after, for instance, the Second World War. Therefore he who would say that these three nations have moved up significantly *in rank* would have to find new evidence to support the statement.

(For example, Moussa says:

The prestige of the Russian model of development rests primarily upon Russia herself. For although her modern development was already adumbrated in 1917, she claims, not without reason, to owe the tremendous acceleration of her growth to her political system.[6]

And Horowitz says: "the Soviet Union demonstrated that historical 'stage skipping' is not only possible but necessary."[7] But neither of these statements is validated by any indicator of development, that is, long-term per capita figures. In fact, they are falsified by the proportionate number of telephone instruments and by a wide variety of other social and economic indicators which show that the place of Russia in comparative development has not changed significantly since the opening of the twentieth century.[8] Just prior to Russia's active involvement in the First World War,

the productive capacity of society as a whole was certainly greater than at any other time in Russian history; and to take again the long view, the economic graphs had all been mounting for Russia as a whole in the late nineteenth and early twentieth centuries, and the progress in trade and production since the abortive revolution of 1905 had been notable.[9]

I conclude from this slight digression that not a single Russian owes anything to his "political system" because in comparative terms his nation has not "stage skipped.")

If we extend our view, to scan a century or more, then and only then do we see large change. Taking this very long view, we see that the lineup of nations has been somewhat reversed: several nations close to the top of the roster before the eighteenth century, and earlier, are now close to the bottom. Marco Polo was born and raised in the most developed area of all the West, yet he pointed to the East when he spoke of a supremely developed place. All the evidence he presented was, of course, in traditional form: gold and diamonds, rubies and jade, gardens and temples; poetical and philosophic works, length of tradition; precious ointments, delicate porcelains, and rare spices; and personal observation of and in public administration, the road system, and diplomacy. For centuries on end, from Herodotus to Adam Smith, the East had been the region of known and admired development. In fact, throughout most of history Europe was a borrower of things Eastern rather than a donor. The plants and animals which made settled life in the West possible came to it from Asia, together with all its basic technologies from smelting to printing.[10]

Regardless of type of change, therefore, small changes occurring in less than a century or large changes occurring over more than a century, the fact of hierarchy persists and may always be observed. Hierarchy has a top, a bottom, and a middle. However inevitable inequalities in development may seem, one thing is certain; rich nations and poor are becoming neither more nor less equal significantly than they have been since the turn of this century.

Explaining World Inequality

That some nations in the last century stood high in the development hierarchy and others low can be explained by their differential exposure and response to the mechanisms of culture, communication, and cohesion at about the same time. The earlier the exposure and the quicker the positive response, the sooner the presently more favored nations entered upon the historical trail of development. This had one paramount effect, it strung out nations on a structure of inequality. That such inequality continues through time can be explained by the application of these mechanisms differentially; the greater the application, the higher a nation's level of development.

Culture, communication, and cohesion are applied differentially by nations before, during, and after war. While war may influence the application of these mechanisms to some degree, its effect does not show up in the development hierarchy in any important way. Perhaps the influence of war is constant and equal for all nations or, more certainly from the long-term perspective, that influence is marginal to world inequality. At any rate, the development hierarchy and the differential application of the mechanisms which condition it have not exhibited any great changes from 1913 through 1952. For war to affect the development hierarchy, it must significantly affect the working of these mechanisms and their differential application by rich nations and poor. But war has brought neither discontinuities nor important increases to world culture; it has created neither insurmountable barriers between nations nor made their borders more permeable to global communication; and, it has led neither to irreparable breakdowns of, nor to differential increments to, the key social processes of centralization, consociation, and cooperation: the cohesiveness of nationalities has sustained the impact.

More formally, the explanation of world inequality can be theoretically rendered as follows. Continuity of the development hierarchy is a function of culture, communication, and cohesion. Differential application of these mechanisms by nations provides for the existing values in rank stability, rank spread, and speed of material improvement. Therefore, continuity of the development hierarchy varies with the values of rank stability or order, rank spread or integration, and speed of material improvement or progress. War does not significantly affect the differential application of the mechanisms of inequality. Therefore, continuity of the development hierarchy in its several aspects—order, integration, and progress—should be anticipated through war.

Inequality in development appears as the central drama of our time. It is, moreover, one of the most mind-disturbing phenomena of scholarship. Authors have been either attracted or repelled by the subject according to their biases, but it has never lacked fascination for them. An indication of this can be seen in the many other explanations offered to account for it.

Huntington presents a theory of inequality based on climate. He says that climate and its fluctuations cause fluctuations in health and the efficiency of physical and mental work; fluctuations in health and in work efficiency lead to corresponding fluctuations of business and economic conditions of a society.[11] Gobineau offers, as the fundamental cause of inequality, the racial factor. He attempts to show that neither religious fervor, nor corruption and licentiousness, nor luxury lead necessarily to inequalities among nations. Neither do the merits of a government influence the historical longevity of nations; nor does the geographical or social environment.[12] And Coste claims that "numerical increase of the members of a society is the primary cause of its whole evolution. The increase of a unified population leads to an increase of social differentiation, and to a division of labor and of social aptitudes, facilitating the communication of various parts of the society, and making possible a better and more powerful coordination of the individual actions, and a more and more accurate representation of the unity of natural laws."[13]

Elegant as these turn-of-the-century explanations are, they have not gained adherents or favor since their first appearance; but then neither have more recently advanced explanations of inequality in development among nations:

toilet training, children's stories, size of family, status loss, entrepreneurship, skill of labor force, accessibility to suitable markets, an acquisitive ethic facilitating capital formation, and type of economy or polity. The theory of differential application is not the only possible explanation of world inequality, to be sure, but it is the only explanation based on hard information about many nations before and after a significant event and over a long period of time.[14]

War has been consistently advanced throughout history as an explanation of inequality in development. But the world wars of this century have neither equalized the development ranks of nations nor increased the inequalities between them. The relationship between war and inequality, therefore, can be characterized as spurious or irrelevant. Inequalities in development among nations continue and remain relatively intact through history whether or not wars occur.

World Satisfaction

While all nations master a portion of the environment, some exercise greater mastery than others; if a handful of nations appear to possess considerable mastery, many more are frequently victimized by the environment. The variability of environmental mastery is probably now the most conspicuous fact of our time. It is conspicuous because up to 1900 the horizon of any one individual was often limited to events occurring within his own nation, if he was sufficiently attuned to them. Perhaps a handful of individuals in any nation outside the foreign service (if such existed) had interests in more than two or three other nations at one time, excluding the interests of migrants. Now with the advances attending the essential mechanisms of development (that is, increases in mass knowledge, transnational contact, and in the number and cohesiveness of nations), even normally educated youth seem to have little trouble locating the more visible nations in a hierarchy when asked.[15]

Nations line up like beads on a string, according to development, and their feelings do not escape the effects of this fact. Awareness of these world inequalities is now a global phenomenon. Awareness has always existed and so has inequality. What is peculiar to this century, and thus new, is the expansion of awareness. Until recent time, low awareness or ignorance of world inequality could be said to have served an integrative function; today, however, awareness of world inequality has expanded to include the political leaders of the newest and least developed nations. "The elites are extremely sensitive to their country's status among their neighbors and in the world at large, and particularly to any slights or humiliations." Intellectual elites, perhaps because of their wider associations, certainly because of their greater awareness, seem more susceptible for "they are often more concerned about the international status of their country than they are about the people in village and bush."[16]

Luard supports this general view of expanded awareness of world inequality by noting its potential as a source of stress. "The most significant phenomenon within contemporary society is the extension of those urges toward equality which have for hundreds of years made themselves felt within states into the international arena."[17] And Worsley, carrying the argument of stress to an effect, says that "a new kind of revolutionary theory" has emerged "in which the major conflict is seen as one between" the underdeveloped and developed nations with violence at its heart and through which it "will rejuvenate the earth and transform former slaves and former masters alike into human beings."[18]

Expanded awareness of world inequalities has become more fundamental to conflict and the dissatisfaction of nations than the actual differences. Hovet has shown that the new awareness of the north-south divergencies in development affects voting in the United Nations Assembly in patterned ways.[19] But this is not to suggest that such dissatisfaction may arise only as the result of new knowledge of inequality between strata, for it also may cause strain between nations within a stratum.[20]

Awareness expands often as not when and where the stress is greatest; that is, under circumstances of war and change.[21] Nothing so awakens one's national feeling as a crisis such as war and by it becoming increasingly aware of members of other nations. Just prior to the First World War, Burckhardt said: "A people actually feels its full strength as a people only in war. It must then endeavor to sustain its power at that level. Its whole standard has been enlarged."[22] And Spengler, writing just after the First World War, expresses a similar opinion. "*A people is only really such in relation to other peoples*, and the substance of this actuality comes out in natural and ineradicable oppositions, in attack and defense, hostility and war."[23] Now war also means change. And as we learned in Chapter 7, poor nations experience proportionately more change than rich nations and so were subject to greater amounts of stress. Given the expansion of awareness to these nations, then, they must bear a bit more stress than they would have otherwise felt in exactly the same circumstances of change.

One way in which nations attempt to reduce the stress that attends change and expanded awareness, is to fashion an ideology to explain away what is and provide a vision of what ought to be. But given a fishbowl world, the dominant ideologies have become less and less helpful. For example, the ideologies of capitalism and communism can neither explain world inequality nor assuage pained feelings about it. So, many nations, particularly those in the lower reaches of development, have rejected or ignored these ideologies as useless in light of their real situation.

All this is not to imply that ideology is dead. Ideology is obviously alive and well in the twentieth century. It is to imply, however, that preexisting ideologies provide little comfort to all those who feel dissatisfied with position in the development hierarchy due to change and increased awareness. But the need that ideology subserves persists. So new, or at least different ideologies emerge to replace the traditional or dominant ones. Thus it should come as no surprise to learn that fresh ideologies have been preeminently fashioned among poor nations. Sigmund, for example, has collected a number of documents showing that a distinctive ideology, peculiar to the developing nations, has arisen.[24]

Dissatisfaction with position is not a new phenomenon for it attends perception of inequality, and inequality, always existing, has always been perceived regionally by some proportion of nations. The one essential requirement is awareness of a neighbor; this provides the occasion for invidious comparison. Stress is provoked by a nation's awareness of its own disadvantage relative to another nation; it is exacerbated under circumstances of awareness-expansion. World inequality alone does not provide a condition for stress or a feeling of dissatisfaction until awareness expands to include the entire development hierarchy: an expansion of awareness among formerly isolated nations, of their inclusion in a system of inequality which insistently and forcefully embraces the world. Awareness, then, may serve as a source of stress to some of the nations all of the time and to all of the nations some of the time. Any nation nowadays can see and measure its own position, draw invidious comparisons with all other nations, and, hence, come to resent and envy those above and despise and fear those below.

For at least a century now, each succeeding generation has gained increased mastery over the environment. The evidence of continuous material improvement is quite impressive. In the past fifty years, for instance, the world's population has nearly doubled while telephone growth has increased twelve-fold. Yet rich nations and poor exhibit dissatisfaction as evidenced by internal disturbances and expressions of outrage in various media. A single example will suffice to exemplify the point. In the fall of 1965, Lin Piao, commander in chief of China's Armed Forces and second in authority only to Mao, made a public pronouncement outlining the shape of the future as he (and presumably Mao) viewed it. Speaking in metaphorical terms, he presented an image of North America and Western Europe as "cities" encircled by the indigent and rebellious "rural areas of the world"–Asia, Africa, and Latin America. Basing his analysis on China's revolutionary experience, the prospects were excellent, according to Lin, that the destitute "country-side," in the not-too-distant future, would envelop the prosperous and "selfish" North Atlantic enclaves. This hoped for change clearly illustrates a sense of profound dissatisfaction with the existing system of inequality, a direct function most probably of an expanded awareness about it which has since the Second World War penetrated the boundaries of all nations in the lower stratum of the development hierarchy.

If the world is on a socioeconomic progress course, and there is nothing on the present horizon which seriously threatens this long-term trend of continuous development short of cosmic disaster or thermonuclear holocaust, then why should dissatisfaction as a phenomenon mount and spread? The answer lies in the fact that the same conditions which promote development also promote

Appendix

Appendix

Table A-1
Population Size in Thousands

Nation	1913	1920	1925	1938	1947	1952
Algeria	5,610	5,804	6,066	7,235[f]	8,302	9,126
Argentina	7,885	8,861	10,358	13,725	15,942	18,040
Australia	4,872	5,360	5,939	6,899	7,579	8,636
Austria	29,193	6,455	6,582	6,753	6,920	6,949
Belgium	7,639	7,552	7,778	8,374	8,450	8,730
Bolivia	2,400	2,136	2,263	2,629	2,916	3,104
Brazil	25,000	27,404	30,332	39,480	48,438	54,477
Bulgaria	4,828	4,825	5,314	6,253	7,064	7,275
Burma	–	–	–	15,797	17,934	18,860
Canada	7,408	8,820	9,559	11,448	12,888	14,459
Ceylon	4,262	4,486	4,847	5,826	7,037	8,074
Chile	3,482	3,785	4,073	4,914	5,748	6,295
China	441,500	443,000+	448,231*	446,930	456,901	568,910
Colombia	5,500	6,089	6,724	8,702	10,609	11,847
Congo	15,000	6,491	7,708	10,309	10,753	11,767
Cuba	2,383	3,000+	3,450*	4,428	5,152	5,725
Czechoslovakia	13,593	12,979	13,537	14,603	12,164	12,683
Denmark	3,000	3,243	3,425	3,777	4,146	4,334
Ecuador	2,000	1,541	1,724	2,355	2,936	3,393
Egypt	12,144	13,222	13,965	16,295	19,068	21,473
Finland	3,250	3,133	3,304	3,656	3,859	4,091
France	39,790	38,750	40,300	41,100	40,644	42,360
Ghana	1,600	2,298	2,300*	3,541	4,081	4,410
Greece	4,810	5,008	5,958	7,122	7,483[h]	7,733
Hungary	21,410	7,950	8,299	9,167	9,079	9,511
India	243,861	249,699	263,071	307,694	345,085	367,530
Indonesia	43,925	52,327	56,371	68,409	73,700[g]	78,300
Iran	9,000	9,000+	9,000*	16,200	17,735	17,067
Iraq	2,250[a]	2,850	3,175*	3,560[e]	4,816	5,611
Ireland	3,110	3,103	2,085	2,937	2,974	2,953
Italy	35,598	37,006	38,533	42,976	45,664	47,321
Japan	55,131	55,391	59,479	70,530	77,490	85,500
Kenya	2,835	–	–	3,366*	5,311	5,760
Korea	15,170	16,850	18,081	21,817	19,886	21,144
Luxemburg	260	261	268	301	289	301
Madagascar	3,288	3,364	3,579	3,882	4,081	4,464

Table A-1 (cont.)

Nation	1913	1920	1925	1938	1947	1952
Malawi	1,065	1,202	1,212	1,674	2,150·	2,380
Malaya	2,070	2,907	3,675*	4,318	4,908	5,439
Mexico	15,527	14,444[b]	15,204	19,071	23,811	27,287
Morocco	5,000	4,500+	4,229*	7,564	8,524	9,268
Mozambique	3,120	3,120+	3,120*	4,814	5,506	5,836
Netherlands	6,213	6,820	7,366	8,684	9,629	10,382
New Zealand	1,147	1,241	1,382	1,604	1,797	1,995
Nigeria	17,500	18,000+	18,470*	19,725*	23,745	29,600
Norway	2,464	2,635	2,747	2,936	3,165	3,328
Paraguay	900	699	785	1,061	1,305	1,462
Peru	4,500	5,212	5,579	6,805	8,032	8,864
Philippines	9,407	10,000+	11,935[c]	15,814	18,762	20,714
Poland	30,700	26,746	29,275	34,682	23,734	25,753
Portugal	5,974	6,000	6,396	7,506	8,190	8,549
Rhodesia	800+	886	964	1,406	1,850	2,430
Romania	7,656	12,340	13,209	15,601	15,849	16,630
South Africa	6,214	6,842	7,664	9,986	11,690	12,938
Soviet Russia	173,203	136,900	147,028[c]	190,678	193,000	200,200[i]
Spain	20,370	21,196	22,292	25,279	27,223	28,306
Sudan	5,825	6,000+	6,469*	6,342*	7,709	10,263[i]
Sweden	5,639	5,876	6,045	6,297	6,803	7,125
Switzerland	3,864	3,881	3,978	4,205	4,547	4,815
Taiwan	3,265	3,736	4,095	5,678	6,293	8,003
Tanganyika	–	–	–	5,258*	7,355	8,015
Thailand	8,357	9,460	10,542	14,755	17,478	19,193
Turkey	19,574	14,000+	14,250[d]	17,016	19,625	22,219
Uganda	2,909	–	–	3,745*	4,818	5,467
United Kingdom	46,000	43,718	45,059	47,494	49,531	50,737
United States	96,512	106,466	115,832	129,969	144,697	157,636
Uruguay	1,279	1,479	1,659	2,108	2,306	2,495
Venezuela	2,756	2,408	2,840	3,513	4,548	5,280
West Germany	66,978	61,794	63,166	68,558	46,940	50,844
Yugoslavia	4,548	11,882	12,796	15,384	15,679	16,798
Zambia	820+	950	1,130	1,460	1,700	1,960

Sources: For 1913, INTERNATIONAL STATISTICAL YEAR-BOOK, 1926 (League of Nations), Table I; for all other years, DEMOGRAPHIC YEAR-BOOK, 1960 (United Nations), Table 4; for Iraq in 1913 and 1920 estimates representing 1900 and 1919 are taken from Doris Goodrich Adams, IRAQ'S PEOPLE AND RESOURCES (Berkeley: University of California Press, 1958), pp. 34-35; for Soviet Russia in 1920, the figure is taken from Dudley Kirk, EUROPE'S POPULATION IN THE INTERWAR YEARS (New York: League of Nations, 1944), Table 4, p. 27; for Soviet Russia in 1947, the figure is

Table A-1 (cont.)

---

taken from DEMOGRAPHIC YEARBOOK, 1949-50 (United Nations), fn. 145; and for Nigeria and Sudan in 1947, the figures are taken from DEMOGRAPHIC YEARBOOK, 1949-50.

*This sign in 1925 means that the information is taken from INTERNATIONAL STATISTI-CAL YEAR-BOOK, 1926 (League of Nations); the same sign in 1938 means that the information is taken from INTERNATIONAL STATISTICAL YEAR-BOOK, 1939.

+This sign means that the information is estimated.

[a]refers to 1900

[b]refers to 1922

[c]refers to 1926

[d]refers to 1927

[e]refers to 1934

[f]refers to 1936

[g]refers to 1948

[h]refers to 1949

[i]refers to 1956

Table A-2
Total Number of Telephones

Nation	1913	1920	1925	1938	1947	1952
Algeria	9,988*	16,800*a	23,618	47,661	75,670	109,220
Argentina	74,296	116,553	189,036	405,474	651,082	928,724
Australia	137,485	224,000	362,949	630,175	905,017	1,342,961
Austria	172,334	133,480	153,043	281,790^d	305,311	448,936
Belgium	65,000	62,867	159,072	415,522	534,780	743,988
Bolivia	2,500	2,517	1,824	2,595	7,800	10,885
Brazil	3,918	8,509	10,298	25,646	46,850	63,631
Bulgaria	3,608	5,000	9,000	29,576	54,347	61,000
Burma	—	—	—	3,379	—	5,208
Canada	499,774	856,266	1,144,095	1,359,417	2,213,400	3,352,000
Ceylon	1,341*	3,692*	7,318*	10,837*	13,484*	20,420
Chile	19,709	29,867	35,164	78,119	119,500	140,769
China	27,009	74,460	117,774	160,000	244,028	264,000
Colombia	3,177	6,843	17,342	38,833	57,300	114,542
Congo	120*	230*a	427*	1,875*	3,104*	9,415
Cuba	16,097	34,376	62,114	54,153	91,800	139,646
Czechoslovakia	—	—	—	207,300*	356,803*	619,100*
Denmark	129,277	252,321	316,397	442,998	617,586	791,096
Ecuador	2,926	3,946	4,518	7,326	10,000	11,500
Egypt	17,259	22,280	35,744	64,823	99,814	133,315
Finland	40,000	45,000	85,000	185,456	281,013	383,985
France	330,000	473,212	737,198	1,589,595	2,108,140	2,644,910
Ghana	155*	337*	915*	2,771*	4,992*	8,519
Greece	3,200	4,700	5,500	49,872	62,900	95,500

Hungary	84,040	57,009	78,451	165,362	106,768	120,000
India	17,697	34,268	43,239	83,378	126,412	199,768
Indonesia	14,843	34,504	40,963	49,361	22,263	63,360
Iran	913*	2,100*a	2,800*	12,000*	18,309*f	31,000
Iraq	40*	—	1,500*c	5,905*	13,740*	25,257
Ireland	—	—	—	43,086	59,753	97,388
Italy	91,720	114,977	200,000	611,254	958,813	1,540,909
Japan	219,551	330,597	636,736	1,367,958	1,195,238	2,250,000
Kenya	—	—	—	4,127*	8,008*	17,009*
Korea	10,883*	15,590*a	32,063*	74,591*	75,134e	16,529
Luxemburg	4,239*	5,941*	7,818*	15,922*	19,654	25,912
Madagascar	360*	612*	1,224*	2,740*	4,220*	6,800
Malawi	1*	39*	40*	349*	573*	1,595
Malaya	1,400*	2,311*	3,907*	8,082*	13,633*	33,487
Mexico	41,861	44,784	54,465	158,569	237,000	312,225
Morocco	1,000*+	5,305*a	7,828*	24,341*	45,153	90,517
Mozambique	320*	900*a	950*	1,949*	2,930*	5,573
Netherlands	86,490	161,933	214,041	433,927	575,995	896,294
New Zealand	49,415	88,439	130,186	206,216	300,552	425,186
Nigeria	498*	833*	1,813*	3,322*	6,331*	13,279
Norway	82,550	135,372	173,752	235,264	376,503	503,223
Paraguay	499	406	461	3,339	4,900	5,627
Peru	4,000	8,552	11,000	29,318	43,000	56,576
Philippines	6,758	12,451	16,966	29,842	6,917	34,616
Poland	—	—	—	294,828	192,156	235,000
Portugal	8,850	15,421	20,956	69,256	114,818	186,154
Rhodesia	781*	1,445*	1,798*	7,339*	16,405*	31,666
Romania	20,000	24,701	41,755	93,314	127,153	140,000

Table A-2 (cont.)

Nation	1913	1920	1925	1938	1947	1952
South Africa	2,888	5,140	8,068	20,589	33,500	55,777
Soviet Russia	246,600*	172,400*a	197,200*	1,272,500*	1,627,500*	2,636,600
Spain	34,000	70,000	113,000	300,000	509,993	819,553
Sudan	300*	560*	794*	2,252*	4,660*	9,658
Sweden	233,008	388,130	436,340	803,228	1,450,476	1,889,353
Switzerland	96,624	152,336	195,525	450,380	744,997	1,012,590
Taiwan	4,822*	8,215*	16,075*	34,289*	–	30,757
Tanganyika	–	–	–	1,530*	3,056*	6,855
Thailand	794*	1,341*	1,756*b	5,277*	5,362*	7,181
Turkey	3,900*	8,000*a	10,325*	25,025*d	46,000	97,176
Uganda	–	–	–	1,219*	2,135*	5,155
United Kingdom	780,512	985,964	1,376,656	3,220,241	4,654,500	5,915,972
United States	9,542,017	13,329,379	16,935,918	19,953,263	34,866,758	48,056,308
Uruguay	13,599	22,381	26,051	46,656	73,367	101,806
Venezuela	5,029	8,896	12,055	23,804	48,800	81,690
West Germany	1,420,100	1,809,574	2,588,016	4,146,489	1,753,000	2,976,953
Yugoslavia	4,900+	16,439	29,943	67,588	80,000	144,508
Zambia	30*	55*	72*	1,000*	2,332*e	4,577

Source: THE WORLD'S TELEPHONES (New York: American Telephone and Telegraph Company). Before and after the First World War, this series is called TELEPHONE AND TELEGRAPH STATISTICS OF THE WORLD; before and after the Second World War, it is called TELEPHONE STATISTICS OF THE WORLD.

*Means that the information is not in published form and has been obtained from the files of the statistical reporting office of the American Telephone and Telegraph Company in New York City.

+This sign next to Morocco and Yugoslavia in 1913 means that the figures are estimated.

arefers to 1921   crefers to 1930   erefers to 1946
brefers to 1924   drefers to 1937   frefers to 1948

Table A-3
Telephones per Thousand

Nation	1913	1920	1925	1938	1947	1952
Algeria	1.780	2.895	3.894	6.588	9.115	11.968
Argentina	9.422	13.153	18.250	29.543	40.841	51.481
Australia	28.219	41.791	61.113	91.343	119.411	155.507
Austria	5.904	20.679	23.252	41.728	44.120	64.604
Belgium	8.509	8.325	20.452	49.620	63.288	85.222
Bolivia	1.042	1.178	0.806	0.987	2.675	3.507
Brazil	1.567	3.105	3.395	6.496	9.672	11.680
Bulgaria	0.747	1.036	1.694	4.730	7.694	8.385
Burma	–	–	–	0.214	–	0.276
Canada	67.464	97.082	119.688	118.747	171.741	231.828
Ceylon	0.315	0.823	1.510	1.860	1.916	2.529
Chile	5.660	7.891	8.633	15.897	20.790	22.362
China	0.061	0.168	0.263	0.358	0.534	0.464
Colombia	0.578	1.124	2.579	4.463	5.401	9.668
Congo	0.008	0.035	0.055	0.182	0.289	0.800
Cuba	6.755	11.459	18.004	12.230	17.818	24.392
Czechoslovakia	–	–	–	14.196	29.333	48.813
Denmark	43.092	77.805	92.379	117.288	148.959	182.533
Ecuador	1.463	2.561	2.621	3.111	3.406	3.389
Egypt	1.421	1.685	2.560	3.978	5.235	6.208
Finland	12.308	14.363	25.726	50.726	72.820	93.861
France	8.294	12.217	18.293	38.676	51.868	62.439
Ghana	0.097	0.147	0.398	0.783	1.223	1.932
Greece	0.665	0.938	0.923	7.003	8.406	12.350
Hungary	3.925	7.171	9.453	18.039	11.760	12.617
India	0.073	0.137	0.164	0.271	0.366	0.544
Indonesia	0.338	0.659	0.727	0.722	0.302	0.809
Iran	0.101	0.233	0.311	0.741	1.032	1.816
Iraq	0.018	–	0.472	1.659	2.853	4.501
Ireland	–	–	–	14.670	20.092	32.979
Italy	2.577	3.107	5.190	14.223	20.997	32.563
Japan	3.982	5.968	10.759	19.395	15.424	26.316
Kenya	–	–	–	1.226	1.508	2.953
Korea	0.717	0.925	1.773	3.419	3.778	0.782
Luxemburg	16.304	22.762	29.172	52.897	68.007	86.086
Madagascar	0.109	0.182	0.342	0.706	1.034	1.523
Malawi	0.001	0.032	0.033	0.208	0.267	0.670
Malaya	0.676	0.795	1.063	1.872	2.778	6.157
Mexico	2.696	3.101	3.582	8.315	9.953	11.442

Table A-3 (cont.)

Nation	1913	1920	1925	1938	1947	1952
Morocco	0.200	1.179	1.851	3.218	5.297	9.767
Mozambique	0.103	0.288	0.304	0.405	0.532	0.955
Netherlands	13.921	23.744	29.058	49.969	59.819	86.332
New Zealand	43.082	71.264	94.201	128.564	167.252	213.126
Nigeria	0.028	0.046	0.098	0.168	0.267	0.449
Norway	33.502	51.375	63.252	80.131	118.958	151.209
Paraguay	0.554	0.581	0.587	3.147	3.755	3.849
Peru	0.889	1.641	1.972	4.308	5.354	6.383
Philippines	0.718	1.245	1.422	1.887	0.369	1.671
Poland	–	–	–	8.501	8.096	9.125
Portugal	1.481	2.570	3.276	9.227	14.019	21.775
Rhodesia	0.976	1.631	1.865	5.220	8.868	13.031
Romania	2.612	2.002	3.161	5.981	8.023	8.419
South Africa	4.649	7.513	10.528	20.618	28.657	43.111
Soviet Russia	1.424	1.259	1.341	6.674	8.433	13.170
Spain	1.669	3.303	5.069	11.868	18.734	28.953
Sudan	0.052	0.093	0.123	0.355	0.604	0.941
Sweden	41.321	66.053	72.182	127.557	213.212	265.172
Switzerland	25.006	39.252	49.152	107.106	163.844	210.299
Taiwan	1.477	2.199	3.926	6.039	–	3.843
Tanganyika	–	–	–	0.291	0.415	0.855
Thailand	0.095	0.142	0.167	0.358	0.307	0.374
Turkey	0.199	0.571	0.725	1.471	2.344	4.374
Uganda	–	–	–	0.326	0.443	0.943
United Kingdom	16.968	22.553	30.619	67.803	93.971	116.601
United States	98.869	125.198	146.211	153.523	240.964	304.856
Uruguay	10.633	15.133	15.703	22.133	31.816	40.804
Venezuela	1.825	3.694	4.245	6.776	10.730	15.472
West Germany	21.202	29.284	40.972	60.481	37.346	58.551
Yugoslavia	1.077	1.384	2.340	4.393	5.102	8.603
Zambia	0.037	0.058	0.064	0.685	1.372	2.335

Note: This information derives from data in Tables A-1 and A-2.

Table A-4
Ranks of Telephones per Thousand

Nation	1913	1925	1938	1952	1952y
Algeria	28	28	34	33	31
Argentina	15	17	17	17	17
Australia	7	7	7	7	7
Austria	19	14	15	14	14
Belgium	16	15	14	13	13
Bolivia	37	47	54	49	46
Brazil	30	30	35	34	32
Bulgaria	40	41	39	41	38
Burma	–	–	67	70	–
Canada	2	2	4	3	3
Ceylon	48	42	50	52	48
Chile	20	23	22	26	24
China	57	56	61	67	61
Colombia	45	34	40	37	35
Congo	62	62	69	63	57
Cuba	18	18	26	25	23
Czechoslovakia	–	–	25	18	–
Denmark	3	4	5	6	6
Ecuador	33	33	47	50	47
Egypt	35	35	43	43	40
Finland	13	13	12	10	10
France	17	16	16	15	15
Ghana	54	52	55	54	50
Greece	44	46	31	32	30
Hungary	23	22	21	31	29
India	56	58	66	66	60
Indonesia	47	48	57	62	56
Iran	53	54	56	55	51
Iraq	61	51	51	45	42
Ireland	–	–	23	21	–
Italy	26	24	24	22	20
Japan	22	20	20	24	22
Kenya	–	–	53	51	–
Korea	42	40	44	64	58
Luxemburg	11	11	11	12	12
Madagascar	51	53	58	57	53
Malawi	63	63	68	65	59
Malaya	43	45	49	44	41

Table A-4 (cont.)

Nation	1913	1925	1938	1952	1952y
Mexico	24	29	30	35	33
Morocco	49	39	45	36	34
Mozambique	52	55	60	58	54
Netherlands	12	12	13	11	11
New Zealand	4	3	2	4	4
Nigeria	60	60	70	68	62
Norway	6	6	8	8	8
Paraguay	46	50	46	47	44
Peru	39	37	42	42	39
Philippines	41	43	48	56	52
Poland	–	–	29	38	–
Portugal	31	31	28	27	25
Rhodesia	38	38	38	30	28
Romania	25	32	37	40	37
South Africa	21	21	19	19	18
Soviet Russia	34	44	33	29	27
Spain	29	25	27	23	21
Sudan	58	59	63	60	55
Sweden	5	5	3	2	2
Switzerland	8	8	6	5	5
Taiwan	32	27	36	48	45
Tanganyika	–	–	65	61	–
Thailand	55	57	62	69	63
Turkey	50	49	52	46	43
Uganda	–	–	64	59	–
United Kingdom	10	10	9	9	9
United States	1	1	1	1	1
Uruguay	14	19	18	20	19
Venezuela	27	26	32	28	26
West Germany	9	9	10	16	16
Yugoslavia	36	36	41	39	36
Zambia	59	61	59	53	49

Notes: These ranks are composed by arraying the information in Table A-3.

y refers to a special 1952 ranking of the 63 nations of 1913 for which data are available; such reranking permits a long-term comparison as seen in Table 7-1.

Table A-5
National Real Income in Millions of International Units

Nation	1913	1920	1925	1938	1947	1952
Argentina				3,335	5,575	6,200[p]
Australia	1,963	1,675	2,692	3,545	4,982	5,815
Austria	4,520		1,477	1,415[j]	1,215	1,870[p]
Belgium	2,414	1,273	2,064[f]	2,881	3,968	4,460
Brazil				5,387	7,100	10,380
Bulgaria	625		581	1,030	1,168[r]	1,623[o,s]
Canada	3,752[b]	4,001	4,905[g]	5,583	10,272	12,726
Chile				1,187	1,320	1,485[o]
Colombia				730[k]	1,028	1,196[o]
Cuba				650[k]	906	975[p]
Czechoslovakia	2,380		2,285	2,635	2,930	4,040[r]
Denmark	1,177	1,468	1,614	2,075	2,303	2,553[p]
Finland	466		486[f]	925	947	1,532
France	9,900	10,900	14,900	14,400	17,200	21,100
Greece	613		1,002[h]	1,271	864	1,100[t]
Hungary	1,910		1,132[r]	1,314	1,271[r]	
Ireland	807[c]		837[g]	995	1,102	1,228[p]
Italy	5,170	5,770	7,010	7,120	7,980	11,250
Japan	7,120	4,860	9,290	15,300	10,800	18,100
Netherlands	2,290[a]	2,400	2,700	3,900	4,040	5,130
New Zealand	262		792	1,137	1,439	1,678
Norway	529	957	766	1,085	1,260	1,547
Peru				697[l]	761	1,092[p]
Poland				5,320	5,620[s]	
Portugal				860	969	1,270[p]
South Africa	762[d]	752	1,100	1,783[k]	2,705	3,114[p]
Soviet Russia	22,300		25,500[i]	34,900		61,800[q]
Spain	7,100	8,700	7,500	6,220	8,940	12,100[p]
Sweden	1,219	1,578	1,714	2,756	3,620	4,405
Switzerland	1,089		1,381	1,827	2,716	2,998[p]
United Kingdom	22,760	20,130	22,750	29,070	28,050	30,010
United States	46,800[e]	58,700	73,500	84,600	143,100	175,900
West Germany	19,950		16,730	35,200[n]	12,630	19,320[p]

[a]1901	[e]1914	[i]1928	[m]1946	[q]1953
[b]1910	[f]1924	[j]1937	[n]1948	[r]real income including imputation
[c]1911	[g]1926	[k]1939	[o]1950	[s]real product
[d]1912	[h]1927	[l]1942	[p]1951	[t]my estimate

Source: Colin Clark, THE CONDITIONS OF ECONOMIC PROGRESS (London: Macmillan, 1957).

Table A-6
Real Income, per Capita

Nation	1913	1920	1925	1938	1947	1952
Argentina				243	350	344
Australia	403	313	453	514	657	673
Austria	155		224	210	176	269
Belgium	316	169	265	344	470	511
Brazil				136	147	191
Bulgaria	130		109	165	165	223
Canada	506	454	513	488	797	880
Chile				242	230	236
Colombia				84	97	101
Cuba				147	176	170
Czechoslovakia	175		169	180	241	319
Denmark	392	453	471	549	555	589
Finland	143		147	253	245	374
France	249	281	370	350	423	498
Greece	127		168	178	115	142
Hungary	89		136	143	140	
Ireland	259		280	339	371	416
Italy	145	156	182	166	175	238
Japan	131	88	157	217	139	212
Netherlands	369	352	367	449	420	494
New Zealand	228		573	709	801	841
Norway	215	363	279	370	398	465
Peru				102	95	123
Poland				153	237	
Portugal				115	118	149
South Africa	123	110	144	179	231	241
Soviet Russia	129		173	183		309
Spain	349	410	336	246	328	427
Sweden	216	269	284	438	532	618
Switzerland	282		347	434	597	623
United Kingdom	495	460	505	612	566	591
United States	485	551	635	651	989	1,116
West Germany	298		265	513	269	380

Note: This information derives from data in Tables A-1 and A-5.

Table A-7
Ranks of Real Income, per Capita

Nation	1913	1925	1938	1952	1952y
Argentina			17	17	
Australia	4	6	5	4	4
Austria	17	16	20	20	19
Belgium	8	14	13	9	9
Brazil			28	27	
Bulgaria	21	25	26	25	22
Canada	1	3	7	2	2
Chile			18	23	
Colombia			31	31	
Cuba			27	27	
Czechoslovakia	16	19	22	18	17
Denmark	5	5	4	8	8
Finland	19	22	15	16	16
France	12	7	12	10	10
Greece	23	20	24	29	24
Hungary	25	24			
Ireland	11	12	14	14·	14
Italy	18	17	25	22	21
Japan	20	21	19	25	23
Netherlands	6	8	8	11	11
New Zealand	13	2	1	3	3
Norway	15	13	11	12	12
Peru			30	30	
Poland					
Portugal			29	28	
South Africa	24	23	23	21	20
Soviet Russia	22	18	21	19	18
Spain	7	10	16	13	13
Sweden	14	11	9	6	6
Switzerland	10	9	10	5	5
United Kingdom	2	4	3	7	7
United States	3	1	2	1	1
West Germany	9	15	6	15	15

Notes: These ranks are composed by arraying the information in Table A-6.

y refers to a special 1952 ranking of the nations of 1913 for which data are available; such reranking permits a long-term comparison as seen in Table 7-1.

Table A-8
Gross Steel Production in Thousand Metric Tons

Nation	1913	1920	1925	1938	1947	1952
Australia	14	219	469	1,199	1,360	1,576
Austria	1,853	198	464	673	357	1,058
Belgium	2,467	1,253	2,549	2,279	2,882	5,067
Brazil				92	387	893
Canada	1,060	1,127	766	1,174	2,672	3,357
China	43	52	150			
Czechoslovakia	1,229	973	1,361	1,873	2,286	3,433
Denmark				20	58	176
Finland	7	6	30	76	77	147
France	4,687	3,050	7,415	6,216	5,733	10,867
Hungary	830	62	231	648	597	1,396
India	63	158	450	982	1,277	1,603
Italy	934	774	1,785	2,323	1,691	3,474
Japan	240	811	1,200	6,472	941	6,988
Korea				66	8	1
Luxemburg	1,336	585	2,084	1,437	1,715	3,002
Mexico				142	290	537
Netherlands				57	196	685
Norway				68	66	98
Poland	1,661	972	782	1,441	1,579	3,183
Romania	140	40 .	101	277	183	698
South Africa				300	603	1,258
Soviet Russia	4,869	163	2,149	18,068		35,000
Spain	242	250	626	574	608	904
Sweden	749	498	518	972	1,191	1,666
Turkey				38	90	153
United Kingdom	7,787	9,212	7,517	10,565	12,929	16,681
United States	31,802	42,807	46,120	28,805	77,015	84,520
West Germany	17,600	7,798	12,194	22,656	3,060	15,806
Yugoslavia	300		100	227	311	442

Source: League of Nations, INTERNATIONAL STATISTICAL YEAR-BOOK, 1926; and United Nations, STATISTICAL YEARBOOK, 1954.

Note: This table covers, as far as possible, the total production of crude steel, both ingots and steel for casting, whether obtained from pig-iron or scrap. (Wrought-puddled-iron is excluded.)

Table A-9
Steel Production, per Capita

Nation	1913	1920	1925	1938	1947	1952
Australia	003	041	079	174	179	182
Austria	063	031	070	100	052	152
Belgium	323	166	328	272	341	580
Brazil				002	008	016
Canada	143	128	080	103	207	232
China	000	000	000			
Czechoslovakia	090	075	101	128	188	271
Denmark				005	014	041
Finland	002	002	009	021	020	036
France	118	079	184	151	141	257
Hungary	039	008	028	071	066	147
India	000	001	002	003	004	004
Italy	026	021	046	054	037	073
Japan	004	015	020	092	012	082
Korea				003	000	000
Luxemburg	5,138	2,241	7,776	4,774	5,934	9,973
Mexico				007	012	020
Netherlands				007	020	066
Norway				023	021	029
Poland	054	036	027	042	067	124
Romania	018	003	008	108	012	042
South Africa				030	052	097
Soviet Russia	028	001	015	095		175
Spain	012	012	028	023	022	032
Sweden	133	085	086	154	175	234
Turkey				002	005	007
United Kingdom	169	211	167	222	261	329
United States	330	402	398	222	532	536
West Germany	263	126	193	330	065	311
Yugoslavia	066		008	015	020	026

Note: This information derives from data in Tables A-1 and A-8. Except for Luxemburg, each figure begins with a decimal point.

Table A-10
Ranks of Steel Production, per Capita

Nation	1913	1925	1938	1952	1952y
Australia	19	10	6	10	10
Austria	11	11	11	12	12
Belgium	3	3	3	2	2
Brazil			28.5	26	
Canada	6	9	10	9	9
China	22	22			
Czechoslovakia	9	7	9	6	6
Denmark			25	20	
Finland	20	18	20	21	18
France	8	5	8	7	7
Hungary	13	13.5	14	13	13
India	21	21	26.5	28	21
Italy	15	12	15	17	16
Japan	18	16	13	16	15
Korea			26.5	29	
Luxemburg	1	1	1	1	1
Mexico			23.5	25	
Netherlands			23.5	18	
Norway			18.5	23	
Poland	12	15	16	14	14
Romania	16	19	21	19	17
South Africa			17	15	
Soviet Russia	14	17	12	11	11
Spain	17	13.5	18.5	22	19
Sweden	7	8	7	8	8
Turkey			28.5	27	
United Kingdom	5	6	4.5	4	4
United States	2	2	4.5	3	3
West Germany	4	4	2	5	5
Yugoslavia	10	20	22	24	20

Notes: These ranks are composed by arraying the information in Table A-9.

y refers to a special 1952 ranking of the nations of 1913 for which data are available; such reranking permits a long-term comparison as seen in Table 7-1.

Notes

Notes

Chapter 1
Argument

1. "War is therefore not a concern between man and man but between State and State." J.J. Rousseau, THE SOCIAL CONTRACT (New York: Hafner, 1951), p. 11. Moral choices are largely within the context of a nation. Individuals alone or collected in groups cannot practice war when a higher authority possesses a monopoly over the means of violence. This is not so among nations. In world politics nations do not acknowledge a higher authority, for the admission would jeopardize the goal of effective independence. In principle, therefore, no nation delegates authority upwardly; in practice, however, nations will occasionally aggregate their resources in order to attain a specific goal.

A less strict definition than the one appearing in the text would include something about the size of armies, the duration of the conflict, the losses of life, and the magnitude of property destroyed. This kind of definition, although necessary at times due to the various types of war it might subsume, is not satisfying primarily because it overlooks the nation as an organized fighting unit with world power interests. For additional and far less strict definitions of war, see Quincy Wright, A STUDY OF WAR (Chicago: University of Chicago Press, 1965), pp. 8-13, 636-37, and 1544; and, J. David Singer and Melvin Small, THE WAGES OF WAR, 1816-1965: A STATISTICAL HANDBOOK (New York: Wiley, 1972).

2. Richard Hartshorne, "The Role of the State in Economic Growth: Contents of the State Area," pp. 287-88 in Hugh G.J. Aitken (ed.), THE STATE AND ECONOMIC GROWTH (New York: Social Science Research Council, 1959).

3. Perhaps the most forceful exposition of this not unreasonable point of view is contained in the work by Fred Cottrel. See his ENERGY AND SOCIETY: THE RELATION BETWEEN ENERGY, SOCIAL CHANGE, AND ECONOMIC DEVELOPMENT (New York: McGraw-Hill, 1955).

4. Lewis Mumford, TECHNICS AND CIVILIZATION (New York: Harcourt, Brace, 1934), p. 91. The quotations that follow are not continuous in the original, pp. 76 ff.

5. Werner Sombart, KRIEG UND KAPITALISMUS (Leipzig: Duncker & Humblot, 1913).

6. A.N. Agarwala, ECONOMIC MOBILIZATION FOR NATIONAL DEFENSE (New York: Asia Publishing House, 1966), p. v.

7. Giichi Ono, EXPENDITURES OF THE SINO-JAPANESE WAR (New York: Oxford University Press, 1922), p. 323.

8. Gotaro Ogawa, EXPENDITURES OF THE RUSSO-JAPANESE WAR (New York: Oxford University Press, 1923), pp. x, 251-52.

9. Giichi Ono, WAR AND ARMAMENT EXPENDITURES OF JAPAN (New York: Oxford University Press, 1922), pp. 255-56.

10. Ushisaburo Kobayashi, THE BASIC INDUSTRIES AND SOCIAL HISTORY OF JAPAN, 1914-1918 (New Haven: Yale University Press, 1930), p. 2; see also pp. 227 ff. for a description of other effects of the war: Japan's increase of shipping, her near tripling of trade, and her entry into money lending abroad. Thus through the First World War, Japan became a creditor and exporting nation.

11. Marshal Foch, THE PRINCIPLES OF WAR (London: Chapman & Hall, 1918), p. 36. This citation forms part of a lecture to the students of the French Staff College entitled: "The Primal Characteristics of Modern War," and published originally in France in 1903.

12. Ibid., p. 37.

13. Eugene Staley, WAR LOSSES TO A NEUTRAL (New York: League of Nations Association, December, 1937), p. 65.

14. J.U. Nef, WAR AND HUMAN PROGRESS (Cambridge: Harvard University Press, 1952), p. 325.

15. W.W. Rostow, THE PROCESS OF ECONOMIC GROWTH (2nd ed.; New York: W.W. Norton, 1962), p. 164.

16. Stanislav Andreski, THE USES OF COMPARATIVE SOCIOLOGY (Berkeley: University of California Press, 1965), p. 114.

17. Achille Viallate, ECONOMIC IMPERIALISM AND INTERNATIONAL RELATIONS DURING THE LAST FIFTY YEARS (New York: Macmillan, 1923), pp. 139-40.

18. J.B. Condliffe, WAR AND DEPRESSION (Boston and New York: World Peace Foundation, 1935), pp. 5-6.

19. R.F. McWilliams, DOES HISTORY REPEAT ITSELF? (London: J.M. Dent, 1932), p. 22. See also pp. 35-37 for a list of other correspondences, e.g., falling prices, impoverishment of peoples, stirring revolutions in the "new" areas of the world, emerging general purpose organizations: the Holy Alliance and the League of Nations, economic nationalism, and so forth.

20. Eugene Staley, WAR LOSSES TO A NEUTRAL (New York: League of Nations Association, December 1937), p. 64.

21. Scott Nearing, WAR OR PEACE (New York: Island Press, 1946), p. 31. By the time he reaches p. 80 he has considered several other factors and sums up: "Historical experience and contemporary observation will bear out this contention. Wars exhaust economically, socially, emotionally and morally. They wipe out the products of labor, cripple, frustrate and kill. Wars are accompanied and followed by starvation and disease. They weaken victor as well as vanquished."

22. Shepherd B. Clough, THE RISE AND FALL OF CIVILIZATION: AN INQUIRY INTO THE RELATIONSHIP BETWEEN ECONOMIC DEVELOPMENT AND CIVILIZATION (New York: McGraw-Hill, 1951), p. 263. On p.

235 he has the following to say on war in Europe in the twentieth century. "The greatest waste of savings has come from preparation for and waging of war—especially the two world wars of the twentieth century. Even though the countries involved were able to regain pre-war levels of production within a decade after the conflicts, thus indicating the recuperative powers of Western culture's economies, the retarding effects of war on Western Europe have been tremendous."

23. ENCYCLOPEDIA METHODIQUE (Paris: 1788), 4, p. 314, cited by J.U. Nef, WAR AND HUMAN PROGRESS, p. 342.

24. Joseph Schumpeter, IMPERIALISM AND SOCIAL CLASSES (New York: Augustus M. Kelly, 1951), p. 23.

25. Auguste Comte, COURS DE PHILOSOPHIE POSITIVE. Summarized by Jules Rig (Paris, 1881), 2, p. 221, cited by J.U. Neff, WAR AND HUMAN PROGRESS, pp. 341-42.

26. Ivan Stanislavovick Bliokh, THE FUTURE OF WAR IN ITS TECHNI-CAL, ECONOMIC, AND POLITICAL RELATIONS (Boston: Ginn, 1902), p. xxxi. And on p. xxxvii, he summarizes the impediments to making modern war: first, "the immense improvement that has been wrought in the mechanism of slaughter"; second, "the unmanageability of the immense masses of men who will be mobilized at the outbreak of war"; and, third, "the economic impossibility of waging war upon the scale on which it must be waged if it is waged at all."

27. Paul Kecskemeti, STRATEGIC SURRENDER: THE POLITICS OF VICTORY AND DEFEAT (Stanford: Stanford University Press, 1958), p. 245.

28. Scott Nearing, WAR OR PEACE (New York: Island Press, 1946), p. 23.

29. Oswald Spengler, THE DECLINE OF THE WEST (New York: Alfred A. Knopf, 1939), vol. 2, pp. 371-72.

30. A.C. Bell, SEA POWER AND THE NEXT WAR (London and New York: Longmans Green and Co., 1938), p. 48.

31. W.W. Rostow, THE STAGES OF ECONOMIC GROWTH (Cambridge: At the University Press, 1960), p. 108; see also pp. 112-14.

32. Arnold J. Toynbee, WAR AND CIVILIZATION (London: Oxford University Press, 1951), pp. viii-ix.

33. For an early statement on postwar population recovery, see John Stuart Mill, PRINCIPLES OF POLITICAL ECONOMY (London: Longmans, Green, 1909), book I, ch. 5; for empirical confirmation of compensatory recovery of populations after the Second World War see W.S. Woytinsky and E.S. Woytin-sky, WORLD POPULATION AND PRODUCTION (New York: The Twentieth Century Fund, 1953), pp. 141-42; and for thoughts on the effect of future population losses from atomic warfare, see Herman Kahn, ON THERMO-NUCLEAR WAR (Princeton: Princeton University Press, 1961).

34. Ralph Linton, "The Prospect of Western Civilization," p. 535 in Willard Waller (ed.), WAR IN THE TWENTIETH CENTURY (New York: Random House, 1940).

35. James Bryce, "War and Human Progress," INTERNATIONAL CON-CILIATION 108 (November, 1916), p. 295.

36. Thomas Babington Macaulay, THE HISTORY OF ENGLAND FROM THE ACCESSION OF JAMES THE SECOND (London: Macmillan, 1913), vol. I, ch. 3, pp. 270-71. (First published in 1848.)

37. Nef, WAR AND HUMAN PROGRESS, p. 302.

38. Simon Kuznets, MODERN ECONOMIC GROWTH (New Haven and London: Yale University Press, 1966), pp. 70-71.

Chapter 2
Development

1. "The daily food of an average Chinese ... would cost 50 francs in France, which is the wage paid for 20 minutes of a day laborer's work. ... If a Frenchman were to offer 120 hours of gratuitous work to a Chinese, he would be able to double the latter's ration; if this same Frenchman were willing to limit himself to the same diet, he would be able to accept the responsibility, in working a normal year, for no less than 19 Chinese, so that, making all due allowance for costs of transportation, the 21 million French workers would be able to double the food allowance of the 400 million Chinese by working 19 out of 20 hours for the Chinese." Jean Fourastie, THE CAUSES OF WEALTH (Glencoe: Free Press, 1960), p. 103. For other detailed descriptions of the average man by level of development, see Frederick H. Harbison and Charles A. Myers, EDUCATION, MANPOWER, AND ECONOMIC GROWTH (New York: McGraw-Hill, 1964); and Robert L. Heilbroner, THE GREAT ASCENT (New York: Harper & Row, 1963), Chapter 2.

2. An example of this method may be found in United Nations, ECONOMIC AND SOCIAL CONSEQUENCES OF DISARMAMENT (New York: 1962), pp. 17 ff.

3. Norton Ginsburg, ATLAS OF ECONOMIC DEVELOPMENT (Chicago: University of Chicago Press, 1961); Arthur S. Banks and Robert B. Textor, A CROSS-POLITY SURVEY (Cambridge: M.I.T. Press, 1963); and Bruce Russett, et al., WORLD HANDBOOK OF POLITICAL INDICATORS (New Haven: Yale University Press, 1964).

4. "According therefore, as this produce, or what is purchased with it, bears a greater or smaller proportion to the number of those who are to consume it, the nations will be better or worse supplied with all the necessaries and conveniences for which it has occasion." Adam Smith, AN INQUIRY INTO THE NATURE AND CAUSES OF THE WEALTH OF NATIONS (London: Methuen, 1930; first published in 1776), vol. I, p. 1.

5. When that is emphasized by anyone other than a statistician it becomes noteworthy. "Owing to the meager character of records previous to the

nineteenth century, historians can do little with the statistical method in exploring early ages, but the immense quantity of authentic data now being accumulated under public and private auspices will make it possible for the historian of the future to draw with a firmer hand the course of social development. For example, is there progress in public health? Indisputable materials warrant the conclusion that in specific areas the death rate is declining. In the year 2000 A.D. it will be possible to answer many fundamental questions concerning which we can merely guess at present. If there is progress it will be mass progress, measurable in averages and susceptible of graphic presentation. Charles A. Beard, "Introduction," p. xxv, in J.B. Bury, THE IDEA OF PROGRESS (New York: Macmillan, 1932).

6. Stacy V. Jones, THE PATENT OFFICE (New York: Praeger, 1970). The ten patents that shaped the modern world, according to Jones, are: the telephone, the airplane, electric light, vacuum tube, plastic, oil cracking, rocket, nylon, streptomycin, and the atomic reactor.

7. Walter Christaller, CENTRAL PLACES IN SOUTHERN GERMANY (Englewood Cliffs: Prentice Hall, 1966, first published in German in 1933), p. 147; M.K. Bennett, "International Disparities in Consumption Levels," AMERICAN ECONOMIC REVIEW 41 (September 1951), p. 647, Table 2; Jean Fourastie, THE CAUSES OF WEALTH (Glencoe: Free Press, 1960, first published in French in 1951), p. 116, Table XXIII; Seymour Martin Lipset, "Some Social Requisites of Democracy: Economic Development and Political Legitimacy," AMERICAN POLITICAL SCIENCE REVIEW 53 (March 1959); Phillips Cutright, "National Political Development: Measurement and Analysis," AMERICAN JOURNAL OF SOCIOLOGY 28, no. 2 (April 1963); Theodore Caplow and Kurt Finsterbusch, DEVELOPMENT RANK (New York: Bureau of Applied Social Research, Columbia University, 1966); and Donald V. McGranahan, "Analysis of Socio-Economic Development through a System of Indicators," THE ANNALS OF THE AMERICAN ACADEMY OF POLITICAL AND SOCIAL SCIENCE 393 (January 1971).

8. For example, there were forty-eight telephones in Ethiopia in 1913 but there was no estimate of the population until long after the Second World War. In fact, the first census of Ethiopia has still to be attempted according to K.M. Barbour and R.M. Protero (eds.), ESSAYS ON AFRICAN POPULATION (New York: Praeger, 1962), p. 3. In the United Nations' DEMOGRAPHIC YEAR-BOOK, 1965 (New York: 1966), Table 4, no population size entry appears from 1920 through 1954 showing that only since 1955 has Ethiopia been able to achieve even a rough estimate of its own population.

9. Oskar Morgenstern, ON THE ACCURACY OF ECONOMIC OBSERVATIONS (Princeton: Princeton University Press, 1963), pp. 242-282.

10. Milton Gilbert and Irving B. Kravis, AN INTERNATIONAL COMPARISON OF NATIONAL PRODUCTS AND THE PURCHASING POWER OF CURRENCIES (Paris: Organisation of European Economic Cooperation, 1954).

11. Erwin K. Scheuch, "Cross-National Comparisons Using Aggregate Data," pp. 142-143 in Richard L. Merrit and Stein Rokkan (eds.), COMPARING NATIONS (New Haven: Yale University Press, 1966). He notes that these multiple exchange rates have been called political prices and further notes that currency may be undervalued (as a means of export-dumping) or overvalued (to benefit capital owners investing abroad).

12. "Some economies, like that of Japan, have a built-in tendency to exhibit high rates of increase in GNP from year to year. Others, like France, have a tendency towards low rates. By an arithmetic miracle, countries with high rates of increase go on compounding them for years and decades without ever catching up to countries with low rates." Caplow and Finsterbusch, DEVELOPMENT RANK, p. 5.

13. For additional discussion on some of the merits and limitations of using the GNP as an index of economic development, by economists, see: Harvey Leibenstein, ECONOMIC BACKWARDNESS AND ECONOMIC GROWTH (New York: John Wiley, 1957), pp. 7-14; Hyman P. Minsky, "Indicators of the Development Status of an Economy," ECONOMIC DEVELOPMENT AND CULTURAL CHANGE 7 (January 1959), pp. 151-172; and Adamantios Pepelasis, Leon Mears, and Irma Adelman, ECONOMIC DEVELOPMENT (New York: Harper and Row, 1961), pp. 3-17.

14. Caplow and Finsterbusch, DEVELOPMENT RANK.

15. In a recent study, by McGranahan, "Socio-Economic Development," pp. 70 and 80, Tables 1 and 2, telephones represent one of eighteen carefully selected measures of development, there called core indicators. The average correlation of telephones with all other measures of development is shown to be 0.902 or the highest of all such correlations after transformation. The number of nations included in the study is forty-seven and the time involved is the year 1960.

16. The first three of these features were adumbrated by Caplow and Finsterbusch, DEVELOPMENT RANK, p. 17.

17. Perhaps Adam Smith was the first to recognize this lack of relationship. "Whatever be the soil, climate, or extent of territory of any particular nation, the abundance or scantiness of its annual supply must, in that particular situation, depend upon" the division of labor and the proportion of those usefully employed to those not so employed. Adam Smith, AN INQUIRY INTO THE NATURE AND CAUSES OF THE WEALTH OF NATIONS (London: Methuen, 1930), vol. I, pp. 1-2.

18. For the evidence that recent independence does not matter economically, see Norton Ginsburg, ATLAS OF ECONOMIC DEVELOPMENT (Chicago: University of Chicago Press, 1961), pp. 116-17, particularly Figure 8; and for an analysis showing that recent independence does not matter politically, see Lucian W. Pye, POLITICS, PERSONALITY, AND NATION BUILDING (New Haven: Yale University Press, 1962), Chapter 2.

19. H.B.G. Casimir claims that if two firms invest the same percentages of total sales in R&D the larger firm will have the advantage. "ATT is the most striking example of this size effect. There are in Europe several high level telecommunication industries. The government organisations operating telecommunication networks—usually the post offices—have in many countries adequate laboratories and an excellent staff; they have often made a significant contribution to the art. But, together, these industries and organisations are dealing with a network smaller than the 70 or 80 percent of the total US telephone system manufactured and operated by ATT. No wonder the European firms have some difficulty in holding their own against Bell Labs, ATT's impressive research and development organisation. . . . If an European firm is of equal size to its US analogue, it must operate on an international market. This may be stimulating, but the complicated political and economic conditions of to-day are not conducive to optimal efficiency." This quotation appears on p. 418 in REVIEWS OF NATIONAL SCIENCE POLICY: UNITED STATES (Paris: Organisation for Economic Co-Operation and Development, 1968).

Chapter 3
War

1. Erich von Ludendorff, THE NATION AT WAR (London: Hutchinson, 1936). See also Raymond Aron, THE CENTURY OF TOTAL WAR (Boston: Beacon, 1955), pp. 19-22; and Peter Calvocoressi and Guy Wint, TOTAL WAR: THE STORY OF WORLD WAR II (New York: Pantheon, 1972).

2. J.F.C. Fuller, ARMAMENT AND HISTORY (London: Eyre & Spottiswoode, 1946), p. 117.

3. R.G. Hawtrey, ECONOMIC ASPECTS OF SOVEREIGNTY (London: Longmans, Green, 1952), p. 59.

4. "The government conscripts able-bodied men and women to fight; conscripts the skilled and the less able-bodied to work; conscripts the tools of production; conscripts income through taxation and expropriation; conscripts the agencies of propaganda; conscripts the emotions and minds of its citizens by horror stories, false statements, and other forms of propaganda. Every available individual and social agency is coordinated behind the war effort. Opponents and dissidents are 'disloyal' and treated accordingly. The war effort is a one hundred percent national effort." Scott Nearing, WAR OR PEACE (New York: Island Press, 1946), p. 19.

5. Sir William H. Beveridge, THE PILLARS OF SECURITY (London: Allen & Unwin, 1943), pp. 28-29.

6. Paul Kecskemeti, STRATEGIC SURRENDER (Stanford: Stanford University Press, 1958), pp. 22,245. The significance of preexisting material resources in wars of attrition has been succinctly put by Hawtrey: "The war of

1914-18 was a conflict between the British and German coal fields. The French and Belgian coal fields were out of action from the beginning, but in the end the American coal field, which is bigger than any, intervened." R.G. Hawtrey, ECONOMIC ASPECTS OF SOVEREIGNTY (London: Longmans, Green, 1952), p. 59.

7. Herbert Spencer, THE PRINCIPLES OF SOCIOLOGY (New York: D. Appleton, 1880), vol. 1, sections 258-63.

8. William Graham Sumner, FOLKWAYS (Boston: Ginn, 1906), pp. 12-13.

9. Giichi Ono, WAR AND ARMAMENT EXPENDITURES OF JAPAN (New York: Oxford University Press, 1922), p. 256.

10. Walter Lippmann, THE GOOD SOCIETY (Boston: Little, Brown, 1943), p. 90.

11. R.W.B. Clarke, THE ECONOMIC EFFORT OF WAR (London: Allen & Unwin, 1940), p. 18. See also Emanuel Stein and Jules Backman (eds.), WAR ECONOMICS (New York: Farrar and Rinehart, 1942), particularly their chapter entitled "Transition from Peace to War."

12. John A. Armstrong (ed.), SOVIET PARTISANS IN WORLD WAR II (Madison: University of Wisconsin Press, 1964), pp. 16, 41, 58-59. For more details, see also George Fischer, SOVIET OPPOSITION TO STALIN: A CASE STUDY IN WORLD WAR II (Cambridge: Harvard University Press, 1952).

13. Paul Kecskemeti, STRATEGIC SURRENDER (Stanford: Stanford University Press, 1958), pp. 58 and 59. As if to confirm Kecskemeti, Maurice Thorez reviews the Communist party view at the time. "The Hitler aggression against the Soviet Union stimulated the Resistance Movement in our country, especially the organisation of armed struggle. The patriots realised that a new balance of strength had taken shape and that now victory was assured for the partisans of the freedom and independence of nations. Until now, many Frenchmen, even those hostile to the occupation forces, were sceptical [sic] of their strength, and doubted that France would ever be liberated. After June 22, 1941, the patriots said to themselves: 'We are not alone; with an ally like the Soviet people we can win freedom, we can vanquish.' " Maurice Thorez, FILS DU PEUPLE (Paris: Editions Sociales, 1960), p. 148; cited by G. Deborin, THE SECOND WORLD WAR (Moscow: Progress Publishers, 1964), p. 165. For a more thorough view of causes and consequences of low integration in France, see William L. Shirer, THE COLLAPSE OF THE THIRD REPUBLIC, AN INQUIRY INTO THE FALL OF FRANCE IN 1940 (New York: Simon and Schuster, 1969).

14. William Graham Sumner, "Conquest of the U.S. by Spain," p. 334 in Albert Galloway Keller (ed.), WAR AND OTHER ESSAYS (New Haven: Yale University Press, 1911).

15. Karl Liebknecht, MILITARISM (New York: B.W. Huebsch, 1917). Incidentally, many of his phrases are used by war protestors today.

16. For trends in cooperation during the early part of the Second World War,

see John Harding, "The Measurement of Civilian Morale," and "Appendix I," pp. 233-58, 261-85 in Hadley Centril, GAUGING PUBLIC OPINION (Princeton: Princeton University Press, 1944). According to Waller, cooperation goes through several stages; that is, from an intense flag-waving period through respecting the might of the enemy to weariness due to mounting costs. Willard Waller (ed.), WAR IN THE TWENTIETH CENTURY (New York: Random House, 1940), pp. 24-29. According to Janowitz and Little, the phenomenon of diminishing cooperation also occurs in small military units. "At some point continued exposure of any military group to stress begins to produce a weakening of primary group solidarity and an undermining of organizational effectiveness." Morris Janowitz and Roger Little. SOCIOLOGY AND THE MILITARY ESTABLISHMENT (New York: Russell Sage Foundation, 1965) pp. 87-88. Perhaps Janowitz and Little are here thinking only of American soldiers; for in a previous study Janowitz and Shils say that German soldiers during World War II did not exhibit weakened primary group solidarity even though they were continuously exposed to stress. Edward A. Shils and Morris Janowitz, "Cohesion and Disintegration in the Wehrmacht in World War II," THE PUBLIC OPINION QUARTERLY 12 (1948).

17. Albert Speer, INSIDE THE THIRD REICH (New York: Macmillan, 1970), p. 256.

18. Ibid., pp. 255, 264; and for much other information, see Chapters 15, 16, and 25. As with Germany, so with Japan: see Sir George Sansom, "Japan's Fatal Blunder," INTERNATIONAL AFFAIRS, no. 4 (October 1948), esp. pp. 545, 549, 551-552.

19. Data have been made available that distinguish nations by number of months in war; see J. David Singer and Melvin Small, THE WAGES OF WAR, 1816-1965: A STATISTICAL HANDBOOK (New York: Wiley, 1972). For purposes of this study, however, such fine discrimination appears unwarranted.

20. C.V. Wedgwood, THE THIRTY YEARS WAR (London: Jonathan Cape, 1938), Chapters 1 and 12; J.H. Clapham, "Charles Louis, Elector Palatine, 1617-1680. An Early Experiment in Liberalism," ECONOMICA 7 (1940), 381-96; Robert Ergang, THE MYTH OF THE ALL DISTINCTIVE FURY OF THE THIRTY YEARS WAR (Pocono Pines, Pa.: 1956); and R. Ludloff, "Industrial Development in 16th-17th Century Germany," PAST AND PRESENT 12 (November 1957), pp. 58-75.

21. E.J. Hamilton, "The Decline of Spain," ECONOMIC HISTORY REVIEW 8 (1938), pp. 168-78; M. Schwarzmann, "Background Factors in Spanish Decline," EXPLORATIONS IN ENTREPRENEURIAL HISTORY 3 (1951), pp. 221-47; W.W. Borah, NEW SPAIN'S CENTURY OF DEPRESSION (Berkeley: University of California Press, 1951).

22. James Bryce, "War and Human Progress," INTERNATIONAL CONCILIATION 108 (November 1916), p. 303. See also Piero Pieri, LA CRISI MILITARA ITALIANA RENASCIMENTO, NELLA SUE RELAZIONE CON

LA CRISI POLITICA ED ECONOMICA (Naples: R. Ricciardi, 1934), for a discussion of the situation from 1492 through 1559; and C.M. Cipolla, "The Decline of Italy: The Case of a Fully Matured Economy," ECONOMIC HISTORY REVIEW 5 (1952), pp. 178-87.

23. There are those, however, who would not hold with this idea of a time-bound effect. Toffler, for example, asserts that once a change gets set into motion, it continues to have its effect throughout all history. The Peloponnesian War changed the course of Greek history; it has affected the course of world history. "By changing the movement of men, the geographical distribution of genes, values, and ideas, it affected later events in Rome, and through Rome, all Europe. Today's Europeans are to some small degree different people because that conflict occurred. . . . Whatever trace of impact the Peloponnesian War left on the genetic structure, the ideas, and the values of today's Europeans is now exported by them to all parts of the world. Thus today's Mexicans and Japanese feel the distant, twice-removed impact of that war even though their ancestors, alive during its occurrence, did not. In this way, the events of the past, skipping as it were over generations and centuries, rise up to haunt and change us today." Alvin Toffler, FUTURE SHOCK (New York: Random House, 1970), pp. 17-18.

Chapter 4
Order

1. Arnold M. Rose, "The Comparative Study of Institutions," p. 26 in Arnold M. Rose (ed.), THE INSTITUTIONS OF ADVANCED SOCIETIES (Minneapolis: University of Minnesota Press, 1958).

2. Lucian W. Pye, "Introduction," p. 19 in Lucian W. Pye (ed.), COMMUNICATIONS AND POLITICAL DEVELOPMENT (Princeton: Princeton University Press, 1963).

3. "So impressed are modern men in Western culture with their own achievements that they seldom recognize the importance of their cultural heritage." Shepard B. Clough, THE ECONOMIC DEVELOPMENT OF WESTERN CIVILIZATION (New York: McGraw-Hill, 1959), p. 19.

4. But it should be identified. On the outgrowth of ideas from other ideas see William F. Ogburn, SOCIAL CHANGE (New York: Viking, 1952); and Clarence Edward Ayres, THE THEORY OF ECONOMIC PROGRESS (Chapel Hill: University of North Carolina Press, 1944), pp. 105-125. On the stimulation of ideas as solutions to problems, see Jacob Schmookler, INVENTION AND ECONOMIC GROWTH (Cambridge: Harvard University Press, 1966), Chapters 3-4; Paul Mantoux, THE INDUSTRIAL REVOLUTION IN THE EIGHTEENTH CENTURY (New York: Macmillan; rev. ed., 1961); and S.C. Gilfillan, THE SOCIOLOGY OF INVENTION (Chicago: Follet, 1935).

5. For data on growth in science and technology, see Derek J. Price, "The

Exponential Curve of Science," in Bernard Barber and Walter Hirsch (eds.), THE SOCIOLOGY OF SCIENCE (New York: The Free Press of Glencoe, 1962); D.C. Coleman, "Technology and Economic History, 1500-1700," ECONOMIC HISTORY REVIEWS 11 (1959), pp. 506-14; and Pitirim A. Sorokin, SOCIAL AND CULTURAL DYNAMICS (New York: American Book Co., 1937), vol. 2, pp. 150-53, 167-68.

6. Clark Kerr, John T. Dunlop, Frederick H. Harbison and Charles A. Meyers, INDUSTRIALISM AND INDUSTRIAL MAN: THE PROBLEM OF LABOR AND MANAGEMENT IN ECONOMIC GROWTH (Cambridge: Harvard University Press, 1960), p. 284.

7. Wassily Leontief, AUTOMATIC CONTROL (New York: Simon and Schuster, 1955), p. 79; see also his FACTORS IN ECONOMIC DEVELOPMENT (London: Allen and Unwin, 1962), p. 175.

8. Alfred Marshall, PRINCIPLES OF ECONOMICS (London: Macmillan, 1938; first published in 1890), pp. 779-80.

9. Stanislav Andreski, THE USES OF COMPARATIVE SOCIOLOGY (Berkeley: University of California Press, 1965), p. 117.

10. Ralph Linton, "The Prospect of Western Civilization," p. 544 in Willard Waller (ed.), WAR IN THE TWENTIETH CENTURY (New York: Random House, 1940).

11. Toynbee's statement reads as follows: "In studying the breakdowns of civilizations, the writer has indeed subscribed to the conclusion—no new discovery!—that War has proved to have been the proximate cause of the breakdown of every civilization which is known for certain to have broken down, in so far as it has been possible to analyze the nature of these breakdowns and to account for their occurrence." Arnold J. Toynbee, WAR AND CIVILIZATION (London: Oxford University Press, 1951), p. vii.

12. Achille Viallate, ECONOMIC IMPERIALISM AND INTERNATIONAL RELATIONS DURING THE LAST FIFTY YEARS (New York: Macmillan, 1923), p. 140.

13. Cyril Black, THE DYNAMICS OF MODERNIZATION: A STUDY IN COMPARATIVE HISTORY (New York: Harper & Row, 1966), p. 11.

14. Scott Nearing, WAR OR PEACE (New York: Island Press, 1946), p. 24.

15. Eugene Staley, WAR LOSSES TO A NEUTRAL (New York: League of Nations Association, December 1937), p. 63.

16. Ibn Khaldoun, THE MUGADIMMAH: AN INTRODUCTION TO HISTORY (New York: Pantheon, 1958); Giambattista Vico, SCIENZE NUOVA, 3rd ed. (Naples, 1744), translated as THE NEW SCIENCE OF GIAMBATTISTA VICO (New York: Doubleday, 1961).

17. Ralph Linton, "The Prospect of Western Civilization," p. 540 in Willard Waller (ed.), WAR IN THE TWENTIETH CENTURY (New York: Random House, 1940). Usually, predictions about the consequences following upon general wars are gloomy or cast in an eschatological framework. Here is one

made in the year 595, when the Dark Ages had supposedly engulfed the Western world. Gregory the Great, writing to the Patriarch at Constantinople, said: "It is the last hour. Pestilence and sword are raging in the world. Nation is rising against nation, the whole fabric of things is being shaken." Cited by J.F.C. Fuller, ARMAMENT AND HISTORY (London: Eyre and Spottiswoode, 1946), p. viii. Since global equalization did not follow those wars, the whole fabric of things was not shaken. This is not to say that breakdown could not have happened, it is only to say that it did not happen, for the Empire of the East continued brilliantly for nearly a thousand years.

18. Adam Smith, AN INQUIRY INTO THE NATURE AND CAUSES OF THE WEALTH OF NATIONS (London: Methuen; first published in 1776; 1930), vol. 2, p. 202. The same thought was advanced 189 years later. "The invention of firearms constituted a turning point, because it gave unquestionable military superiority to the urban civilizations, capable of mustering skilled craftsmen, mathematicians and workshops, and made nomad invasions impossible." Stanislav Andreski, THE USES OF COMPARATIVE SOCIOLOGY (Berkeley: University of California Press, 1965), p. 115. Another author sees the same difference. "Nations skilled in modern military techniques have an overwhelming advantage over those not so skilled." Quincy Wright, A STUDY OF WAR (Chicago: University of Chicago Press, 1942), vol. I, p. 313. Lastly, "The nation which makes the greatest use of peace intervals to advance its mechanical and engineering potentials for war, and which possesses the greatest number of skilled workers as well as of trained soldiers, and the most abundant supplies of raw materials as well as of arms, is the nation upon whom victory smiles." J.F.C. Fuller, ARMAMENT AND HISTORY (London: Eyre & Spottiswoode, 1946), p. 117; see also pp. 31-32.

19. James Bryce, "War and Human Progress," INTERNATIONAL CONCILIATION 108 (November 1916), pp. 304-305.

20. Henry Simon Bloch and Bert F. Hoselitz, ECONOMICS OF MILITARY OCCUPATION (Chicago: The Foundation Press, 1944), p. 2.

21. John A. Armstrong, SOVIET PARTISANS IN WORLD WAR II (Madison: University of Wisconsin Press, 1964), p. 6.

22. Gerhard von Glahn, THE OCCUPATION OF ENEMY TERRITORY. . . A COMMENTARY ON THE LAW AND PRACTICE OF BELLIGERENT OCCUPATION (Minneapolis: University of Minnesota Press, 1957), pp. 106, 132.

23. See, for example, James Bryce, "War and Human Progress," INTERNATIONAL CONCILIATION 108 (November 1916), p. 307; Charles A. Beard, "Introduction," pp. xxv-xxvi in J.B. Bury, THE IDEA OF PROGRESS (New York: Macmillan, 1932); W.S. Woytinsky and E.S. Woytinsky, WORLD POPULATION AND PRODUCTION (New York: Twentieth Century Fund, 1953), p. lxi; Jean Fourastie, THE CAUSES OF WEALTH (Glencoe: Free Press, 1960), p. 17; and Cyril Black, THE DYNAMICS OF MODERNIZATION: A STUDY IN COMPARATIVE HISTORY (New York: Harper & Row, 1966), pp. 11-12.

24. W. Rupert MacLaurin, "The Sequence from Invention to Innovation and Its Relation to Economic Growth," QUARTERLY JOURNAL OF ECONOMICS 67 (February 1953), pp. 97-111.

25. Sir Edward Smith, "The Critical Importance of Higher Technological Education in Relation to Productivity," AMERICAN SCIENTIST 39 (1951), pp. 279 and 284.

26. On France, see Henry E. Guerlac, "Science and French National Strength," p. 82 in Edward Mead Earle (ed.), MODERN FRANCE (Princeton: Princeton University Press, 1950); and on the United Kingdom, see J.G. Crowther, SCIENCE AND MODERN SOCIETY (New York: Schocken Books, 1968).

27. Ronald S. Edwards, "The Future of Industrial Research and Development in Great Britain," LLOYDS BANK REVIEW (January 1952), p. 42.

28. Joseph Ben-David, "Scientific Productivity and Academic Organization in Nineteenth Century Medicine," AMERICAN SOCIOLOGICAL REVIEW 25 (December 1960), pp. 828-43; Joseph Ben-David and Randall Collins, "Social Factors in the Origin of a New Science: The Cast of Psychology," AMERICAN SOCIOLOGICAL REVIEW 31 (August 1966), pp. 451-65.

29. A relatively minor technological shift, an improvement rather than an invention, such as the substitution of a steel plow for a wooden one, may have far-reaching effects. White argues that as steel plows came to be adopted in Europe beginning around the tenth century, the weight of the tool encouraged the substitution of horses for oxen—with a long train of consequences, including the whole technology of harnessing and the selective breeding of horses for specialized uses. The deeper furrow cut by the steel plow increased soil productivity and was a major factor in changes in land allotments and distributions. See Lynn White, Jr., MEDIEVAL TECHNOLOGY AND SOCIAL CHANGE (Oxford: Clarendon Press, 1962), pp. 41-76.

30. E.H. Carr, WHAT IS HISTORY? (New York: Knopf, 1962), p. 199.

31. On this subject, see Jack Goody and Ian Watt, "The Consequences of Literacy," COMPARATIVE STUDIES IN SOCIETY AND HISTORY 5 (April 1963), pp. 308-309.

32. Hans Kohn, THE IDEA OF NATIONALISM (New York: Macmillan, 1944), p. vii.

33. James Bryce, "War and Human Progress," INTERNATIONAL CONCILIATION 108 (November 1916), p. 307.

34. Taking a very long view, Guido Panciroli, writing in the 1500s, claims that many things have been lost. Scanning his work, I could detect nothing that was lost; in fact, everything listed, either in technique or product, has been improved upon since. The original appeared in Latin and so the title may be an unfortunate English rendering. See Guido Panciroli, THE HISTORY OF MANY MEMORABLE THINGS LOST.... (London: J. Nicholson, 1715). I am inclined, therefore, to accept the following summary statement. "No important technique for producing goods, either agricultural or industrial, no solution of

mathematical or engineering problems, and no important information regarding the earth has been permanently lost." Shepard B. Clough, THE ECONOMIC DEVELOPMENT OF WESTERN CIVILIZATION (New York: McGraw-Hill, 1959), p. 20.

35. "This list of new scientific development comprises the various kinds of new airplanes—the helicopter, rockets, missiles, jet propulsion engines, turbo-jet power plants—armored tanks, motored guns, bacteria bombs, poison gases, discoveries in nutrition, sanitation, surgery and medicine, proximity fuses, high octane fuels, fractionated motors, television, radar, the magnetic wire recorder, facsimile transmission, point-to-point radio-telephones, photoprinting, photographic mapping, microfilm, artificial rubber, gasoline from coal. Diesel engines, plastics, plywood, magnesium, aluminum, and steel alloys." William Fielding Ogburn, "Preface," p. v in William Fielding Ogburn (ed.), TECHNOLOGY AND INTERNATIONAL RELATIONS (Chicago: University of Chicago Press, 1949).

Chapter 5
Integration

1. Edward Hallett Carr, THE TWENTY YEARS CRISIS, 1919-1939 (London: Macmillan, 1940), p. 292.

2. "The long-run trend from the Middle Ages to the 20th century has been, on the whole, towards social and political and economic adjustments in line with the long-run pressure of technology. But in the last few years a sharp reversal of that trend has seemed to be dominant. No one can yet tell whether the march towards *world integration* will be resumed ... or whether the course of the world is really set, and has been since 1914, towards a new localism. A clear view of the situation cannot give hope that a permanent reversal towards localism will be a successful adjustment, unless it succeeds by destroying or severely limiting a technology that still presses in the opposite direction. The conflict between technology and politics is already producing symptoms of strain that are only too evident to all." Eugene Staley, WORLD ECONOMY IN TRANSITION (New York: Council on Foreign Relations, 1939). Italics supplied.

3. Lucian W. Pye, POLITICS, PERSONALITY, AND NATION BUILDING (New Haven: Yale University Press, 1962), p. 10.

4. James Bryce, "War and Human Progress," INTERNATIONAL CONCILIATION 108 (November 1916), p. 308.

5. Marshall D. Sahlins, p. 37 in Marshall D. Sahlins and Elman R. Service (eds.), EVOLUTION AND CULTURE (Ann Arbor: University of Michigan Press, 1960).

6. Marion J. Levy, "Social Patterns (structures) and Problems of Modernization," p. 190 in Wilbert E. Moore and Robert M. Cook (eds.), READINGS ON SOCIAL CHANGE (Englewood Cliffs: Prentice-Hall, 1967).

7. UNESCO, HANDBOOK OF INTERNATIONAL EXCHANGES (Paris: IES./VI.I/AFSR, 1965), p. 7. For some recent studies indicating the trend of contact between nations, see Robert C. Angell, "The Growth of Transnational Participation," JOURNAL OF SOCIAL ISSUES 23 (January 1967), pp. 108-129; Karl W. Deutsch, "The Propensity to International Transactions," POLITICAL STUDIES 8 (1960), pp. 147-155; and W. Phillips Davison, INTERNATIONAL POLITICAL COMMUNICATION (New York: Frederick A. Praeger, for the council on Foreign Relations, 1965).

8. Achille Viallate, ECONOMIC IMPERIALISM AND INTERNATIONAL RELATIONS DURING THE LAST FIFTY YEARS (New York: Macmillan, 1923), p. 140.

9. Shepard B. Clough, THE ECONOMIC DEVELOPMENT OF WESTERN CIVILIZATION (New York: McGraw-Hill, 1959), p. 409.

10. Raul Prebisch, TOWARDS A NEW TRADE POLICY FOR DEVELOPMENT (New York: United Nations, E/Conf. 46/3, 1964), p. 6; Aurelio Peccei, THE CHASM AHEAD (New York: Macmillan, 1969), pp. 179-80.

11. Ralph Linton, "The Prospects of Western Civilization," p. 547, in Willard Waller (ed.), WAR IN THE TWENTIETH CENTURY (New York: Random House, 1940).

12. Winthrop W. Case, "Economic Problems of U.S. Neutrality in War Time," FOREIGN REPORTS 15 (April 15, 1939), p. 24. A large part of the story of Malta throughout the nineteenth century, by the way, can be told in terms of its rise and decline in prosperity during times of war and peace respectively. To cite only one example, when Napoleon introduced the continental blockade it "set off a trade boom in Malta and a few other centres which were well placed to serve as bases for vessels trading with Europe by circuitous routes." Brian Blouet, A SHORT HISTORY OF MALTA (New York: Frederick A. Praeger, 1967), p. 167.

13. W.N. Medlicott, THE ECONOMIC BLOCKADE (London: His Majesty's Stationery Office, 1952), vol. 1, pp. 587 and 589. Also mines were laid in Norway territorial waters by both England and Germany (vol. 1, pp. 49-50) and in general Scandinavian ships were controlled by both English and German naval forces (vol. 1, p. 141).

14. Paul Kecskemeti, STRATEGIC SURRENDER (Stanford: Stanford University Press, 1958), p. 12.

15. As Gunnar Myrdal remarks, "the Japanese must be credited with creating indigenous military forces, accelerating the political organization of local nationalist movements, and providing greater administrative experience and opportunities to persons previously denied positions of responsibility by their European masters. During the interlude of the Japanese occupation, therefore, many nationalist leaders ... suddenly acquired greater status and power within their own societies. Naturally enough, they were not prepared to abdicate when the European colonial rulers returned after the defeat and withdrawal of the

Japanese." Gunnar Myrdal, ASIAN DRAMA (New York: The Twentieth Century Fund, 1968), vol. 1, pp. 133-34.

16. Herodotus, THE PERSIAN WARS (New York: Modern Library, 1942), bks. 3-4, p. 7.

17. Paul Hermann, CONQUEST BY MAN (New York: Harper, 1954), pp. 346, 137. Around the first century, a window shopper in China could observe all the imported goods of the world, the influx of commerce to his shores was so great. From the Spice Islands came camphor, nutmeg, cinnamon, benzoin, parrots, coconuts, and pepper; from Ceylon came gems and spices; from India came diamonds, pearls, attar of roses, hemp, sandalwood, drugs, cotton, and pepper; from Persia, the Parthian caravans brought quicksilver, beeswax, rock-crystal, coral and storex; and from Africa, the Arabs brought ivory, rhinoceros horn, and black slaves. The Romans brought goods from everywhere: from Italy, metals, glass, wool, linen and gold coin; from Syria, cloth dyed purple and interwoven with gold; from Egypt, wheat, corn and cotton; from the Hadhramaut in Arabia, gold and frankincense; from Germany, goose down, furs, and women's hair; from the Baltic, amber and animal skins, and from Cos, an island at the mouth of the Ceramic Gulf in the Aegean, Chinese silk. This last item, actually a reimportation back to China, demands an immediate comment. The Chinese exported a thickly-woven silk called brocade. On the Island of Cos, the women picked apart this brocade into its individual threads and rewove it into a gossamer-thin gauze (Cos?). Perhaps the Chinese window-shopper felt it and then marveled at those inscrutable women of Cos. Most of these items appear in Paul Hermann (1954: 153-54). For more details on the interchange between East and West, see Martin Percival Charlesworth, TRADE-ROUTES AND COMMERCE OF THE ROMAN EMPIRE (Cambridge: University Press, 1924), Chapters 4, 6; C.P. Fitzgerald, CHINA: A SHORT CULTURAL HISTORY (London: Cresset Press, 1954), pp. 196-201; Sir Mortimer Wheeler, ROME BEYOND THE IMPERIAL FRONTIERS (London: G. Bell, 1954), all of Part III; and Sir Mortimer Wheeler, IMPACT AND IMPRINT: GREEKS AND ROMANS BEYOND THE HIMALAYAS (Newcastle upon Tyne: King's College, 28th May, 1959). This last citation is a lecture which reviews some of the evidence for interchange between East and West from the fourth century B.C. to the second century A.D.

18. The concept of technological diffusion is perhaps most associated with Thorstein Veblen who used it to explain the supposedly rapid strides made by Germany in the middle of the nineteenth century, see his IMPERIAL GERMANY AND THE INDUSTRIAL REVOLUTION (New York: Viking, 1939), p. 86. (The book was published originally in 1915.)

19. The following quotation illustrates a special view of the matter. "The inhabitant of London could order by telephone, sipping his morning tea in bed, the various products of the whole earth, in such quantity as he might see fit, and reasonably expect their early delivery upon his doorstep. . . . He could secure

forthwith, if he wished it, cheap and comfortable means of transit to any country or climate without passport or other formality, could dispatch his servant to the neighboring office of a bank for such supply of the precious metals as might seem convenient, and could then proceed abroad to foreign quarters, without knowledge of their religion, language, or customs, bearing coined wealth upon his person, and would consider himself greatly aggrieved and much surprised at the least interference." John M. Keynes, THE ECONOMIC OF THE PEACE (London: Macmillan, 1920), p. 11.

20. Bliokh, for instance, considers war an impossible form of conflict not because the world supply network would shrivel and shatter during its course but because the exchangeable products of the enemy would be reduced. "What is the use of talking about the past when you are dealing with an altogether new set of considerations? Consider for a moment what nations were a hundred years ago and what they are to-day. In those days before railways, telegraphs, steamships, etc., were invented, each nation was more or less a homogeneous, self-contained, self-sufficing unit.... All this is changed.... Every year the interdependence of nations upon each other for the necessaries of life is greater than it ever was before.... Hence the first thing that war would do would be to deprive the Powers that made it of all opportunity of benefiting by the products of the nations against whom they were fighting." Ivan Stanislavovich Bliokh, THE FUTURE OF WAR IN ITS TECHNICAL, ECONOMIC, AND POLITICAL RELATIONS (Boston: Ginn, 1902), pp. xlii-xliii.

21. Dean Acheson, PRESENT AT THE CREATION (New York: W.W. Norton, 1969), p. 48.

22. W.N. Medlicott, THE ECONOMIC BLOCKADE (London: His Majesty's Stationery Office, 1952), vol. 1, pp. 405, 667-71, and vol. 2, pp. 665-68.

23. Jacob Viner, "Power Versus Plenty as Objectives of Foreign Policy in the Seventeenth and Eighteenth Centuries," WORLD POLITICS 1 (October 1948), 22, n. 53.

24. Eli F. Heckscher, MERCANTILISM (London: Allen & Unwin, 1935), vol. 2, p. 99.

25. W.W. Rostow, THE PROCESS OF ECONOMIC GROWTH (New York: W.W. Norton, 1962), p. 164.

26. Robert C. Binkley, REALISM AND NATIONALISM, 1852-1871 (New York: Harper, 1935), p. 176.

27. Georg Cohn, NEO-NEUTRALITY (New York: Columbia University Press, 1939), p. 13.

28. W.N. Medlicott, THE ECONOMIC BLOCKADE (London: His Majesty's Stationery Office, 1952), vol. 1, p. 495.

29. Frederick J. Teggart, ROME AND CHINA: A STUDY OF CORRELATIONS IN HISTORICAL EVENTS (Berkeley: University of California Press, 1939), pp. vii-viii.

30. A.K. Cairncross, FACTORS IN ECONOMIC DEVELOPMENT (New York: Praeger, 1962), pp. 21-22.

31. W. Paul Strassmann, TECHNOLOGICAL CHANGE AND ECONOMIC DEVELOPMENT (Ithaca: Cornell University Press, 1968), p. 57.

Chapter 6
Progress

1. Friedrich List, THE NATIONAL SYSTEM OF POLITICAL ECONOMY (New York: Augustus M. Kelly, 1966), pp. 174-75.

2. Lord Robbins, THE THEORY OF ECONOMIC DEVELOPMENT (New York: St. Martin's Press, 1968), p. 158.

3. "That is the organization of *actual* States in contradistinction to those conceived on paper and in the minds of pedants. There is no best, or true, or right State that could possibly be actualized according to plan. Every State that emerges in history exists as it is but once and for a moment; the next moment it has, unperceived, become different, whatever the rigidity of its legal-constitutional crust. Therefore, words like 'republic,' 'democracy,' mean something different in every instance, and what turns them into catch-words is their use as definite concepts by philosophers and ideologues. A history of States is physiognomic and not systematic. Its business is not to show how 'humanity' advances to the conquest of its eternal rights, to freedom and equality, to the evolving of a super-wise and super-just State, but to describe the political units that really exist in the fact-world, how they grow and flourish and fade, and how they are really nothing but actual life 'in form.' " Oswald Spengler, THE DECLINE OF THE WEST (New York: Knopf, 1928), vol. 2, p. 370.

4. Milovan Djilas, THE UNPERFECT SOCIETY (New York: Harcourt, Brace & World, 1969).

5. Harlan Cleveland, THE OBLIGATIONS OF POWER (New York: Harper & Row, 1966), p. 14.

6. S. Whittemore Boggs, INTERNATIONAL BOUNDARIES (New York: Columbia University Press, 1940), p. 203.

7. Norman Hill, CLAIMS TO TERRITORY (New York: Oxford University Press, 1945), pp. 23 and 29.

8. Harlan Cleveland, THE OBLIGATIONS OF POWER (New York: Harper & Row, 1966), p. 14.

9. L. Hobhouse, G. Wheeler, and M. Ginsberg, THE MATERIAL CULTURE AND SOCIAL INSTITUTIONS OF THE SIMPLER PEOPLES (London: Chapman & Hall, 1930), pp. 231 ff.

10. In the peaceful years prior to the First World War: "There were the June Days of 1848; the resistance to the Coup d'Etat of 1851; the Commune of 1871. There were the less dramatic or less dramatized days of 1848 in Berlin and Vienna; there were riots and risings in the Romagna, in Valencia; there were the great strikes—and their bloody consequences, Fetherstonhaugh and the battle

between the steel workers and the Pinkerton gunmen hired by Carnegie and Frick. There were Moscow and Petersburgh in 1905; Paterson and Lowell; the 'Wobblies' and the mutineers of the 17th Infantry at Montpellier; all the tradition of insurrection and defiance that runs continuously from the first Fourteenth of July." Dennis W. Brogan, THE PRICE OF REVOLUTION (New York: Harper, 1952), pp. 19-20. Moreover: "Between independence and World War I the Spanish-American republics experienced 115 successful revolutions and many times that number of abortive revolts." Edwin Lieuwen, ARMS AND POLITICS IN LATIN AMERICA (New York: Frederick Praeger, 1960), p. 21. In Mexico alone, according to Lieuwen on p. 101, there were over 1,000 military uprisings between 1821 and 1914.

11. The reference is to E.H. Carr, THE TWENTY YEARS' CRISIS (London: Macmillan, 1940); and to H.F. Armstrong, WHEN THERE IS NO PEACE (New York: Macmillan, 1939).

12. C.P. Kindleberger, "Group Behavior and International Trade," THE JOURNAL OF POLITICAL ECONOMY 59 (February 1951), p. 45.

13. Simon Kuznets, MODERN ECONOMIC GROWTH (New Haven: Yale University Press, 1966), p. 215.

14. This paragraph stems from Emanuel Stein and Jules Backman, "Transition from Peace to War," pp. 3-5, in their edited work WAR ECONOMICS (New York: Farrar & Rinehart, 1942).

15. "In most non-Western societies political activities are not part of any single general process; rather there are several distinct and nearly unrelated political processes. The most conspicuous division is that between the dominant national politics of the more urban elements and the more traditional village level of politics. Those who participate in the political life of the village are not an integral part of the national politics, and they can act without regard to developments at the national level. Possibly even more significant, all the various village groups have their own separate and autonomous political processes." Lucian W. Pye, POLITICS, PERSONALITY, AND NATION BUILDING (New Haven: Yale University Press, 1962), p. 20. See also Dankwart A. Rustow, A WORLD OF NATIONS (Washington, D.C.: Brookings Institution, 1967), pp. 91-92.

16. Auguste Comte, SYSTEM OF POSITIVE POLITY, vol. 2, "Social Statics" (London: Longmans, Green, 1875), p. 243.

17. Gamal Abdul Nasser, EGYPT'S LIBERATION (Washington, D.C.: Public Affairs Press, 1955), pp. 244-45.

18. Gunnar Myrdal, ASIAN DRAMA: AN INQUIRY INTO THE POVERTY OF NATIONS (New York: Twentieth Century Fund, 1968), vol. 2, p. 895. He is thinking here of the duties of villagers regarding the construction and upkeep of roads, bridges, and waterworks; the prevention and control of forest fires; policing the local community; participation in the nation's defense, and so on.

19. Daniel Lerner, "Modernization, Social Aspects," p. 387 in INTER-

NATIONAL ENCYCLOPEDIA OF THE SOCIAL SCIENCES, vol. 10 (New York: Macmillan, 1968).

20. Gino Germani, "Democratie representative et classes populaires en Amerique Latine," SOCIOLOGIE DU TRAVAIL (Octobre-Decembre, 1961), 3e Annee: pp. 408-425.

21. Quincy Wright, A STUDY OF WAR (Chicago: University of Chicago Press, 1942), vol. 1, p. 271.

22. Ralph Linton, "The Prospects of Western Civilization," p. 548 in Willard Waller (ed.), WAR IN THE TWENTIETH CENTURY (New York: Random House, 1940).

23. J.B. Condliffe, WAR AND DEPRESSION (Boston: World Peace Foundation, 1935), p. 9.

24. Shortages created during the course of war led the participants to engage in controlling socioeconomic activity and in governmental planning. Prior to 1914 little thought had been given to such war measures, except as regarded transportation, the mobilization of men, and the production of war material, for political and military leaders until then thought only in terms of short campaigns. Hence national planning, which was to become so important in later years, came into being piecemeal during the war. But early during the war many representative men became convinced that there would be severe shortages of strategic raw materials. So administrative boards were created: the Germans created the Kriegs-Rohstoff Abteilung (War Raw Materials Department); the English created the British Control Boards; and the Americans created the War Production Board. These various boards tried not only to increase the production of those goods in short supply, but also to develop substitutes for materials which could not be obtained abroad, to control the allocation of goods, and subsequently to determine the very uses to which these materials should be put. Food control boards were also created: food prices were regulated, and some foods were rationed either by limiting the amounts available to individuals or by forbidding the sale of a given product except on specific days.

25. A rise of cooperation through war does not come automatically; it requires considerable and systematic persuasion. "Technologists and scientists readily develop new weapons; preachers and rabbis and priests bless the great endeavor; newsmen disseminate the official definitions of world reality, labeling for their public the shifting line-up of friends and enemies; publicists elaborate the 'reasons' for the coming war and the 'necessity' for the causes of it. They do not set forth alternative policies; they do not politically oppose and politically debate the thrust toward war. . . . They have generally become the Swiss Guard of the power elite." C. Wright Mills, THE CAUSES OF WORLD WAR III (New York: Ballantine Books, 1963), p. 85. Of course more detached views of the process of mobilizing cooperation abound; see Harold W. Lasswell, PROPAGANDA TECHNIQUE IN THE WORLD WAR (New York: Knopf, 1938); Louis Wirth, "Consensus and Mass Communication," AMERICAN SOCIOLOGICAL

REVIEW 13 (February 1948), pp. 1-14; and Joseph T. Klapper, "Mass Media and the Engineering of Consent," AMERICAN SCHOLAR 17 (October 1948), pp. 419-29.

26. This may be seen in the growth of national and per capita product. The handiest reference is Colin Clark, THE CONDITIONS OF ECONOMIC PROGRESS (London: Macmillan, 1957).

27. Emanuel Stein and Jules Backman (eds.), WAR ECONOMICS (New York: Farrar & Rinehart, 1942), pp. 20-21.

28. Henry Simon Bloch and Bert F. Hoselitz, ECONOMICS OF MILITARY OCCUPATION (Chicago: Foundation Press, 1944), pp. 126-27. The authors provide several examples of this; here is one appearing on p. 117. "Aluminum production for instance was greater than ever before in French history." Other authors view the scene of occupation far more pessimistically; for details on consumer goods and services, health and welfare, prices and wages, see Louis Baudin, L'ECONOMIE FRANCAISE SOUS L'OCCUPATION ALLEMANDE (Paris: Librairie De Medicis, 1945); Francesco Capotorti, L'OCCUPAZIONE NEL DIRITTO DI GUERRA (Napoli: Casa Editrice Dott. Eugenio Jovene, 1949); and Odile Debbasch, L'OCCUPATION MILITAIRE (Aix-en-Provence: La Pensee Universitaire, 1960).

29. Henry Simon Bloch and Bert F. Hoselitz, ECONOMICS OF MILITARY OCCUPATION (Chicago: Foundation Press, 1944), p. 4. The problem of maintaining the cohesion of the occupied nation has been discussed in Edwin M. Martin, THE ALLIED OCCUPATION OF JAPAN (Stanford: Stanford University Press, 1948); Lord Rennell of Rodd, BRITISH MILITARY ADMINISTRATION OF OCCUPIED TERRITORIES IN AFRICA: 1941-1947 (London: His Majesty's Stationery Office, 1948); Sydney Connor and Carl J. Friedrich (eds.), MILITARY GOVERNMENT, a special issue of THE ANNALS 267 (January 1950); and C.R.S. Harris, ALLIED MILITARY ADMINISTRATION OF ITALY: 1943-1945 (London: Her Majesty's Stationery Office, 1957).

30. Paul Kecskemeti, STRATEGIC SURRENDER (Stanford: Stanford University Press, 1958), p. 245.

31. The literature on the subject of early nation forming is enormous; here is a handful of citations. Max Weber, "Citizenship," Chapter 28 in his GENERAL ECONOMIC HISTORY (New York: Collier Books, 1961); Karl Mannheim, "The History of the Concept of the State," Chapter 11 in his ESSAYS IN SOCIOLOGY AND SOCIAL PSYCHOLOGY (London: Routledge and Kegan Paul, 1953); Carl J. Friedrich, "Nation-building?" in Karl W. Deutsch and William J. Foltz (eds.), NATION-BUILDING (New York: Atherton Press, 1963); T.H. Marshall, CLASS, CITIZENSHIP AND SOCIAL DEVELOPMENT (Garden City: Doubleday, 1964); Reinhard Bendix, NATION BUILDING AND CITIZENSHIP (New York: John Wiley, 1964); and Dankwart A. Rustow, A WORLD OF NATIONS (Washington, D.C.: The Brookings Institution, 1967), Chapters 3, 4, and 8.

32. Gustav Schmoller, THE MERCANTILE SYSTEM AND ITS HISTORI-
CAL SIGNIFICANCE (New York: Macmillan, 1896), pp. 50-51.

33. For the quotation on the sixteenth century, see L. Stone, "State Control
in Sixteenth-Century England," ECONOMIC HISTORY REVIEW 17 (1947), p.
110; and for the quotation on the nineteenth century, see Edmond Silberner,
THE PROBLEMS OF WAR IN NINETEENTH CENTURY ECONOMIC
THOUGHT (Princeton: Princeton University Press, 1946), p. 286.

34. The quotation is from George Beckmann, THE MAKING OF THE MEIJI
CONSTITUTION (Lawrence: University of Kansas Press, 1957), pp. 131-32.

35. And in the ARTE DELLA GUERRA, he says: "Many are now of the
opinion that no two things are more discordant and incongruous than a civil and
military life. But if we consider the nature of government, we shall find a very
strict and intimate relation betwixt these two conditions; and that they are not
only compatible and consistent with each other, but necessarily connected and
united together." G. Mazzoni and M. Casella (eds.), TUTTE LE OPERE
STORICHE E LETTERARIE DI NICCOLO MACHIAVELLI (Florence: 1929),
pp. 224 and 265; cited by Felix Gilbert, "Machiavelli: The Renaissance of the
Art of War," p. 3, in Edward Mead Earle (ed.), MAKERS OF MODERN
STRATEGY (Princeton: Princeton University Press, 1943).

36. Adam Smith, AN INQUIRY INTO THE NATURE AND CAUSES OF
THE WEALTH OF NATIONS (London: Methuen, 1930), vol. 2, p. 200. For
more recent views on this peculiar role of the military in development, see Hans
Speier, "Preface," p. v, and Lucian W. Pye, "Armies in the Process of Political
Modernization," p. 86, in John J. Johnson (ed.), THE ROLE OF THE
MILITARY IN UNDERDEVELOPED COUNTRIES (Princeton: Princeton
University Press, 1962); Frank Keenan Sloan, "The Role of the Military in
Development," in William R. Polk (ed.), DEVELOPMENTAL REVOLUTION
(Washington, D.C.: Middle East Institute, 1963); Morris Janowitz, THE MILI-
TARY IN THE POLITICAL DEVELOPMENT OF NEW NATIONS (Chicago:
University of Chicago Press, 1964); John J. Johnson, THE MILITARY AND
SOCIETY IN LATIN AMERICA (Stanford: Stanford University Press, 1964), p.
260; and Harlan Cleveland, THE OBLIGATIONS OF POWER (New York:
Harper & Row, 1966), pp. 111-12.

37. Oswald Spengler, THE DECLINE OF THE WEST (New York: Knopf,
1939), vol. 2, p. 367.

38. E.R. Hughes (ed. and trans.), CHINESE PHILOSOPHY IN CLASSICAL
TIMES (London: Dent, 1950), p. 23.

39. Here is a clue why nations in the lower stratum cannot mobilize cohesion
more. "Their society in itself is inchoate. To emerge from tutelage is a
sufficiently traumatic experience, but to emerge from technological innocence
into the twentieth century is a shock so violent that it can hardly be appreciated
by anybody who has not suffered it. Old customs, habits, beliefs, values, and
rules become irrelevant; an *elite* gropes for new ones, while the mass is left with

none. A great gulf opens between the *elite* and the rest, greater perhaps—because more unacceptable—than the old gap between colonial masters and subject races. And pervading the whole scene are poverty and inexperience, sometimes on a staggering scale." Peter Calvocoressi, WORLD ORDER AND NEW STATES (New York: Praeger, 1962), p. 35.

40. Ralph Linton, "The Prospect of Western Civilization," p. 537, in Willard Waller (ed.), WAR IN THE TWENTIETH CENTURY (New York: Random House, 1940).

Chapter 7
Satisfaction

1. Much has been written on this topic of loss. In the field of world order, see Gustavo Lagos, INTERNATIONAL STRATIFICATION AND UNDER-DEVELOPED COUNTRIES (Chapel Hill: University of North Carolina Press, 1963); in the field of social order, see Chester I. Barnard, "Functions and Pathology of Status Systems in Formal Organizations," in William F. Whyte (ed.), INDUSTRY AND SOCIETY (New York: McGraw-Hill, 1949); and, in the field of personal order, see Gregory Rocklin, GRIEFS AND DISCONTENTS (Boston: Little, Brown, 1965).

2. Quincy Wright, A STUDY OF WAR (Chicago: University of Chicago Press, 1942), vol. 2, p. 1112.

3. This relationship between change and reaction to change, interestingly, has been observed before in another context. In World War II, the Research Branch, Information and Education Division, of the United States Army, carried out a series of studies on the attitudes of American soldiers. Among other things, the investigators studied attitudes toward promotion, and they found, for instance, that soldiers in the Air Force were much less satisfied with promotions than were soldiers in the Military Police, in spite of the fact that the actual chances of promotion were far greater in the former than in the latter. Judging from the average satisfaction among the men interviewed, comparisons occurred more frequently to men in the Air Force who saw more of their buddies promoted, than to men in the Military Police where the chances for promotion were less. See Samuel A. Stouffer and Leland C. DeVinney, THE AMERICAN SOLDIER: ADJUSTMENT DURING ARMY LIFE (Princeton: Princeton University Press, 1949), vol. 1, pp. 250-53.

4. Oliver Edmund Clubb, TWENTIETH CENTURY CHINA (New York: Columbia University Press, 1964).

5. The quotation is cited by Robert Strausz-Hupe, GEOPOLITICS (New York: G.P. Putnam, 1942), p. 29.

6. Jawaharlal Nehru, THE DISCOVERY OF INDIA (London: Meridian Books, 1956), p. 458.

7. Alexis de Tocqueville, THE OLD REGIME AND THE FRENCH REVOLUTION (Garden City: Doubleday, 1955), p. 176. De Tocqueville further says (pp. 37 and 264) that France prior to 1789 enjoyed a relatively higher level of socioeconomic development than did neighboring nations such as the German principalities. Seeley, attempting to account for dissatisfaction, in this case that of India, claims that it also relates to rising expectations. "I find great populations cowering in abject misery for centuries together, but they do not rise in rebellion; no, if they cannot live they die, and if they can only just live, then they just live, their sensibilities dulled and their very wishes crushed out by want. A population that rebels is a population that is looking up, that has begun to hope and to feel its strength." J.R. Seeley, THE EXPANSION OF ENGLAND (London: Macmillan, 1883), pp. 233-34.

8. Raymond Aron, THE CENTURY OF TOTAL WAR (Boston: Beacon Press, 1955), p. 63. I should hasten to add that M. Aron is here taking issue with many German publicists who are using these data for other purposes; nevertheless, articles did appear.

9. The quotation is cited by Scott Nearing, WAR OR PEACE (New York: Island Press, 1946).

10. Thucydides, THE PELOPONNESIAN WAR (New York: Random House, 1934), p. 15.

11. MEMOIRES DE RICHELIEU (ed. by Petitot), vol. 4, p. 245; cited by Bertrand de Jouvenal, ON POWER: ITS NATURE AND THE HISTORY OF ITS GROWTH (New York: Viking, 1949), p. 145. For further details, see C.V. Wedgwood, THE THIRTY YEARS WAR (New York: Anchor Books, 1961), Chapter 1.

12. Shepard B. Clough, THE RISE AND FALL OF CIVILIZATION: AN INQUIRY INTO THE RELATIONSHIP BETWEEN ECONOMIC DEVELOPMENT AND CIVILIZATION (New York: McGraw-Hill, 1951), p. 263.

13. Lionel Robbins, THE ECONOMIC CAUSES OF WAR (London: Jonathan Cape, 1939), p. 84.

14. W.W. Rostow, THE STAGES OF ECONOMIC GROWTH (Cambridge: At The University Press, 1960), p. 121.

15. The application of the idea, of course, is limitless. See Robert K. Merton and Alice S. Kitt, "Contributions to the Theory of Reference Group Behavior," in Robert K. Merton and Paul S. Lazarfeld (eds.), STUDIES IN THE SCOPE AND METHOD OF "THE AMERICAN SOLDIER," (Glencoe: Free Press, 1950).

16. William Fielding Ogburn, "Introductory Ideas on Inventions and the State," p. 3, in William Fielding Ogburn (ed.), TECHNOLOGY AND INTERNATIONAL RELATIONS (Chicago: University of Chicago Press, 1949). Adam Smith also erroneously assumed that a material gain is directly and linearly related to satisfaction. "It deserves to be remarked, perhaps, that it is in the progressive state, while the society is advancing to the further acquisition, rather

than when it has acquired its full complement of riches, that the condition of the labouring poor, of the great body of the people, seems to be the happiest and the most comfortable. It is hard in the stationary, and miserable in the declining state. The progressive state is in reality the cheerful and the hearty state, to all the different orders of the society. The stationary is dull; the declining, melancholy." Adam Smith, AN INQUIRY INTO THE NATURE AND CAUSES OF THE WEALTH OF NATIONS (London: Methuen, 1930), vol. 1, p. 83.

17. That rank change tends to vary inversely with hierarchy has been observed by others. "Below the elite universities, the scores of similarly ranked institutions were very close for both periods, and, therefore, as one would expect, there were more marked changes in rank among them than among the elite. Among the top five in 1965-68, the mean change from 1960-64 was only 2 rank positions, whereas for the next lower ten it was 6.6, for the next lower ten it was 16.0, and so forth. Only one institution was displaced from the top five, and it dropped only to sixth place. In contrast, three were displaced from the top ten, and these dropped to thirteenth, twenty-fifth, and thirty-fourth places. Upward movements were equally dramatic. The top twenty in 1965-68 included universities that had risen from thirty-first, thirty-fifth, fifty-second, and fifty-seventh places. In short, there was little movement into and out of the elite but a great deal of upward and downward movement below that level." Norval D. Glenn and Wayne Villemez, "The Productivity of Sociologists at 45 American Universities," AMERICAN SOCIOLOGIST 5 (August 1970), pp. 248-49.

18. After noting that in the eight years through late 1966 there were one hundred and sixty-four internationally significant outbreaks of violence, each of them directly challenging the authority or the existence of eighty-two different governments, Robert McNamara, overlooking change and stress, states that "there is a direct and constant relationship between the incidence of violence and the economic status of the countries afflicted." To prove this statement, McNamara first sorts nations on the basis of per capita income into four categories: rich, middle-income, poor, and very poor. Then he determines the percent distribution of violence for the last three categories, excluding the rich because only one of the rich twenty-seven nations has suffered an important internal upheaval on its own territory. "Since 1958, 87 percent of the very poor nations, 69 percent of the poor nations, and 48 percent of the middle-income nations suffered serious violence. There can be no question but that there is a relationship between violence and economic backwardness, and the trend of such violence is up, not down." Robert S. McNamara, THE ESSENCE OF SECURITY (New York: Harper & Row, 1968), pp. 145 and 146.

19. Louis De Jong, "Foreword," in Werner Warmbrunn, THE DUTCH UNDER GERMAN OCCUPATION (Stanford: Stanford University Press, 1963). Generally the literature on occupation is not as objective in appraising the situation. This may be accounted for by early publication and sympathy for the

occupied inhabitants because the emphasis is most often on economic exploitation and human horror. For example, in Shuhsi Hsu, THE WAR CONDUCT OF THE JAPANESE (Shanghai: Kelly and Walsh, 1938), the emphasis is on atrocities; in Robert S. Ward, ASIA FOR THE ASIATICS? THE TECHNIQUES OF JAPANESE OCCUPATION (Chicago: University of Chicago Press, 1945), an American consul in Hong Kong describes the story of its surrender in terms of human brutalization; in OCCUPIED EUROPE (London: Royal Institute of International Affairs, 1944), the emphasis is on economic and human exploitation; in Fernand Baudhuin, L'ECONOMIE BELGE SOUS L'OCCUPATION, 1940-1944 (Bruxelles: Etablissments Emil Bruylant, 1945), the author discusses first the incompetence, collusion, and arrogance of traitors who contributed to a reign of police terror, and then the economic hard times during the famine with the few figures at his disposal; in Louis Baudin, L'ECONOMIE FRANCAISE SOUS L'OCCUPATION ALLEMANDE (Paris: Librairie De Medicis, 1945), the division of France, repression, assassination, pillaging, and the retention of workmen in Germany are mentioned as well as the removal of industrial, agricultural, and mining products; and, in Amanda Johnson, NORWAY, HER INVASION AND OCCUPATION (Decatur, Ga.: Bowen Press, 1948), the author describes economic exploitation and the reprisals against the resistance movement and its heroes.

20. I am speaking here quite generally and am not for the moment considering complementary evaluation between pairs of nations. Essentially, satisfaction can only be understood in comparative terms. Thus it is not enough to say with Bismarck that nations are either "satiated or unsatiated"; one must take into account other nations, particularly other nations in similar circumstances: a set of nations active in war, those two nations immediately adjacent in the development hierarchy, or any nation to which the evaluator has reference.

21. "Basically the new imperialism was a nationalistic phenomenon. It followed hard upon the national wars which created an all-powerful Germany and a united Italy, which carried Russia within sight of Constantinople, and which left England fearful and France eclipsed. It expressed a resulting psychological reaction, an ardent desire to maintain or recover national prestige." Carlton J.H. Hayes, A GENERATION OF MATERIALISM, 1871-1900 (New York: Harper, 1941). For even more detail, see Parker Thomas Moon, IMPERIALISM AND WORLD POLITICS (New York: Macmillan, 1929); and Harry Elmer Barnes, WORLD POLITICS IN MODERN CIVILIZATION (New York: Alfred Knopf, 1930).

Chapter 8
Conflict

1. For the details not only in the sense of absolute figures but also in a relative sense of the number of war casualties per one million of the population

in all the wars of Greco-Roman and the Western nations from 600 B.C. to present time, see Pitirim Sorokin, SOCIAL AND CULTURAL DYNAMICS (New York: Bedminster Press, 1962), vol. 3, pp. 259-380; L.F. Richardson, STATISTICS OF DEADLY QUARRELS (Pittsburgh: Boxwood Press, 1960); B.L. Urlanis, VOYNY I NARODONASELENIE EVROPY (Moscow, 1960); and Quincy Wright, "The Study of War," INTERNATIONAL ENCYCLOPEDIA OF THE SOCIAL SCIENCES (New York: Macmillan, 1968), vol. 16, pp. 453-68.

2. Hans Delbruck, GESCHICHTE DER KRIEGSKUNST, IM RAHMEN DER POLITISCHER GESCHICHTE (Berlin: 1900); and Ferdinand Lot, L'ART MILITAIRE ET LES ARMÉES AU MOYEN AGE (Paris: 1946). References to active armies of 30,000 and more men in Western Europe in the later Middle Ages (for example, Werner Sombart, KRIEG UND KAPITALISMUS (Leipzig: Duncker & Humblot, 1913, p. 38) are challenged by Lot. Sombart's statement that Edward III had an army of 32,000 men at Calais in 1347, on the eve of the battle of Crecy, for example, is refuted by J.H. Ramsay, "The Strength of English Armies in the Middle Ages," ENGLISH HISTORICAL REVIEW 29 (1914), pp. 223-24. Contrary to what might be general impression on relative size, in the Persian Wars, the Greek citizen armies outnumbered the Persian (Delbruck, vol. 1, p. 10); and, in the celebrated victory at Agincourt, celebrated in both history books and plays, the English army outnumbered the French (Lot, vol. 2, pp. 13-14, 441).

3. See Hubert G.R. Reade, SIDELIGHTS ON THE THIRTY YEARS' WAR (London: 1924); C.V. Wedgwood, THE THIRTY YEARS WAR (London: Jonathan Cape, 1938), Chapter 1; and, Robert Ergang, THE MYTH OF THE ALL DESTRUCTIVE FURY OF THE THIRTY YEARS WAR (Pocono Pines, Pa.: 1956). This last work systematically attempts to correct a persistingly exaggerated view of the effect of the Thirty Years War; it is a concise work showing clearly that the economic decline of Germany had begun long before the outbreak of the war. Oddly enough, commentators on this war tend to omit any mention of the considerable gains made by other participants in the war; I am thinking here of France, but one could go down the roster and identify all the others. Obviously, the case of the Thirty Years War begs reinterpretation.

4. For example, James Shotwell oversaw well over one hundred monographs on the subject of the consequences of the First World War and the experience hardly impinged upon his view that war proceeds with disastrous socioeconomic results. "The generation that has endured the World War has at last come to grips with the problem of war itself. The movement to eliminate it from international dealings is not based upon sentiment nor emotion, although they may fortify its purpose; it is gaining rather than losing in strength as the poignant memories of the war grow fainter, because it embodies the major lesson of the whole vast tragic experience, that as between the highly civilized nations war has become a futile instrument incapable of direction and therefore criminal in use. A new attitude is forcing its way in international politics—as it also is

revealing itself in the world of business and internal economics—one which seeks to substitute for ruthless competition some measure of cooperation, so that each member of the community of nations may have a larger share in an increasing common good. This change in attitude is itself a fact of history." James T. Shotwell, WAR AS AN INSTRUMENT OF NATIONAL POLICY (New York: Harcourt, Brace, 1929), p. v.

5. Of course, attempts at explaining war abound: for a controlled speculative effort, see Luther L. Bernard, WAR AND ITS CAUSES (New York: Holt, 1944), Chapters 8-9; and, for a multidimensional approach, see J. David Singer, "Modern International War: From Conjecture to Explanation," pp. 47-71, in Albert Lepawsky, et al. (eds.), THE SEARCH FOR WORLD ORDER: ESSAYS IN HONOR OF QUINCY WRIGHT (New York: Appleton-Century-Crofts, 1971).

6. R.G. Hawtrey, ECONOMIC ASPECTS OF SOVEREIGNTY (London: Longmans, Green, 1952), p. 65. The desire to settle this question of relative strength seems so urgent and pervasive that not a few nations will fight, supposedly, even when foresight dictates that costs will outstrip gains. For example, "wars are not usually fought to raise absolutely the power of a single nation; they are fought to determine the relative power of two or more nations. Victory can be meaningful even if it involves lower economic strength for the victorious nation." W.W. Rostow, THE PROCESS OF ECONOMIC GROWTH (New York: W.W. Norton, 1962), p. 150. Such an argument engages considerable attention apparently for even knowledgable pacifists find themselves seduced by it. "Since inequality in position is one of the outstanding causes of war, each victory carries with it a guarantee of further hostilities. In addition, victory provides one more proof of the superiority of the winning side, thus justifying its domination and exploitation of its neighbors. Assertions of superiority, domination and exploitation lead to antagonism, unrest, and a new appeal to arms." Scott Nearing, WAR OR PEACE (New York: Island Press, 1946), p. 78.

7. Fortunately, there is at least one precedent for the opinion. "Apprehension of the loss of political prestige and relative power has been a major cause of popular anxiety. . . . This apprehension may arise because of differential rates of population growth, economic development, of political unification, or of military development. While these changes are watched closely by statesmen, their influence upon war is mainly indirect, through their influence in creating popular apprehension and in inducing a rise in tension levels." Quincy Wright, A STUDY OF WAR (Chicago: University of Chicago Press, 1942), vol. 2, p. 1114.

8. "Of all states, from the smallest to the biggest, one can safely say that the fundamental rule of government is the principle of extending their territories. . . . The passions of rulers have no other curb but the limits of their power. Those are the fixed ideas of European politics to which every politician submits. If a ruler were to tend his own interests less carefully than his

neighbors', then the latter would only grow stronger; and it would leave him more virtuous but also weaker. . . . To tell the truth, treaties are only affirmations of deception and faithlessness." This quotation is cited by Frederick Menecke, MACHIAVELLISM (New Haven: Yale University Press, 1957), p. 301. On p. 228 he quotes Frederick to similar effect: "The policy of the great monarchies has always been the same. Their fundamental principle has constantly been to grasp at everything in order to increase their territory continually; and their wisdom has consisted in forestalling the tricks of their enemies, and playing the subtler game."

9. For a thorough elaboration of this statement, see Lewis F. Richardson, ARMS AND INSECURITY: A MATEHMATICAL STUDY OF THE CAUSES AND ORIGIN OF WAR (Pittsburgh: Boxwood Press, 1960).

10. For a concise introduction to the subject, see Raymond Aron, WAR AND INDUSTRIAL SOCIETY (London: Oxford University Press, 1958).

11. Harold Lasswell, "The Garrison-State Hypothesis Today," p. 51 in Samuel P. Huntington (ed.), CHANGING PATTERNS OF MILITARY POLITICS (Glencoe: Free Press of Glencoe, 1962).

12. Thus William James in his popular essay, the moral equivalent of war, notes the following. "Every up-to-date dictionary should say that 'peace' and 'war' mean the same thing, now *in posse*, now *in actu*. It may even reasonably be said that the intensely sharp competitive *preparation* for war by the nation *is the real war*, permanent, unceasing; and that battles are only a sort of public verification of mastery gained during the 'peace' intervals." William James, MEMORIES AND STUDIES (New York: Longmans, Green, 1911), pp. 273-74. Twenty-eight years later, Speier and Kahler, independently, take up the theme. "Every technological improvement applied to the machinery of destruction tightens the grip which modern war has on the common man's life. The scope of war has become as large as that of peace, or indeed even larger, since under modern conditions it is the interest of efficient war to militarize peace." Hans Speier and Alfred Kahler (eds.), WAR IN OUR TIME (New York: W.W. Norton, 1939), p. 13.

13. Plato, LAWS (London: William Heinemann, 1926), vol. 1, bk. 1, vol. 2, bks. 7-8, and 12.

14. Pitirim Sorokin, SOCIAL AND CULTURAL DYNAMICS (New York: Bedminster Press, 1962), p. 352.

15. For a recent study on peacemaking, see Robert Randle, THE ORIGINS OF PEACE, (New York: Free Press, 1973).

16. "Acceleration of technological and economic progress came simultaneously on both sides of the Atlantic in the second half of the nineteenth century, especially the latter part of this period." W.S. Woytinsky and E.S. Woytinsky, WORLD POPULATION AND PRODUCTION (New York: Twentieth Century Fund, 1953), p. lx. As a matter of fact, "during the greater part of history the normal condition of the world has been one of scarcity . . .[but] as a result of

the modernization of production and transport . . . mere scarcity ceased, after the middle of the nineteenth century, to be, except in . . . [parts of the Far East] , the haunting terror which till recently it had been." R.H. Tawney, "The Abolition of Economic Controls, 1918-1921," ECONOMIC HISTORY REVIEW 13 (1943), p. 24. This idea of continuous development prior to the First World War can be established quantitatively, for example, by figures on income and hours worked. The real income per person gainfully employed improved 75 percent or more from 1870 to 1914, while the hours of work were substantially reduced in such nations as France, Germany, Great Britain, Norway, Sweden, United States, and Canada. Colin Clark, THE CONDITIONS OF ECONOMIC PROGRESS (London: Macmillan, 1940), pp. 79, 83, 87, 91, 144, and Charts facing pp. 147-48.

17. Dewey Anderson, FINAL REPORT OF THE EXECUTIVE SECRETARY TO THE TEMPORARY NATIONAL ECONOMIC COMMITTEE ON THE CONCENTRATION OF ECONOMIC POWER IN THE UNITED STATES (Washington: U.S. Government Printing Office. 1941), p. 105.

18. J.B. Bury, THE IDEA OF PROGRESS (New York: Macmillan, 1932), p. 332.

19. Alfred N. Whitehead, SCIENCE AND THE MODERN WORLD (New York: Macmillan, 1926), p. 136.

20. See Derek J. de Solla Price, LITTLE SCIENCE, BIG SCIENCE (New York: Columbia University Press, 1963), Chapters 1-2.

21. William Ashworth, A SHORT HISTORY OF THE INTERNATIONAL ECONOMY 1850-1950 (London: Longmans, Green, 1952), pp. 163-64.

22. Achille Viallate, ECONOMIC IMPERIALISM AND INTERNATIONAL RELATIONS DURING THE LAST FIFTY YEARS (New York: Macmillan, 1923), Chapter I.

23. Kingsley Davis, "Population and Power in the Free World," p. 195 in Philip M. Hauser (ed.), POPULATION AND WORLD POLITICS (Glencoe: Free Press, 1958).

24. See Eli F. Heckscher, MERCANTILISM (London: Allen & Unwin, 1936), vol. 2, "Mercantilism As a System of Power," pp. 16 ff. The overarching requirement of national economy to meet competition from other nations has been recognized by others. Details of the process may be obtained from Barrington Moore, SOCIAL ORIGINS OF DICTATORSHIP AND DEMOCRACY: LORD AND PEASANT IN THE MAKING OF THE MODERN WORLD (Boston: Beacon Press, 1966).

25. This quotation is cited by Georg Schwarzenberger, POWER POLITICS (London: Stevens, 1964), p. 54.

26. For recent considerations on the profound influence of colonialism, its capacity to diffuse the concept of contemporary nationhood as well as current technology and science, see Rupert Emerson, FROM EMPIRE TO NATION (Cambridge: Harvard University Press, 1960); John Plamenatz, ALIEN RULE

AND SELF-GOVERNMENT (London: Longmans, Green, 1960); David C. Gordon, Self Determination and History in the Third World (Princeton: Princeton University Press, 1971); and, Elie Kedourie (ed.), NATIONALISM IN ASIA AND AFRICA (New York: World Publishing Co., 1971).

27. Kingsley Davis, "Population and Power in the Free World," p. 196 in Philip M. Hauser (ed.), POPULATION AND WORLD POLITICS (Glencoe: Free Press, 1958).

Chapter 9
Inequality

1. "We know . . . that most of this disparity is the product of the last hundred years or so." A.K. Cairncross, FACTORS IN ECONOMIC DEVELOP-MENT (New York: Praeger, 1962), p. 18. The advantage of the more developed nations was much smaller "before they started to develop rapidly a century or more ago." Gunnar Myrdal, RICH LANDS AND POOR (New York: Harper & Brothers, 1957), p. 3. Prior to that time, according to Fourastie, the material situation was nearly the same for everyone. "Everywhere the level of living was controlled by the level of agricultural production. Everywhere the expansion of population was periodically checked by famine that imposed upon the population the Draconian and capricious rhythm of climatic disasters." Jean Fourastie, THE CAUSES OF WEALTH (Glencoe: Free Press, 1960), p. 60. This idea pervades the work as it appears in several contexts; see pp. 23, 101, 115, 118, 215, and 224-25.

2. Gunnar Myrdal, RICH LANDS AND POOR (New York: Harper, 1957), p. 6; and Geoffrey Crowther, THE WEALTH AND POVERTY OF NATIONS (Claremont, Calif.: Claremont College, 1957), p. 7.

3. Karl Marx, CAPITAL (Chicago: C.H. Kerr, 1906), pp. 13-15; and W.W. Rostow, THE STAGES OF ECONOMIC GROWTH (Cambridge: At The University Press, 1960), pp. 4 and 148.

4. Thornstein Veblen, IMPERIAL GERMANY AND THE INDUSTRIAL REVOLUTION (New York: Viking, 1939), p. 86; see also his article, "The Opportunity of Japan" in ESSAYS IN OUR CHANGING ORDER (New York: Viking, 1934), for a similar application; Ralph Linton, "The Prospects of Western Civilization," p. 545 in Willard Waller (ed.), WAR IN THE TWENTIETH CENTURY (New York: Random House, 1940); and, A.K. Cairncross, FAC-TORS IN ECONOMIC DEVELOPMENT (New York: Praeger, 1962), p. 18.

5. N.S. Khrushchev, CONTROL FIGURES FOR THE ECONOMIC DEVEL-OPMENT OF THE U.S.S.R. FOR 1959-1965 (Moscow: Foreign Language Publishing House, 1959), p. 77.

6. Pierre Moussa, THE UNDERPRIVILEGED NATIONS (Boston: Beacon Press, 1963), p. 181.

7. Irving Louis Horowitz, THREE WORLDS OF DEVELOPMENT: THE THEORY AND PRACTICE OF INTERNATIONAL STRATIFICATION (New York: Oxford University Press, 1966), p. 126.

8. For a detailed examination of the available statistical series see Cyril E. Black, "Soviet Society: A Comparative View," esp. pp. 40-43 in Allen Kassof (ed.), PROSPECTS FOR SOVIET SOCIETY (New York: Praeger, 1968).

9. Crane Brinton, THE ANATOMY OF REVOLUTION (New York: W.W. Norton, 1938), p. 43; also relevant, on growth prior to the Revolution of 1917, is N.S. Timasheff, THE GREAT RETREAT (New York: Dutton, 1946). That Russia was making significant progress prior to the outbreak of the First World War can be seen in the following table.

Russian Exports and Imports per Capita: 1895-1913

Period	Exports (in Rubles)	Imports (in Rubles)
1895-99	5.5	4.7
1900-04	6.3	4.6
1905-09	7.4	5.1
1910-13	9.1	7.1

Source: Anatole G. Mazour, RUSSIA: TSARIST AND COMMUNIST (New York: Van Nostrand, 1962), p. 323.

10. An intimate relationship exists between a political unit and its road system. The dissolution of empires or city-states is often followed by the decay of the roads, which cannot be maintained without an efficient centralized government. I believe, therefore, that this is a good way as any to show the differences between nations in another historical epoch. "In India," relates an early fourteenth century traveller from Tangier, "there is an express post, the *Ulak*, which is as swift as the falcon and can traverse the immense distance from the northern mountains to the southern sea in a few days, by means of a highly organized system of relays; besides this there is the ordinary *Berid*, and also a state service used exclusively by the Sultan and operated by relay runners." H.A.R. Gibb, SELECTIONS FROM THE TRAVELS OF IBN BATUTA (London: Routledge, 1929). Prescott tells us that "all the difficulties that beset a wild and mountainous region, and which might appall the most courageous engineer of modern times, were encountered and successfully overcome," in building the road from Quito to Cuzco, 2,000 miles long. And Pizarro found that "nothing in Christendom equals the magnificence of this road across the sierra." William H. Prescott, HISTORY OF THE CONQUEST OF MEXICO and HISTORY OF THE CONQUEST OF PERU (New York: Modern Library, 1936), pp. 763 and 954. These notes are significant in light of the fact that the Taxis Post had only gotten under way in Europe in the sixteenth century according to

Eli F. Heckscher, MERCANTILISM (London: Allen & Unwin, 1935), vol. 1, p. 34, n. 1. A British author studying the eighteenth century remarks that "besides the Delhi of the Moguls the London of 1715 must have seemed in many respects a country town." John Strachey, THE END OF EMPIRE (London: Gollancz, 1959), p. 16. See also K.M. Panikkar, ASIA AND WESTERN DOMINANCE: A SURVEY OF THE VASCO DA GAMA EPOCH OF ASIAN HISTORY 1498-1945 (London: Allen & Unwin, 1959).

11. "A high death rate (as an index of health) regularly precedes hard times, while a low death rate precedes prosperity. Health is a cause far more than an effect (of business prosperity). Health in its turn is determined by the weather." Ellsworth Huntington, WORLD POWER AND EVOLUTION (New Haven: Yale University Press, 1919), pp. 29 ff. See also pp. 190-92 for an example of how climate is interpreted as influencing the rise and fall of a civilization. In a much later work, probably his last, he modifies this powerful view somewhat, see "The Geography of Human Productivity," ANNALS OF THE ASSOCIATION OF AMERICAN GEOGRAPHERS 33 (1943), pp. 1-31.

12. "Then passing from one induction to another, I was gradually penetrated by the conviction that the racial question overshadows all other problems of history, that it holds the key to them all, and that the inequality of the races from whose fusion a people is formed is enough to explain the whole course of its destiny." Arthur de Gobineau, THE INEQUALITY OF HUMAN RACES (New York: G.P. Putnam, 1915; first published in 1854), p. xiv.

13. Adolphe Coste, L'EXPERIENCE DES PEUPLES ET LES PREVISIONS QU'ELLE AUTORISE (Paris: S. Alcan, 1900), pp. 588 ff. The effect of size on the division of labor is also noted by Durkheim. Competition is the sharpest among members of the same occupation when there is a superabundance of membership. Hence, an increase in the density of a population leads to an increase in the division of labor. This is how he formulates it: "The progress of the division of labor is in direct ratio to the moral or dynamic density of society." Emile Durkheim, THE DIVISION OF LABOR IN SOCIETY (Glencoe: Free Press, 1949), p. 257.

14. Other explanations of world inequality or comparative development abound. See Joseph J. Spengler, "Theories of Socio-Economic Growth," p. 53 for a list of twenty factors in Universities-National Bureau Committee on Economic Research, PROBLEMS IN THE STUDY OF ECONOMIC GROWTH (New York: National Bureau of Economic Research, 1949), pp. 52-53; W.W. Rostow, THE PROCESS OF ECONOMIC GROWTH (New York: W.W. Norton, 1952), pp. 13-14 for a list of six factors therein called propensities; A.K. Cairncross, FACTORS IN ECONOMIC DEVELOPMENT (New York: Praeger, 1962), for a list of four factors; Robert L. Heilbroner, THE GREAT ASCENT (New York: Harper & Row, 1963), Chapter 6 for a list of three factors; C.E. Black, THE DYNAMICS OF MODERNIZATION (New York: Harper & Row, 1966), p. 67 for a list of four factors therein called phases; and, Lauchlin Currie,

OBSTACLES TO DEVELOPMENT (East Lansing: Michigan State University Press, 1967), p. 7 for a list of three factors.

15. For an illustration of this new awareness, see Michiya Shimbori, et al., "Measuring a Nation's Prestige," AMERICAN JOURNAL OF SOCIOLOGY 69, no. 1, (July 1963).

16. Edward Shils, "The Military in the Political Development of the New States," pp. 11 and 19 in John J. Johnson (ed.), THE ROLE OF THE MILITARY IN UNDERDEVELOPED COUNTRIES (Princeton: Princeton University Press, 1962).

17. Evan Luard, NATIONALITY AND WEALTH (London: Oxford University Press, 1964), p. 357.

18. Peter Worsley, THE THIRD WORLD (Chicago: University of Chicago Press, 1964), pp. 242-43.

19. Thomas Hovet, Jr., BLOC POLITICS IN THE UNITED NATIONS (Cambridge: Harvard University Press, 1960).

20. Peccei, for example, notes a growth in strain between the more developed nations of the West. "There is no wisdom in concealing the fact that in our part of the world two different societies are rapidly emerging and progressively becoming estranged from each other. . . . Constructive dialogue between the banks of the chasm would then become as difficult as it is now between the advanced West and the Underdeveloped peoples of the world." Aurelio Peccei, THE CHASM AHEAD (New York: Macmillan, 1969), p. 69.

21. The general statement on the expansion of awareness is eloquently expressed by W.I. Thomas as an awakening of *attention.* "Attention is the mental attitude which takes note of the outside world and manipulates it; it is the organ of accommodation. But attention does not operate alone; it is associated with habit on the one hand and with crisis on the other. When the habits are running smoothly, the attention is relaxed; it is not at work. But when something happens to disturb the run of habit, the attention is called into play and devises a new mode of behavior which will meet the crisis." The quotation is drawn from the Introduction which Thomas wrote for his SOURCE BOOK OF SOCIAL ORIGINS (Chicago: University of Chicago Press, 1909).

22. Jacob Burckhardt, FORCE AND FREEDOM (New York: Pantheon Books, 1943), p. 260.

23. Oswald Spengler, THE DECLINE OF THE WEST (New York: A. Knopf, 1928), vol. 2, p. 363.

24. Paul E. Sigmund (ed.), THE IDEOLOGIES OF THE DEVELOPING NATIONS (New York: Praeger, 1963).

Bibliography

Bibliography

Acheson, Dean. PRESENT AT THE CREATION. New York: W.W. Norton, 1969.

Adams, Doris Goodrich. IRAQ'S PEOPLE AND RESOURCES. Berkeley: University of California Press, 1958.

Agarwala, A.N. ECONOMIC MOBILIZATION FOR NATIONAL DEFENSE. New York: Asia Publishing House, 1966.

American Telephone and Telegraph Company. THE WORLD'S TELEPHONES; TELEPHONE STATISTICS OF THE WORLD; TELEPHONE AND TELEGRAPH STATISTICS OF THE WORLD. New York: American Telephone and Telegraph Company, January 1st 1914, 1921, 1926, 1939, 1948, and 1953.

Anderson, Dewey. FINAL REPORT OF THE EXECUTIVE SECRETARY TO THE TEMPORARY NATIONAL ECONOMIC COMMITTEE ON THE CONCENTRATION OF ECONOMIC POWER IN THE UNITED STATES. Washington: U.S. Government Printing Office, 1941.

Andreski, Stanislav. THE USES OF COMPARATIVE SOCIOLOGY. Berkeley: University of California Press, 1965.

Angell, Robert C. "The Growth of Transnational Participation," JOURNAL OF SOCIAL ISSUES 23 (January 1967).

Armstrong, H.F. WHEN THERE IS NO PEACE. New York: Macmillan, 1939.

Armstrong, John A. SOVIET PARTISANS IN WORLD WAR II. Madison: University of Wisconsin Press, 1964.

Aron, Raymond. WAR AND INDUSTRIAL SOCIETY. London: Oxford University Press, 1958.

_____ . THE CENTURY OF TOTAL WAR. Boston: Beacon Press, 1955.

Ashworth, William. A SHORT HISTORY OF THE INTERNATIONAL ECONOMY 1850-1950. London: Longmans Green, 1952.

Ayres, Clarence Edward. THE THEORY OF ECONOMIC PROGRESS. Chapel Hill: University of North Carolina Press, 1944.

Bagehot, Walter. PHYSICS AND POLITICS. Boston: Beacon Press, 1956.

Banks, Arthur S., and Textor, Robert B. A CROSS-POLITY SURVEY. Cambridge: M.I.T. Press, 1963.

Barbour, K.M., and Protero, R.M., eds. ESSAYS ON AFRICAN POPULATION. New York: Frederick A. Praeger, 1962.

Barnes, Harry Elmer. WORLD POLITICS IN MODERN CIVILIZATION. New York: Alfred Knopf, 1930.

Batuta, Ibn. SELECTIONS FROM THE TRAVELS OF IBN BATUTA. Edited by H.A.R. Gibb. London: Routledge, 1929.

Baudhuin, Fernand. L'ECONOMIE BELGE SOUS L'OCCUPATION, 1940-1944. Bruxelles: Establissments Emil Bruylant, 1945.

Bauduin, Louis. L'ECONOMIE FRANCAISE SOUS L'OCCUPATION ALLE-MANDE. Paris: Librairie De Medicis, 1945.

Beard, Charles A. "Introduction," in J.B. Bury, THE IDEA OF PROGRESS. New York: Macmillan, 1932.

Beckmann, George. THE MAKING OF THE MEIJI CONSTITUTION. Lawrence: University of Kansas Press, 1957.

Bell, A.C. SEA POWER AND THE NEXT WAR. London and New York: Longmans Green, 1938.

Ben-David, Joseph. "Scientific Productivity and Academic Organization in Nineteenth Century Medicine." AMERICAN SOCIOLOGICAL REVIEW 25 (December 1960).

_____, and Collins, Randall. "Social Factors in the Origin of a New Science: The Case of Psychology." AMERICAN SOCIOLOGICAL REVIEW 31 (August 1966).

Bendix, Reinhard. NATION BUILDING AND CITIZENSHIP. New York: John Wiley, 1964.

Bennett, M.K. "International Disparities in Consumption Levels." AMERICAN ECONOMIC REVIEW 41 (September 1951).

Bernard, L.L. WAR AND ITS CAUSES. New York: Henry Holt, 1944.

Beveridge, Sir William H. THE PILLARS OF SECURITY. London: Allen & Unwin, 1943.

Binkley, Robert C. REALISM AND NATIONALISM, 1852-1871. New York: Harper, 1935.

Black, Cyril E. THE DYNAMICS OF MODERNIZATION. New York: Harper & Row, 1966.

_____. "Soviet Society: A Comparative View." PROSPECTS FOR SOVIET SOCIETY. Edited by Allen Kassof. New York: Frederick A. Praeger, 1968.

Bliokh, Ivan Stanislavovich. THE FUTURE OF WAR IN ITS TECHNICAL, ECONOMIC, AND POLITICAL RELATIONS. Boston: Ginn, 1902.

Block, Henry, and Hoselitz, Bert F. ECONOMICS OF MILITARY OCCUPATION. Chicago: The Foundation Press, 1944.

Blouet, Brian. A SHORT HISTORY OF MALTA. New York: Frederick A. Praeger, 1967.

Boggs, S. Whittemore. INTERNATIONAL BOUNDARIES. New York: Columbia University Press, 1940.

Borah, W.W. NEW SPAIN'S CENTURY OF DEPRESSION. Berkeley: University of California Press, 1951.

Brogan, Dennis W. THE PRICE OF REVOLUTION. New York: Harper, 1952.

Bryce, James. "War and Human Progress." INTERNATIONAL CONCILIATION 108 (November 1916).

Burckhardt, Jacob. FORCE AND FREEDOM. New York: Pantheon Books, 1943.

Bury, J.B. THE IDEA OF PROGRESS. New York: Macmillan, 1932.

Cairncross, A.K. FACTORS IN ECONOMIC DEVELOPMENT. New York: Frederick A. Praeger, 1962.

Calvocoressi, Peter. WORLD ORDER AND NEW STATES. New York: Frederick A. Praeger, 1962.

_____, and Wint, Guy. TOTAL WAR: THE STORY OF WORLD WAR II. New York: Pantheon, 1972.

Caplow, Theodore, and Finsterbusch, Kurt. DEVELOPMENT RANK. New York: Bureau of Applied Social Research, Columbia University, 1966.

Capotorti, Francisco. L'OCCUPAZIONE NEL DIRITTO DI GUERRA. Napoli: Casa Editrice Dott. Eugenio Jovene, 1949.

Carr, E.H. WHAT IS HISTORY? New York: Alfred A. Knopf, 1962.

_____. THE TWENTY YEARS' CRISIS, 1919-1939. London: Macmillan, 1940.

Case, Winthrop W. "Economic Problems of U.S. Neutrality in Wartime." FOREIGN REPORTS 15 (April 15, 1939).

Casimir, H.B.G. In REVIEWS OF NATIONAL SCIENCE POLICY: UNITED STATES. Paris: Organisation for Economic Co-operation and Development, 1968.

Charlesworth, Martin Percival. TRADE-ROUTES AND COMMERCE OF THE ROMAN EMPIRE. Cambridge: University Press, 1924.

Christaller, Walter. CENTRAL PLACES IN SOUTHERN GERMANY. Englewood Cliffs: Prentice Hall, 1966.

Cipolla, C.M. "The Decline of Italy: The Case of a Fully Matured Economy." ECONOMIC HISTORY REVIEW 5 (1952).

Clapham, J.H. "Charles Louis, Elector Palatine, 1617-1680. An Early Experiment in Liberalism." ECONOMICS 7 (1940).

Clark, Colin. THE CONDITIONS OF ECONOMIC PROGRESS. London: Macmillan, 1940 (also 1957 edition).

Clarke, R.W.B. THE ECONOMIC EFFORT OF WAR. London: Allen & Unwin, 1940.

Cleveland, Harlan. THE OBLIGATIONS OF POWER. New York: Harper & Row, 1966.

Clough, Shepherd B. THE RISE AND FALL OF CIVILIZATION: AN INQUIRY INTO THE RELATIONSHIP BETWEEN ECONOMIC DEVELOPMENT AND CIVILIATION. New York: McGraw-Hill, 1951.

_____. THE ECONOMIC DEVELOPMENT OF WESTERN CIVILIZATION. New York: McGraw-Hill, 1959.

Clubb, Oliver Edmund. TWENTIETH CENTURY CHINA. New York: Columbia University Press, 1964.

Cohn, Georg. NEO-NEUTRALITY. New York: Columbia University Press, 1939.

Coleman, D.C. "Technology and Economic History, 1500-1700." ECONOMIC HISTORY REVIEW 11 (1959).

Comte, Auguste. COURS DE PHILOSOPHIE POSITIVE. 2. Paris: 1881.

Condliffe, J.B. WAR AND DEPRESSION. Boston and New York: World Peace Foundation, 1935.

Connor, Sydney, and Friedrich, Carl J., eds. MILITARY GOVERNMENT. A special edition of the ANNALS 267 (January 1950).

Coste, Adolphe. L'EXPERIENCE DES PEUPLES ET LES PREVISIONS QU'ELLE AUTORISE. Paris: S. Alcan, 1900.

Cottrel, Fred. ENERGY AND SOCIETY: THE RELATION BETWEEN ENERGY, SOCIAL CHANGE, AND ECONOMIC DEVELOPMENT. New York: McGraw-Hill, 1955.

Crowther, J.G. SCIENCE AND MODERN SOCIETY. New York: Schocken Books, 1968.

Crowther, Geoffrey. THE WEALTH AND POVERTY OF NATIONS. Claremont, California: Claremont College, 1957.

Currie, Lauchlin. OBSTACLES TO DEVELOPMENT. East Lansing: Michigan State University Press, 1967.

Cutright, Phillips. "National Political Development: Measurement and Analysis." AMERICAN JOURNAL OF SOCIOLOGY 28, no. 2 (April 1963).

Davis, Kingsley. "Population and Power in the Free World." POPULATION AND WORLD POLITICS. Edited by Philip M. Hauser. Glencoe: Free Press, 1958.

Davison, W. Phillips. INTERNATIONAL POLITICAL COMMUNICATION. New York: Frederick A. Praeger, 1965.

Debbasch, Odile. L'OCCUPATION MILITAIRE. Aix-en-Provence: La Pensee Universitaire, 1960.

Deborin, G. THE SECOND WORLD WAR. Moscow: Progress Publishers, 1964.

Delbruck, Hans. GESCHICHTE DER KRIEGSKUNST, IM RAHMEN DER POLITISCHER GESCHICHTE. Berlin, 1900.

de Solla Price, Derek J. LITTLE SCIENCE, BIG SCIENCE. New York: Columbia University Press, 1963.

de Tocqueville, Alexis. THE OLD REGIME AND THE FRENCH REVOLUTION. Garden City: Doubleday, 1955.

Deutsch, Karl W. "The Propensity to International Transactions." POLITICAL STUDIES 8 (1960).

Djilas, Milovan. THE UNPERFECT SOCIETY. New York: Harcourt, Brace, 1969.

Durkheim, Emile. THE DIVISION OF LABOR IN SOCIETY. Glencoe: Free Press, 1949.

Edwards, Ronald S. "The Future of Industrial Research and Development in Great Britain." LLOYDS BANK REVIEW. (January 1952).

Emerson, Rupert. FROM EMPIRE TO NATION. Cambridge: Harvard University Press, 1960.

ENCYCLOPEDIA METHODIQUE. 4. Paris: 1788.

Ergang, Robert. THE MYTH OF THE ALL DESTRUCTIVE FURY OF THE THIRTY YEARS WAR. Pocono Pines, Pa.: 1956.

Fischer, George. SOVIET OPPOSITION TO STALIN: A CASE STUDY IN WORLD WAR II. Cambridge: Harvard University Press, 1952.

Fitzgerald, C.P. CHINA: A SHORT CULTURAL HISTORY. London: Cresset Press, 1954.

Fourastie, Jean. THE CAUSES OF WEALTH. Glencoe: Free Press, 1960.

Foch, Marshal. THE PRINCIPLES OF WAR. London: Chapman & Hall, 1918.

Friedrich, Carl J. "Nation-building?" NATION-BUILDING. Edited by Karl W. Deutsch and William J. Foltz. New York: Atherton Press, 1963.

Fuller, J.F.C. ARMAMENT AND HISTORY. London: Eyre & Spottiswoode, 1946.

Germani, Gino. "Democratie representative et classes populaires en Amerique Latine." SOCIOLOGIE DU TRAVAIL, (Octobre-Decembre, 1961).

Gilbert, Felix. "Machiavelli: The Renaissance of the Art of War." MAKERS OF MODERN STRATEGY. Edited by Edward Mead Earle. Princeton: Princeton University Press, 1943.

Gilbert, Milton, and Kravis, Irving B. AN INTERNATIONAL COMPARISON OF NATIONAL PRODUCTS AND THE PURCHASING POWER OF CURRENCIES. Paris: Organisation of European Economic Cooperation, 1954.

Gilfillan, S.C. THE SOCIOLOGY OF INVENTION. Chicago: Follett, 1935.

Ginsburg, Norton. ATLAS OF ECONOMIC DEVELOPMENT. Chicago: University of Chicago Press, 1961.

Glahn, Gerhard von. THE OCCUPATION OF ENEMY TERRITORY . . . A COMMENTARY ON THE LAW AND PRACTICE OF BELLIGERENT OCCUPATION. Minneapolis: University of Minnesota Press, 1957.

Glenn, Norval D., and Villemez, Wayne. "The Productivity of Sociologists at 45 American Universities." AMERICAN SOCIOLOGIST, 5 (August 1970).

Gobineau, Arthur de. THE INEQUALITY OF HUMAN RACES. New York: G.P. Putnam, 1915.

Goody, Jack, and Watt, Ian. "The Consequences of Literacy." COMPARATIVE STUDIES IN SOCIOLOGY AND HISTORY 5 (April 1963).

Gordon, David C. SELF DETERMINATION AND HISTORY IN THE THIRD WORLD. Princeton: Princeton University Press, 1971.

Guerlac, Henry E. "Science and French National Strength." MODERN FRANCE. Edited by Edward Mead Earle. Princeton: Princeton University Press, 1950.

Gumplowicz, Ludwig. OUTLINES OF SOCIOLOGY. New York: Paine-Whitman, 1963.

Hamilton, E.J. "The Decline of Spain." ECONOMIC HISTORY REVIEW 8 (1938).

Harbison, Frederick H., and Myers, Charles A. EDUCATION, MANPOWER, AND ECONOMIC GROWTH. New York: McGraw-Hill, 1964.

Harding, John. "The Measurement of Civilian Morale." GAUGING PUBLIC OPINION. Hadley Cantril. Princeton: Princeton University Press, 1944.

Harris, C.R.S. ALLIED MILITARY ADMINISTRATION OF ITALY: 1943-1945. London: Her Majesty's Stationery Office, 1957.

Hartshorne, Richard. "The Role of the State in Economic Growth: Contents of the State Area." THE STATE AND ECONOMIC GROWTH. Edited by Hugh G.J. Aitken. New York: Social Science Research Council, 1959.

Hawtrey, R.G. ECONOMIC ASPECTS OF SOVEREIGNTY. London: Longmans Green, 1952.

Hayes, Carlton J.H. A GENERATION OF MATERIALISM, 1871-1900. New York: Harper, 1941.

Heckscher, Eli F. MERCANTILISM. London: Allen & Unwin, 1935.

Heilbroner, Robert L. THE GREAT ASCENT. New York: Harper & Row, 1963.

Hermann, Paul. CONQUEST BY MAN. New York: Harper, 1954.

Herodotus. THE PERSIAN WARS. New York: Modern Library, 1942.

Hill, Norman. CLAIMS TO TERRITORY. New York: Oxford University Press, 1945.

Hobhouse, L., et al. THE MATERIAL CULTURE AND SOCIAL INSTITUTIONS OF THE SIMPLER PEOPLES. London: Chapman & Hall, 1930.

Horowitz, Irving Louis. THREE WORLDS OF DEVELOPMENT: THE THEORY AND PRACTICE OF INTERNATIONAL STRATIFICATION. New York: Oxford University Press, 1966.

Hovet, Thomas, Jr. BLOC POLITICS IN THE UNITED NATIONS. Cambridge: Harvard University Press, 1960.

Hsu, Shuhsi. THE WAR CONDUCT OF THE JAPANESE. Shanghai: Kelly and Walsh, 1938.

Hughes, E.R., ed. and trans. CHINESE PHILOSOPHY IN CLASSICAL TIMES. London: Dent, 1950.

Huntington, Ellsworth. WORLD POWER AND EVOLUTION. New Haven: Yale University Press, 1919.

_____. "The Geography of Human Productivity." ANNALS OF THE ASSOCIATION OF AMERICAN GEOGRAPHERS 33 (1943).

James, William. "The Moral Equivalent of War." MEMORIES AND STUDIES. New York: Longmans Green, 1911.

James, Stacy V. THE PATENT OFFICE. New York: Praeger, 1970.

Janowitz, Morris. THE MILITARY IN THE POLICITAL DEVELOPMENT OF NEW NATIONS. Chicago: University of Chicago Press, 1964.

_____, and Little, Roger. SOCIOLOGY AND THE MILITARY ESTABLISHMENT. New York: Russell Sage Foundation, 1965;

Johnson, Amanda. NORWAY, HER INVASION AND OCCUPATION. Decatur, Ga.: Bowen Press, 1948.

Johnson, John J. THE MILITARY AND SOCIETY IN LATIN AMERICA. Stanford: Stanford University Press, 1964.

Jong, Louis de. "Foreword." THE DUTCH UNDER GERMAN OCCUPATION. Werner Warmbrunn. Stanford: Stanford University Press, 1963.

Jouvenal, Bertrand de. ON POWER: ITS NATURE AND THE HISTORY OF ITS GROWTH. New York: Viking, 1949.

Kahn, Herman. ON THERMONUCLEAR WAR. Princeton: Princeton University Press, 1961.

Kecskemeti, Paul. STRATEGIC SURRENDER: THE POLITICS OF VICTORY AND DEFEAT. Stanford: Stanford University Press, 1958.

Kedourie, Elie, ed. NATIONALISM IN ASIA AND AFRICA. New York: World Publishing Co., 1971.

Kerr, Clark; Dunlop, John T.; Harbison, Frederick H.; and Meyers, Charles A. INDUSTRIALISM AND INDUSTRIAL MAN: THE PROBLEM OF LABOR AND MANAGEMENT IN ECONOMIC GROWTH. Cambridge: Harvard University Press, 1960.

Keynes, John M. THE ECONOMICS OF PEACE. London: Macmillan, 1920.

Khrushchev, N.S. CONTROL FIGURES FOR THE ECONOMIC DEVELOPMENT OF THE U.S.S.R. FOR 1959-1965. Moscow: Foreign Languages Publishing House, 1959.

Kindleberger, C.P. "Group Behavior and International Trade." THE JOURNAL OF POLITICAL ECONOMY 59 (February 1951).

Kirk, Dudley. EUROPE'S POPULATION IN THE INTERWAR YEARS. New York: League of Nations, 1944.

Klapper, Joseph T. "Mass Media and the Engineering of Consent." AMERICAN SCHOLAR 17 (October 1948).

Kobayashi, Ushisaburo. THE BASIC INDUSTRIES AND SOCIAL HISTORY OF JAPAN, 1914-1918. New Haven: Yale University Press, 1930.

Kohn, Hans. THE IDEA OF NATIONALISM. New York: Macmillan, 1944.

Kuznets, Simon. MODERN ECONOMIC GROWTH. New Haven and London: Yale University Press, 1966.

Lasswell, Harold D. PROPAGANDA TECHNIQUE IN THE WORLD WAR. New York: A. Knopf, 1938.

_____. "The Garrison-State Hypothesis Today." CHANGING PATTERNS OF MILITARY POLITICS. Edited by Samuel P. Huntington. Glencoe: Free Press, 1962.

League of Nations. INTERNATIONAL STATISTICAL YEAR-BOOK 1926 and 1939. 1926, 1939.

Leibenstein, Harvey. ECONOMIC BACKWARDNESS AND ECONOMIC GROWTH. New York: John Wiley, 1957.

Leontief, Wassily. AUTOMATIC CONTROL. New York: Simon and Schuster, 1955.

_____. FACTORS IN ECONOMIC DEVELOPMENT. London: Allen and Unwin, 1962.

Lerner, Daniel. "Modernization, Social Aspects." INTERNATIONAL ENCY-

CLOPEDIA OF THE SOCIAL SCIENCES. Vol. 10. New York: Macmillan, 1968.

Levy, Marion J. "Social Patterns (Structures) and Problems of Modernization." READINGS ON SOCIAL CHANGE. Edited by E. Moore and Robert M. Cook. Englewood Cliffs: Prentice-Hall, 1967.

Liebknecht, Karl. MILITARISM. New York: B.W. Huebsch, 1917.

Lieuwen, Edwin. ARMS AND POLITICS IN LATIN AMERICA. New York: Frederick Praeger, 1960.

Linton, Ralph. "The Prospect of Western Civilization." WAR IN THE TWENTIETH CENTURY. Edited by Willard Waller. New York: Random House, 1940.

Lippmann, Walter. THE GOOD SOCIETY. Boston: Little Brown, 1943.

Lipset, Seymour Martin. "Some Social Requisites of Democracy: Economic Development and Political Legitimacy." AMERICAN POLITICAL SCIENCE REVIEW 53 (March 1969).

List, Friedrich. THE NATIONAL SYSTEM OF POLITICAL ECONOMY. New York: Augustus M. Kelly, 1966.

Lot, Ferdinand. L'ART MILITAIRE ET LES ARMEES AU MOYEN AGE. Paris: 1946.

Luard, Evan. NATIONALITY AND WEALTH. London: Oxford University Press, 1964.

Ludendorff, Erich von. THE NATION AT WAR. London: Hutchinson, 1936.

Ludloff, R. "Industrial Development in 16th-17th Century Germany." PAST AND PRESENT 12 (November 1957).

Macaulay, Thomas Babington. THE HISTORY OF ENGLAND FROM THE ACCESSION OF JAMES THE SECOND. Edited by C.H. Firth. London: Macmillan, 1913, vol. I.

Maclaurin, W. Rupert. "The Sequence from Invention to Innovation and its Relation to Economic Growth." QUARTERLY JOURNAL OF ECONOMICS 67 (February 1953).

Mannheim, Karl. "The History of the Concept of the State." ESSAYS IN SOCIOLOGY AND SOCIAL PSYCHOLOGY. London: Routledge and Kegan Paul, 1953.

Mantoux, Paul. THE INDUSTRIAL REVOLUTION IN THE EIGHTEENTH CENTURY. Rev. ed. New York: Macmillan, 1961.

Marshall, Alfred. PRINCIPLES OF ECONOMICS. London: Macmillan, Eighth ed., 1938.

Marshall, T.H. CLASS, CITIZENSHIP AND SOCIAL DEVELOPMENT. Garden City: Doubleday, 1964.

Martin, Edwin M. THE ALLIED OCCUPATION OF JAPAN. Stanford: Stanford University Press, 1948.

Marx, Karl. CAPITAL. Chicago: Charles H. Kerr, 1906.

_____ . A CONTRIBUTION TO THE CRITIQUE OF POLITICAL ECONOMY. Chicago: Charles H. Kerr, 1903.

Mazour, Anatole G. RUSSIA: TSARIST AND COMMUNIST. New York: Van Nostrand, 1962.

McGranahan, Donald V. "Analysis of Socio-Economic Development through a System of Indicators." THE ANNALS OF THE AMERICAN ACADEMY OF POLITICAL AND SOCIAL SCIENCE 393 (January 1971).

McNamara, Robert S. THE ESSENCE OF SECURITY. New York: Harper & Row, 1968.

McWilliams, R.F. DOES HISTORY REPEAT ITSELF? London: J.M. Dent, 1932.

Medlicott, W.N. THE ECONOMIC BLOCKADE. London: His Majesty's Stationery Office, 1952.

Meinecke, Friedrich. MACHIAVELLISM. New Haven: Yale University Press, 1957.

Merton, Robert K., and Kitt, Alice S. "Contributions to the Theory of Reference Group Behavior." STUDIES IN THE SCOPE AND METHOD OF "THE AMERICAN SOLDIER." Edited by Robert K. Merton and Paul S. Lazarfeld. Glencoe: Free Press, 1950.

Mill, John Stuart. PRINCIPLES OF POLITICAL ECONOMY. London: Longmans Green, 1909.

Mills, C. Wright. THE CAUSES OF WORLD WAR III. New York: Ballantine Books, 1963.

Minsky, Hyman P. "Indicators of the Development Status of an Economy." ECONOMIC DEVELOPMENT AND CULTURAL CHANGE 7 (January 1959).

Moon, Parker Thomas. IMPERIALISM AND WORLD POLITICS. New York: Macmillan, 1929.

Morgenstern, Oskar. ON THE ACCURACY OF ECONOMIC OBSERVATIONS. Princeton: Princeton University Press, 1963.

Moussa, Pierre. THE UNDERPRIVILEGED NATIONS. Boston: Beacon Press, 1963.

Mumford, Lewis. TECHNICS AND CIVILIZATION. New York: Harcourt, Brace, 1934.

Myrdal, Gunnar. RICH LANDS AND POOR. New York: Harper, 1957.

_____. ASIAN DRAMA: AN INQUIRY INTO THE POVERTY OF NATIONS. New York: The Twentieth Century Fund, 1968.

Nasser, Gamal Abdul. EGYPT'S LIBERATION. Washington, D.C.: Public Affairs Press, 1955.

Nearing, Scott. WAR OR PEACE. New York: Island Press, 1946.

Nef, J.U. WAR AND HUMAN PROGRESS. Cambridge: Harvard University Press, 1952.

Nehru, Jawaharlal. THE DISCOVERY OF INDIA. London: Meridian Books, 1956.

OCCUPIED EUROPE. London: Royal Institute of International Affairs, 1944.

Ogawa, Gotaro. EXPENDITURES OF THE RUSSO-JAPANESE WAR. New York: Oxford University Press, 1923.

Ogburn, William F. SOCIAL CHANGE. New York: Viking, 1952.

_____. "Preface." TECHNOLOGY AND INTERNATIONAL RELATIONS. Edited by William Fielding Ogburn. Chicago: University of Chicago Press, 1949.

Ono, Giichi. EXPENDITURES OF THE SINO-JAPANESE WAR. New York: Oxford University Press, 1922.

_____. WAR AND ARMAMENT EXPENDITURES OF JAPAN. New York: Oxford University Press, 1922.

Panciroli, Guido. THE HISTORY OF MANY MEMORABLE THINGS LOST . . . London: J. Nicholson, 1715 (originally published in Latin in mid-sixteenth century in Italy).

Panikkar, K.M. ASIA AND WESTERN DOMINANCE: A SURVEY OF THE VASCO DA GAMA EPOCH OF ASIAN HISTORY 1498-1945. London: Allen & Unwin, 1959.

Peccei, Aurelio. THE CHASM AHEAD. New York: Macmillan, 1969.

Pepelasis, Adamantios; Mears, Leon; and Adelman, Irma. ECONOMIC DEVELOPMENT. New York: Harper and Row, 1961.

Pieri, Piero. LA CRISI MILITARA ITALIANA RENASCIMENTO, NELLA SUE RELAZIONE CON LA CRISI POLITICA ED ECONOMICA. Naples: R. Ricciardi, 1934.

Plomenatz, John. ALIEN RULE AND SELF-GOVERNMENT. London: Longmans Green, 1960.

Plato. LAWS. Edited by R.G. Bury. London: William Heinemann, 1926.

Prebisch, Raul. TOWARDS A NEW TRADE POLICY FOR DEVELOPMENT. New York: United Nations, E/Conf. 46/3, 1964.

_____. NUEVA POLITICA COMERCIAL PARA EL DESARROLLO. Mexico and Buenos Aires: Fondo de Cultural Economica, 1964.

Prescott, William H. HISTORY OF THE CONQUEST OF MEXICO and HISTORY OF THE CONQUEST OF PERU. New York: Modern Library, 1936.

Price, Derek J. "The Exponential Curve of Science." THE SOCIOLOGY OF SCIENCE. Edited by Bernard Barber and Walter Hirsch. New York: The Free Press of Glencoe, 1962.

PROCEEDINGS OF THE INTERNATIONAL CONFERENCE ON THE PEACEFUL USES OF ATOMIC ENERGY, HELD IN GENEVA, 8 AUGUST–20 AUGUST 1955, VOLUME I, THE WORLD'S REQUIREMENTS FOR ENERGY: THE ROLE OF NUCLEAR ENERGY. New York: United Nations, 1956 [X].

Pye, Lucian W. "Introduction." COMMUNICATIONS AND POLITICAL DEVELOPMENT. Edited by Lucian W. Pye. Princeton: Princeton University Press, 1963.

_____. POLITICS, PERSONALITY, AND NATION BUILDING. New Haven: Yale University Press, 1962.

_____, "Armies in the Process of Political Modernization." THE ROLE OF THE MILITARY IN UNDERDEVELOPED COUNTRIES. Edited by John J. Johnson. Princeton: Princeton University Press, 1962.

Ramsay, J.H. "The Strength of English Armies in the Middle Ages." ENGLISH HISTORICAL REVIEW 29 (1914).

Randle, Robert. The ORIGINS OF PEACE: A STUDY OF PEACEMAKING AND THE STRUCTURE OF PEACE SETTLEMENTS. New York: Free Press, 1973.

Reade, Hubert G.R. SIDELIGHTS ON THE THIRTY YEAR'S WAR. London: Jonathan Cape, 1938.

Renn, Ludwig. WARFARE: THE RELATION OF WAR TO SOCIETY. New York: Oxford University Press, 1939.

Rennell, Lord, of Rodd. BRITISH MILITARY ADMINISTRATION OF OCCUPIED TERRITORIES IN AFRICA: 1941-1947. London: His Majesty's Stationery Office, 1948.

Richardson, Lewis F. ARMS AND INSECURITY: A MATHEMATICAL STUDY OF THE CAUSES AND ORIGIN OF WAR. Edited by Nicholas Rashevsky and Ernesto Trucco. Pittsburgh: Boxwood Press, 1960.

_____. STATISTICS OF DEADLY QUARRELS. Pittsburgh: Boxwood Press, 1960.

Robbins, Lionel. THE ECONOMIC CAUSES OF WAR. London: Jonathan Cape, 1939.

Robbins, Lord. THE THEORY OF ECONOMIC DEVELOPMENT. New York: St. Martin's Press, 1968.

Rocklin, Gregory. GRIEFS AND DISCONTENTS. Boston: Little, Brown, 1965.

Rose, Arnold M. "The Comparative Study of Institutions." THE INSTITUTIONS OF ADVANCED SOCIETIES. Edited by Arnold M. Rose. Minneapolis: University of Minnesota Press, 1958.

Rostow, W.W. THE PROCESS OF ECONOMIC GROWTH. New York: W.W. Norton, 1952, 1962.

_____. THE STAGES OF ECONOMIC GROWTH. Cambridge: At The University Press, 1960.

Rousseau, J.J. THE SOCIAL CONTRACT. New York: Hafner, 1951.

Russett, Bruce, et al. WORLD HANDBOOK OF POLITICAL INDICATORS. New Haven: Yale University Press, 1964.

Rustow, Dankwart A. A WORLD OF NATIONS. Washington, D.C., The Brookings Institution, 1967.

Sahlins, Marshall D., and Service, Elman R., eds. EVOLUTION AND CULTURE. Ann Arbor: University of Michigan Press, 1960.

Scheuch, Erwin K. "Cross-National Comparisons Using Aggregate Data." COMPARING NATIONS. Edited by Richard L. Merritt and Stein Rokkan. New Haven: Yale University Press, 1966.

Schmoller, Gustav. THE MERCANTILE SYSTEM AND ITS HISTORICAL SIGNIFICANCE. New York: Macmillan, 1896.

Schmookler, Jacob. INVENTION AND ECONOMIC GROWTH. Cambridge: Harvard University Press, 1966.

Schumpeter, Joseph A. IMPERIALISM AND SOCIAL CLASSES. New York: Augustus M. Kelly, 1951.

Schwarzenberger, Georg. POWER POLITICS. London: Stevens, 1964.

Schwarzmann, M. "Background Factors in Spanish Decline." EXPLORATIONS IN ENTREPRENEURIAL HISTORY 3 (1951).

Seeley, J.R. THE EXPANSION OF ENGLAND. London: Macmillan, 1883.

Shils, Edward. "The Military in the Political Development of the New States." THE ROLE OF THE MILITARY IN UNDERDEVELOPED COUNTRIES. Edited by John J. Johnson. Princeton: Princeton University Press, 1962.

_____, and Janowitz, Morris. "Cohesion and Disintegration in the Wehrmacht in World War II." PUBLIC OPINION QUARTERLY 12 (1948).

Shimbori, Michiya, et al. "Measuring a Nation's Prestige." AMERICAN JOURNAL OF SOCIOLOGY 69, no. 1 (July 1963).

Shirer, William L. THE COLLAPSE OF THE THIRD REPUBLIC, AN INQUIRY INTO THE FALL OF FRANCE IN 1940. New York: Simon and Schuster, 1969.

Shotwell, James T. WAR AS AN INSTRUMENT OF NATIONAL POLICY. New York: Harcourt, Brace, 1929.

Sigmund, Paul E., ed. THE IDEOLOGIES OF THE DEVELOPING NATIONS. New York: Praeger, 1963.

Silberner, Edmond. THE PROBLEMS OF WAR IN NINETEENTH CENTURY ECONOMIC THOUGHT. Princeton: Princeton University Press, 1946.

Singer, J. David. "Modern International War: From Conjecture to Explanation." THE SEARCH FOR WORLD ORDER: ESSAYS IN HONOR OF QUINCY WRIGHT. Edited by Albert Lepawsky et al. New York: Appleton-Century-Crofts, 1971.

_____, and Small, Melvin. THE WAGES OF WAR, 1816-1965: A STATISTICAL HANDBOOK. New York: Wiley, 1972.

Sloan, Frank Keenan. "The Role of the Military in Development." DEVELOPMENTAL REVOLUTION. Edited by William R. Polk. Washington, D.C.: Middle East Institute, 1963.

Smith, Adam. AN INQUIRY INTO THE NATURE AND CAUSES OF THE WEALTH OF NATIONS. London: Methuen, 1930.

Smith, Sir Edward. "The Critical Importance of Higher Technological Education in Relation to Productivity." AMERICAN SCIENTIST 39 (1951).

Sombart, Werner. KRIEG UND KAPITALISMUS. Leipzig: Duncker & Humblot, 1913.

Sorokin, Pitirim A. SOCIAL AND CULTURAL DYNAMICS. New York: American Book Co., 1937, vol 11.

Speer, Albert. INSIDE THE THIRD REICH. New York: Macmillan, 1970.

Speier, Hans. "Preface." THE ROLE OF THE MILITARY IN UNDERDEVEL-OPED COUNTRIES. Edited by John J. Johnson. Princeton: Princeton University Press, 1962.

_____, and Kahler, Alfred, eds. WAR IN OUR TIME. New York: W.W. Norton, 1939.

Spencer, Herbert. THE PRINCIPLES OF SOCIOLOGY. New York: D. Appleton, 1880, vol I.

Spengler, Joseph J. "Theories of Socio-Economic Growth." PROBLEMS IN THE STUDY OF ECONOMIC GROWTH. Universities-National Bureau Committee on Economic Research. New York: National Bureau of Economic Research, 1949.

Spengler, Oswald. THE DECLINE OF THE WEST. New York: Alfred A. Knopf, 1928, vol II.

Staley, Eugene. WAR LOSSES TO A NEUTRAL. New York: League of Nations Association, December 1937.

_____. WORLD ECONOMY IN TRANSITION. New York: Council on Foreign Relations, 1939.

Stein, Emanuel, and Backman, Jules. "Transition from Peace to War." WAR ECONOMICS. Edited by Emanuel Stein and Jules Backman. New York: Farrar & Rinehart, 1942.

Stone, L. "State Control in Sixteenth-Century England." ECONOMIC HISTORY REVIEW 17 (1947).

Stouffer, Samuel A., and DeVinney, Leland C. THE AMERICAN SOLDIER: ADJUSTMENT DURING ARMY LIFE. Princeton: Princeton University Press, 1949, vol I.

Strachey, John. THE END OF EMPIRE. London: Gollancz, 1959.

Strassman, W. Paul. TECHNOLOGICAL CHANGE AND ECONOMIC DEVELOPMENT. Ithaca: Cornell University Press, 1968.

Strausz-Hupe, Robert. GEOPOLITICS. New York: G.P. Putnam, 1942.

Sumner, William Graham. FOLKWAYS. Boston: Ginn, 1906.

_____. "Conquest of the U.S. by Spain." WAR AND OTHER ESSAYS. Edited by Albert Galloway Keller. New Haven: Yale University Press, 1911.

Tawney, R.H. "The Abolition of Economic Controls, 1918-1921." ECONOMIC HISTORY REVIEW 13 (1943).

Teggart, Frederick J. ROME AND CHINA: A STUDY OF CORRELATIONS IN HISTORICAL EVENTS. Berkeley: University of California Press, 1939.

Thomas, W.I. SOURCE BOOK OF SOCIAL ORIGINS. Chicago: University of Chicago Press, 1909.

Thorez, Maurice. FILS DU PEUPLE. Paris: Editions Sociales, 1960.

Thucydides, THE PELOPONNESIAN WAR. New York: Random House, 1934.

Timasheff, N.S. THE GREAT RETREAT. New York: Dutton, 1946.

Toffler, Alvin. FUTURE SHOCK. New York: Random House, 1970.

Toynbee, Arnold J. WAR AND CIVILIZATION. London: Oxford University Press, 1951.

Twain, Mark. "The Mysterious Stranger." THE MYSTERIOUS STRANGER AND OTHER STORIES. New York: Harper & Row, 1916.

UNESCO. HANDBOOK OF INTERNATIONAL EXCHANGES. Paris: IES./ VI.I/AFSR, 1965.

United Nations. ECONOMIC AND SOCIAL CONSEQUENCES OF DISARMA-MENT. New York: 1962.

_____. DEMOGRAPHIC YEARBOOK, 1965. New York: 1966.

_____. STATISTICAL YEARBOOK, 1954. New York: 1955.

Urlanis, B.L. VOYNY I NARODONASELENIE EVROPY. Moscow, 1960.

Veblen, Thorstein. IMPERIAL GERMANY AND THE INDUSTRIAL REVOLU-TION. New York: Viking, 1939.

_____. "The Opportunity of Japan." ESSAYS IN OUR CHANGING ORDER. New York: Viking, 1934.

Viallate, Achille. ECONOMIC IMPERIALISM AND INTERNATIONAL RELA-TIONS DURING THE LAST FIFTY YEARS. New York: Macmillan, 1923.

Viner, Jacob. "Power versus Plenty as Objectives of Foreign Policy in the Seventeenth and Eighteenth Century." WORLD POLITICS 1 (October 1948).

Ward, Robert S. ASIA FOR THE ASIATICS? THE TECHNIQUES OF JAPAN-ESE OCCUPATION. Chicago: University of Chicago Press, 1945.

Weber, Max. "Citizenship." GENERAL ECONOMIC HISTORY. New York: Collier Books, 1961.

Wedgwood, C.V. THE THIRTY YEARS WAR. London: Jonathan Cape, 1938; and New York: Anchor Books, 1961.

Wheeler, Sir Mortimer. ROME BEYOND THE IMPERIAL FRONTIERS. London: G. Bell, 1954.

_____. IMPACT AND IMPRINT: GREEKS AND ROMANS BEYOND THE HIMALAYAS. Newcastle-upon-Tyne: King's College, 28th May, 1959.

White, Jr., Lynn. MEDIEVAL TECHNOLOGY AND SOCIAL CHANGE. Oxford: Clarendon Press, 1962.

Whitehead, Alfred N. SCIENCE AND THE MODERN WORLD. New York: Macmillan, 1926.

Wirth, Louis. "Consensus and Mass Communication." AMERICAN SOCIOLOGI-CAL REVIEW 13 (February 1948).

Worsley, Peter. THE THIRD WORLD. Chicago: University of Chicago Press, 1964.

Woytinsky, W.S., and Woytinsky, E.S. WORLD POPULATION AND PRODUC-TION. New York: The Twentieth Century Fund, 1953.

Wright, Quincy. A STUDY OF WAR. Chicago: University of Chicago Press, 1942; 1965.

_____. "The Study of War." INTERNATIONAL ENCYCLOPEDIA OF THE SOCIAL SCIENCES. New York: Macmillan, 1968, vol. 16.

Index

About the Author

Henry Barbera received the Ph.D. from Columbia University. He teaches social stratification and political sociology at City College, CUNY, and is an active member of the curriculum, faculty research, and communications committees as well as being a senator of the college.

He has taught sociology at Hunter College, CUNY, and has gained research experience at the National Opinion Research Center, the University of Chicago, and at the Bureau of Applied Social Research, Columbia University.

He serves as a consultant to the Center for Advanced Studies and Analyses, the Westinghouse Electric Corporation, and is a Fellow of the Inter-University Seminar on Armed Forces and Society.

Professor Barbera's interests include war and society, international inequality, and the military and diplomatic professions and organization.